WAR AND A CHILD

Trapped between the Allied and German Forces in the Battle of Monte Cassino

ALBERTO PANETTA

Copyright © 2013 Alberto Panetta

The moral right of the author has been asserted.

Any part of this book cannot be used without express permission of the author.

Apart from any fair dealing for the purposes of research or private study, or criticism or review, as permitted under the Copyright, Designs and Patents Act 1988, this publication may only be reproduced, stored or transmitted, in any form or by any means, with the prior permission in writing of the publishers, or in the case of reprographic reproduction in accordance with the terms of licences issued by the Copyright Licensing Agency. Enquiries concerning reproduction outside those terms should be sent to the publishers.

Matador
9 Priory Business Park
Kibworth Beauchamp
Leicestershire LE8 0RX, UK
Tel: (+44) 116 279 2299
Fax: (+44) 116 279 2277
Email: books@troubador.co.uk
Web: www.troubador.co.uk/matador

ISBN 978 1780885 124

British Library Cataloguing in Publication Data.
A catalogue record for this book is available from the British Library.

Printed and bound in the UK by TJ International, Padstow, Cornwall
Typeset in 11pt Book Antiqua by Troubador Publishing Ltd, Leicester, UK

Durham County Council Libraries, Learning and Culture	
C0 1 71 64971 B4	
Askews & Holts	
940.5421	

I dedicate this book to the memory of my mother and father for their determination and courage, risking their lives amidst the German army for the family's survival. Their struggles and suffering were horrendous. The pain of seeing my brother and me suffer must have broken their hearts a million times and more. I think too, or should I say I know, that they dedicated their lives to the well-being of my brother and myself and gave so much love to so many. They lived to the ages of over ninety-seven and ninety years respectively. Their names were Delisa and Crescenzo.

*Delisa and Crescenzo Panetta
Photograph taken before the war*

Alberto (Berto) Panetta
Photograph taken two years after the war

Enio Panetta
Photograph taken two years after the war

Childhood memories of terror, suffering, death. There are scars that never heal.

A World in Turmoil

Over a period of six years, from 1939 to 1945, the Second World War took place. Battle upon battle was fought in different parts of the world, destroying man's achievements and in some cases the very earth itself. Opposing armies killed one another by the tens of thousands and civilians of all ages suffered injuries, death and unimaginable atrocities – all because of one evil man, Adolph Hitler, the German dictator whose aim was to conquer the world and inflict his twisted ideology on the human race. This included the extermination of races he considered inferior and the creation of a German master race, an obsession that allowed neither justice nor compassion to stand in its way.

Italy too was being ruled by a dictator, Benito Mussolini. The nation was under his absolute command, as much of the population had little knowledge of either domestic politics or international events. It was a country with little industry, where a large number of people struggled for survival by working farmland, a country that had been unified for about eighty years yet whose people remained insular, a population easy to dominate. Sadly, Benito Mussolini was induced by Hitler to take his side in this war, so the Italian army was obliged to fight against the Allied Forces. Italians are not a warmongering people nor did they have the resources to fight such a war, but above all most of the population were resentful and confused as to why the dictator had taken sides with Germany. For these reasons, there came a time when the Italian population abandoned fighting and turned against the German army. This was in early September 1943, when the Italian forces were disbanded and Italian soldiers joined the Allied Forces in their thousands. Benito Mussolini, aware that most of the Italian population had been against his alliance with Germany, went into hiding, but such was the anger of the Italian people that they hunted him down and he was publicly hanged.

Towards the end of 1943 the German army had occupied much of the area south of Rome called Valle di Comino as well as the town of Cassino and its surroundings. It was a mountainous region, with towns and villages both in the lowlands and perched on mountain plateaux. Cassino was a small town with an imposing mountain immediately above it called Monte Cassino, steep and rocky and with a huge monastery on its peak. The German army took up strategic positions in many of these towns, embedding themselves particularly strongly with their guns and ammunition on top of Monte Cassino. It was almost impossible for the Allied Forces to conquer or break through this area and the battle was long and ferocious, the carnage and suffering continuing not only for the Allied Forces but also for the civilians. It is known as the Battle of Monte Cassino, the hardest fought battle of the Second World War.

The following story is a record of what I suffered and witnessed as an eight-year-old boy under the German army during this battle.

Still standing in front of the town hall in Cassino today. Armoured tank left by the Allied Forces and a gun from the Italian army. Both were used in ousting the German army from Monte Cassino

All illustrations in this book are by Ivan Allen

Prologue

It is mainly due to others' requests and encouragement that I come to write this short piece of history more than sixty years on. It is what I remember so clearly myself, with no input from any other person, and its purpose is to give an account of what I and my family were forced to endure during one year of my life, from the age of eight to nine years, from September 1943 to August 1944.

The story tells of my parents, my six-year-old brother, me and other family members and our struggle to survive under the German occupation during the Second World War.

Before entering upon my story, I would like to give a glimpse of the town and environment in which I was born and brought up, a small country town south of Rome called Villa Latina. It was a place that pleased and comforted the eye, whose fertile land supplied its inhabitants' homes with everything they needed, and whose community lived in harmony together, relying upon and caring for each other; all this I was aware of and rejoiced in. It was amongst this community, this benevolent way of life, in this graceful and pleasing landscape with its fruitful abundance, its security and beauty, that my formative years were shaped. It was a natural life, safe, simple and profound – a contrast to the terrible events about to be unleashed.

How it Was

Life in my small country town was good, peaceful and full of joy. Groups of houses maintained the closeness of their inhabitants, the roads were flanked by hedges full of flowers and the music of clear brooks accompanied you on your way. Sunny days, blue skies and cool mountain breezes were taken for granted. Fields of colour delighted the eye: the mellow gold of ripened wheat, green fields of vegetables, and fruit trees laden with their own unique colours – peaches, pears, apples, figs, cherries, and many, many others. Savouring their delicious flavours felt like receiving gifts from nature. It was a land surrounded by undulating hills with vines and olive groves, all in the embrace of a chain of receding, ever-higher mountains, most wooded, some tall and bold with rocky surfaces where the sun blazed down until the twilight hours.

It felt good to be living near my grandparents, uncles and aunts and many other members of our family, among a community that cared for and relied on one another. Each morning I knew when it was almost time to get up by the sounds of cockerels calling one another, then the bleat of sheep and the cheep, cheep of birds, followed by human voices starting a new day.

Sometimes I took my breakfast in my china bowl with the boiled milk and boiled water from the roasted barley, lots of sugar and chunks of toasted bread and ate it sitting on the balcony watching the morning sun slowly rising behind the mountain amidst a sea of golden red. I waited for the rays of the sun to reach the telegraph wire above the roadside, when suddenly hundreds of swallows would leave their nests under the eaves and perch on the wire, filling the air with their cheeping as they faced and rejoiced in the warmth of the morning sun.

Soon the sun rises high above the mountain and pours its bright rays on everyone and everything, lighting up the pink blossoms of the peach tree beside the house. Then, as I sat on my tiny chair softly singing my favourite songs, I waited to see them all go by: farmers, their carts loaded with equipment pulled by donkeys or cows, off to cultivate their land; shepherds taking their flocks to pastures on the hills; lumberjacks and charcoal makers on their way to the mountains; the blacksmith, his clothes darkened by the forge and anvil, going to his work; the man in flour-dusted clothing and cap on his way to the mill, where a vast water reservoir has been filling throughout the night to power and turn the huge stone grinding wheels; the clerks to the town hall and post office; the cobbler, the tailor, the carpenter, the builder, all peacefully and happily off to their workplaces. A community in motion, serving each other's needs. The old man with his shirt sleeves rolled up, his hat on and puffing his pipe, pushes his wheelbarrow to his kitchen garden. The housewife returns, having picked the fruit before the heat of the day and carrying a basket full of everything in season, apples, pears, peaches, plums, figs, cherries, grapes, melons, tomatoes, cucumbers and bunches of herbs, all to enrich the daily family reunion around the dinner table. The portly postman passes with his large leather case strapped over his shoulder, calling the names of recipients of letters in his deep, resonant voice. Soon the aroma of foods being prepared to welcome and nourish the workers begins to rise out of the kitchens. Together with the mountains that surround them and the fertile earth, they are all a part of this productive community.

This was a town full of people whose hearts overflowed with benevolence towards one another, sensitive to others' needs and ready to give a helping hand. There was always time: time to speak, time to listen, time to praise. Never would two people pass without engaging in conversation, not about outside events but matters of their own lives, speaking of their achievements, their losses and, above all, their families. Having been able to express their feelings, having received encouragement and support, they would then part to resume their daily tasks, each grateful for the other's existence.

Since the majority of the community were farmers, it was the custom for everyone to help the one whose harvest was in greatest need of attention: picking grapes, reaping wheat, picking olives, making wine, and many other tasks. So, it was not unusual to see eight, ten or more people working side by side in various fields. Walking along the road, one could hear their interchanges from afar: a story being told, laughter from a joke, but most of all, lovely harmonious singing from the whole group. Beautiful sounds thrown into the open sky for their own delight, expressing their contentment and unity to anyone there to hear them.

I vividly recall when Grandfather used to take my brother and me to the piazza to buy chocolate. On the way, if he saw a farmer working his field, Grandfather would say to him, "The fruits of your labour look good and plentiful, may God preserve it", and the farmer would answer, "The same be with yours". When we met men with their cows or flocks of sheep, Grandfather would greet them and say, "The cows or sheep look well, may God bless them", and they answered, "Thank you". Whenever we met the parish priest, Grandfather always slightly raised his hat and said, "The Lord be praised". The priest touched his large, round-rimmed hat and answered, "Always be praised". This way of expressing goodwill was normal practice. Older men and women were always referred to as uncle or aunt, even by people who were twenty or thirty years old.

We all looked forward to Sundays, the day no one worked and everyone dressed in their best clothes, the day everyone went to church. A day to relax, to rejoice in meeting relatives and friends, the day when there were special preparations for the dinner table. There were also the feasts of saints, when the whole community joined together in making the day special, householders brought out pots of flowers to line the roadside and colourful bedspreads were hung on balconies to decorate the streets. Festoons of lights arched the road, creating a magic tunnel to the church.

Baskets of rose petals were prepared, ready for throwing from balconies on the statues of the saints as the procession passed by. The town band played as it marched around the streets and sometimes an orchestra would also come to play. Music was always to be heard as people played during the evenings. I savoured it, rejoicing, and when Father wound up the record player and put a record on I would listen, not moving from its side. When Father left the room I stood on a chair to look inside the funnel-like amplifier, wanting to be close to the beautiful sounds, imagining there was a little man singing with his arms spread out at the bottom of the funnel.

Autumn, I remember, brought its own unique quality; everything became quieter and less active. There was a feeling of coolness and cleanliness in the air, a special scent, as nature gently displayed a variety of different colours, all giving a sense of tranquillity, peacefulness and beauty. It is the end of the productive cycle of nature, when farmers see the fruits of their labour realised and take stock with pride of their achievements, when man and nature, both having given so much, take a rest together. People had more time to visit their relatives and friends, more time for social gatherings, comfortable in the security of the harvest stored up to sustain their families for another year. Man was at peace with himself and his fellow men. Alas, we were to be robbed of all this.

Uncertain Times

It was springtime 1943 and I was about seven and a half years old. It was then that I started to become more aware of the war because of the way people's conversations had changed from general chat about everyday matters to serious discussions about the war. It was the only thing people were concerned with now. The conversations were too serious for me to take part in, so I just listened.

I used to hear people curse Mussolini, the dictator of Italy, saying: "Mussolini ha rovinato l'Italia" (Mussolini has ruined Italy), "l'avvenire sarà triste" (the future will be bleak). I remember people gathering in Grandfather's house, talking angrily, saying: "The majority of us didn't want to go into war, taking sides with the Germans", "Mussolini ci ha tradito" (Mussolini has betrayed us), "Hitler e Mussolini sono assassini" (Hitler and Mussolini are assassins). Their discussions were noisy, filled with fury. They seemed to have forgotten I was there.

Father was a soldier in the army. I remember when he returned home on leave people immediately came to greet him and asked how the war was going. He answered, "Male, molto male" (Bad, very bad). He too kept repeating that most of the population didn't want to be on the Germans' side, and said there was even conflict between soldiers and regiments in the armed forces because they differed so strongly in their political views on this subject. Father also said that thousands and thousands of soldiers had deserted from the armed forces and joined the underground movement called 'I Partigiani', fighting against the Germans and in many cases even against their own armies. "Fratelli contra fratelli" (Brothers against brothers), said Father, "because of Mussolini." Their discussions went on and on while they cursed Hitler and Mussolini, but I wanted them to go so we would have Father all to ourselves.

Each morning people came out of their houses to ask one another if they had heard any news or a particular announcement on the radio. All the adults looked lost, helpless, dejected. There was so much anxiety in mothers' and wives' faces as they anxiously waited each morning for the postman, hoping he might bring a letter from their sons or husbands who were away fighting the war. We knew when Father would come home on leave and towards evening I would wait and wait by the roadside for the daily coach which carried people and brought the post to our town; we called it 'La postala'. I listened for the sound of the engine coming from far away and prepared to be alert, as when it passed by me Father would always be standing looking out of the window and would throw the hat of his uniform to me. The coach would carry on to the piazza where the church and post office were and I would wait eagerly for him to walk back, as Mother always prepared a special meal for that evening. After only a few days with us Father had to go back. Mother would cry, and it was always sad.

Our small peaceful town had now become a place of

gloom and insecurity. People's faces were sad, robbed of their men, robbed of the family unit and then robbed of their goods. Women were told to give their wedding rings to support the war, then each family was ordered to hand in some of their copper pots and pans and other metals. I watched women reluctantly carrying their pots and pans to the blacksmith's works. Fear of the few who supported the dictator made people obey the orders.

Mother and I had to take some of ours too. We had to line up and our names and addresses were taken. Mother made sure they had taken our address correctly because she feared being accused of not obeying the order. I watched as each item was handed over. It was placed upside down on the huge anvil and immediately the blacksmith hit it with a big pointed hammer, damaging the copper pots to render them unusable, so they would make their way to the ammunition factory. I saw Mother's parents sorrowfully watching men ruthlessly dismantling the ornate cast iron railing along the frontage of their house. It brought gloom to the face of the house and gloom to Grandfather's face.

Days passed and the uncertainty and insecurity increased. People's eyes were full of fear, confusion and suspicion. They spoke to one another quietly and out of sight, fearful their views might be overheard by those who did not share the same political allegiance. It was those who supported the dictator who were always feared.

One morning Mother and I stood by the roadside waiting for the postman, hoping he would bring a letter from Father. The woman next door joined us and began to discuss the war and the dictator. When they saw a man coming along the road who had an official job and was known to be a strong supporter of the dictator, they immediately changed the subject as if they had been committing a crime. As the man passed us he was greeted with a smile and told, "Good morning, we are waiting for the postman, hoping for good news." The man answered "Good morning" as he continued to walk. When he was some way from us, Mother and the woman looked at one another and said quietly, "He is not to be trusted. Good thing we saw him coming." Such was the fear. What I used to hear was that the minority who supported the dictator were fanatics, who tried to convince others and were willing to report those who did not share their views to people in high positions in government offices, with the result that if the need arose for a document or any other matter, the request would fall on stony ground. People had therefore to be careful of what they said in front of these fanatics, be evasive, act stupid. Freedom of speech came at a very high cost; fear of the few was a reality. Hypocrisy was essential for survival.

The fanatics adopted a dictatorial attitude, worked relentlessly towards their cause and were full of their own importance. They even wasted time trying to convince boys of my age, seven years old. At school, not only were we taught about the dictator's ideology and how great he was, we were also supplied with black shirts and hats with tassels on like the one the dictator wore, and a cravat that we tied loosely in front of our shirts. We had to parade in the school playground like soldiers, marching very fast while shouting "Duce,

Duce, Duce, e viva Mussolini" in praise of the dictator.

The teacher was very solemn and kept telling us to shout louder, but when he couldn't see our faces we laughed and laughed and laughed, because we didn't know what we were doing or why. As a seven-year-old with no understanding of politics, I went home wearing the hat and cravat as the other boys did. I felt I looked smart and thought Mother would like it too and compliment me, but as I entered the kitchen I saw her eyes looking with such disapproval at my hat. She just murmured, "You look nice" and turned away. I was so disappointed.

Now that I know what Mother knew then, I understand her spontaneous reaction. The next day I heard other boys say how their mothers had been annoyed at what the teacher had made us do instead of teaching us to read and write, but we had not to let the teacher know this.

As each day passed, news of the war worsened. Squadrons upon squadrons of English and American warplanes passed over us. At night we heard the muted sounds of the exploding bombs and watched the flashing lights in the sky somewhere far away. People became more and more worried. No more smiles, no more happiness, as we were borne into bleaker and bleaker times and then into days, weeks and months of events we could never have imagined.

I was almost eight years old. Now I could really sense people's concern about what was going on in the war because of the drastic changes in our way of life. There was a shortage of food. Salt was scarce. People spoke to one another with sad faces and in sorrowful voices in which I sensed fear. It was total misery. It made me sad too, particularly because I felt Mother's anxiety. Father being away in the army, all responsibilities fell on her. My brother Enio was younger than me, six years old, and I felt it was up to me to help Mother and stand by her, carrying the wood for the fire from where it was stored, keeping an eye on what she was cooking and going to the shop in the piazza or Via Roma to buy what we needed. When Mother felt unwell I went to the chemist to buy medicine. I looked after my brother. I listened to what people were saying about the war and reported it to Mother, feeling her worries were mine too. At the end of each day we locked the door and Mother, my brother and I stayed safely inside, wishing for better news the next day and that Father would soon return.

Since all the eligible men were away fighting the war, the people left in the town were generally the older men, women and boys and girls of various ages. It was difficult, therefore, for families to cope with the day-to-day running of their businesses, their farms, attending to the animals and dealing with the necessities of life. I could see how each family faced a heavy burden without the usual manpower, but worse was the anxiety, the uncertainty and sorrow in people's faces, longing to see again their husbands, sons or brothers, who had been away for so long and no news from them. Now my father too was one of the soldiers we had not heard from for some time. Were they still alive? Were they prisoners of war? Would we ever see them again? That was what people thought and spoke about.

Every morning, about the time the postman was due, I would see wives, mothers and sisters come out of their houses and gather by the roadside, chatting maybe but all anxiously waiting for the postman in the hope he might bring news from their men. As the postman passed without any letters they gave each other hope by saying, "Perhaps tomorrow we will get some news", then slowly dispersing to their houses with pensive, disappointed faces. A neighbour who had already lost a son in the war and had received no communication from her two other sons walked towards the postman but he looked at her and shook his head, indicating there was no post for her. No words were spoken. She turned and slowly walked back to her house, head bowed, looking as if there was no life left in her body to go on. Many times I would see the postman pass earlier than his usual time, walking quickly as if he wanted to avoid seeing people so disappointed when he had no news for them. Soon after, people would come out enquiring among themselves if anyone had seen the postman go by or they had heard from their loved ones.

Armistice

It was towards the end of the afternoon and the sun was still shining when I suddenly saw people gathering in our neighbour's house, all listening to the radio. The room had become so packed that some had to remain outside the front door. They looked agitated, moving around, craning their necks, trying to hear the radio announcements. As each statement was made they nodded at each other in acknowledgement and their faces became increasingly apprehensive, their expressions fixed as if hypnotised. So absorbed were they all in listening to the radio that there was no other sound, but the anxiety was as present as the air one breathed. After a while the silence suddenly broke and I heard the excited voices repeating "Armistizio, armistizio, armistizio, armistizio". They sounded relieved, their eyes and faces alight as if they had received a present. I sensed that there was good news in the word armistizio (armistice), but I didn't know what it meant, so I ran across the road to my grandparents' house where I knew Mother was. I found her and Grandmother at the rear of the house, sitting enjoying the evening sun while hand-sewing a garment. "What does the word armistizio mean?" I asked Mother and they both stood up, looking at me in surprise. "Where have you heard this word?" Mother demanded. I told her about the people listening to the radio, then Grandmother took the material out of Mother's hands and said, "Quickly, you go and see what is happening."

As Mother and I approached the people, there was complete silence. A neighbour moved towards Mother and told her what was being said by the radio announcer. Each time a new person came and broke the silence by asking for the latest news there was a spontaneous "Sh, sh" and they placed their finger against their nose, indicating they should be quiet. All communication was carried on by facial, head and hand gestures, but it was enough to indicate that the situation seemed to have got better.

Later that evening I remember Mother giving me and my brother our evening meal then wanting us to go to bed but I objected, saying I wanted to be with her. My brother did go to bed and my mother and I rejoined the people and continued to listen to the radio. I sat on the stone step outside the door near to everyone, wanting to be part of them. It was now dark, and I was feeling cold, so Mother put a shawl over my shoulders and my legs. The radio broadcast went on and on and on. I fought not to fall asleep, but I think I did.

Then I suddenly became aware of a commotion, disappointed voices, sighs and gestures of hopelessness. I heard them say that the radio announcer had repeated over and over again that the war would continue, that it was going to be much, much worse and that the people would have much to suffer. A drone of sounds emerged from the room: "Che disastro, che disastro, chi sa che ci succeede?" (What a disaster, what a disaster, who knows what will happen to us?). Every statement that followed only confirmed this forecast, destroying all their hopes, replacing them with dismay, hopelessness and more fear. I felt sad because they were all sad.

A few days later, in the late afternoon, there was an influx of about fifty carabinieri (Italian police) in their uniforms. They were unshaven, and looked sad, tired and hungry. They asked for shelter, food and civilian clothing, saying they had escaped from towns occupied by the Germans and how cruel the Germans were to them and civilians alike. They spoke angrily, saying: "Sparano, uccidono senza nessuna ragione" (They shoot and kill for no reason), "They take all they want, including pigs, cows and sheep, for their food and donkeys to carry ammunition". Their accents were very different from ours and it amused me to hear them speak. The townspeople were under so much fear that at first they didn't know whether to trust them in case they were on the side of the Germans. However, a man from our town hall reassured everyone that the carabinieri were speaking the truth and families then invited them into their houses and fed them. It was almost dark when they returned, some already wearing civilian clothing people had given them, all carrying a bundle of straw under their arms to sleep on the floor of our schoolrooms and corridor.

The next morning they had all gone, as it was felt that any day the Germans would reach our town. Days passed in an atmosphere of insecurity and fear. When people met, all they wanted to know from each other was whether they had heard anything – in the hope that they might have some good news!

But the news I always heard was that the Germans were getting nearer and nearer to our town, aggressively entering houses, taking goods, cows for their food, donkeys to carry ammunition to the battlefront and men at gunpoint to dig trenches and carry ammunition up the mountains.

The atmosphere of my joyous town was now one of mourning. So much secrecy, pessimistic faces, lamenting voices, minds already given up to the horrors of war. It felt as if everyone was a criminal, fearful of being caught.

Better Not to Know

Each day only brought more bad news. Fear and anxiety hung over everyone. One sunny morning, about ten o'clock, Mother and our next-door neighbour were talking outside the house near the roadside, waiting for the postman. I went and stood near them. A woman came by with a donkey loaded with two sacks full of goods, stopped and said, "Buon giorno, do you have any news of how things are going?" Mother answered, "That's what we were saying, we haven't heard anything this morning", but no sooner had she finished the sentence than a man began to approach us. "Perhaps he will know something," said Mother. When the man reached us, he began to speak in a serious, nervous voice. "Buon giorno, go back into your houses and lock your doors. I have just been to the town hall, what they are saying there doesn't sound good, it won't be long before they arrive here. Go inside, go inside and lock your doors."

The woman with the donkey couldn't decide what to do next, saying, "I have people working on my land, I need to go there, but I don't know what to do. I am frightened; there's no one at home and I don't want to find my house looted." Eventually she decided to continue and go to her workers. She went about a hundred metres or so then returned with her donkey and said, "The workers I employed are waiting for me but I don't want to abandon my house, do you think the man was exaggerating?" Mother and our neighbour shrugged their shoulders, opened their arms and said, "Chi lo sà" (Who knows). The woman turned, pulled the donkey's lead and started to walk towards her land again. After about fifty metres she returned, having worked herself into a nervous and confused state. She said hurriedly, "I need to be with my workers, I don't know what to do." She went on and on about her dilemma, becoming angry and increasingly confused about what she should do. She stood by the head of her donkey, looking tensely up and down the road, eyes full of fear, as if at any moment a catastrophe was about to happen, while she passed the donkey's lead from one hand to the other, over and over again. The donkey stood by her side as still as an oak tree, its face showing complete calmness and obedience, void of any thought, the only sign of life being that every now and then its eyelids blinked over its big translucent deep brown eyes in which I could see my own reflection. A total contrast to its owner's tormented face, but little did it know that it too was wanted by the enemy, to be heavily loaded with explosives, to carry them up difficult mountain tracks, under stress, danger and horrible sounds in order for human beings to inflict cruelties on one another, a thought that would never have entered its docile mind. Sometimes it's good not to know.

It was only seconds later that we heard the sound of screeching brakes and bicycle tyres as a cyclist suddenly stopped by the side of two men about fifty metres away from us. The cyclist spoke to the men without dismounting from his bicycle. A third man was about to join them, but the cyclist swiftly left and stopped by us. Speaking very quickly in a strained, gasping voice charged with fear, he warned, "The Germans are coming, they are entering houses, taking all they want, they want donkeys to carry ammunition and men to dig trenches near to the front line." He set off again, saying, "I am going to warn others", turned his head, gave us one last glance, said "Look after yourselves", then disappeared like a frightened fox. Mother, our neighbour and the woman with the donkey were now visibly terrified, making agitated gestures to each other, discussing what they should do, interrupting each other as they spoke of the frightening situation, while the donkey and I maintained our silence, looking on at the traumatic scene. Then we quickly parted as they said to each other, "Fate attenzione, speriamo che non succede niente di male" (Be careful, let's hope that nothing bad will happen). The woman gave the poor loaded donkey a slap with the palm of her hand on its hind leg, saying "Ah, Ah, Ah" to hurry it along as they went back home.

We rushed back into our house and I quickly took my brother to Mother's parents across the road. Mother collected her jewellery, money and documents, placed them in a small leather travelling case and we went to hide it where we stored the firewood, buried it under a pile of logs and spread a few bunches of twigs on the top so as to make the place untidy and not arouse suspicion. On the way back, Mother realised she had lost the key of the leather case. We looked for it for a while, but fear

made us return home. It was then that I became fully aware of Mother's terror. She pushed the door almost closed leaving a few centimetres gap, leant against the door frame and stopped there, looking out. I went in front of her, she placed her arms over my shoulders from behind, resting her hands on my stomach, holding me close to her, and we stayed there, our eyes fixed on the road. More than once Mother said, "Don't be afraid, no one will come to us", but from the sound of her voice and movements of her body, so close to mine, I sensed a deep fear, a sense of desolation as if she had been abandoned.

There we stood, watching the empty road, not a soul nor a sound anywhere. The only sign of life was the movement of Mother's body as she breathed in and out and I felt the warmth of her deep breath on the side of my face. After some time she said, "Are you hungry? I will cook lunch soon", but neither of us moved from our position, waiting and waiting. It was probably about two hours now since the man on the bicycle had come to warn us when we heard the sound of a motorbike getting nearer and nearer. Mother closed the door a little more, reducing the view of the road to only a few metres. A motorbike with a sidecar appeared and slowly passed along the road. The rider was a German soldier wearing a helmet and goggles, the passenger in the sidecar a soldier with a peaked cap. It was only a glimpse, but it was a scene that imprinted itself on my mind with its immense significance, a sign of horror.

The road remained desolate. We stayed in our position, still keeping the door almost closed. Were there more motorbikes to come? Was our town going to be invaded that day? Were they going to enter our houses? Thoughts that made us so fearful; no one to ask, nor anyone to answer. Mother then attempted to prepare our lunch while I stayed watching the road. About an hour later I heard the sound of the motorbike again. I called Mother and she joined me, watching through the gap of the doorway. We saw the motorbike with the sidecar pass; what a relief! People reappeared outside their houses and on the road, all talking, talking, talking. We learned that they had spent the time looking at lists of men's names in our town hall. At last we had our lunch, which was much later that day.

That afternoon, people were frantically going backwards and forwards, carrying goods to hide in barns and other places thought to be safe. Those who owned cows or sheep moved them to more isolated areas or to the mountains. It was a hustle and bustle such as I had never seen before. Mother too tried to hide some of our possessions, but not being a country woman found this difficult as she wasn't as practised as the country women in lifting and carrying, and I sensed her dismay in all of this. She felt responsible for her parents too, particularly as Grandfather had not been well for some time and, obviously, she was missing Father's support and protection in these difficult and dangerous times.

Mother particularly worried about hiding all the things in our home that related to England, because she was born and brought up in Scotland. If the Germans saw that we had goods from England and found out that

Mother spoke English, it could have been catastrophic for us. So, we packed our fine English bone china cups and saucers, vases and trays with pictures of England. One of the items, which is still in my possession, was a small tin tea caddy with pictures of King Edward VII, his Queen Consort and Queen Victoria and Prince Albert. We carefully hid all these things away from our home, where we stored our firewood and amongst the straw where I kept my rabbit. Afterwards we went across the road to Mother's parents to collect my brother. As we were about to leave, Grandfather said to Mother, "Are you sure you have hidden everything pertaining to England?" Mother answered, "Yes, yes, I am sure." Grandfather then said, "You have hidden the English books?" Like an arrow Mother sped from the room and I followed. We placed the books in wicker baskets and hid them under the pile of logs for the fire, which had now become much, much bigger.

From now on we spent our evenings with Mother's parents and went back at bedtime. Grandfather always stood by his doorway watching until we were inside our home. Days went by, everyone talking about what was happening in the occupied towns nearby. We were all living in a fearful atmosphere of insecurity and danger, as if at any moment the tyrannical enemy would engulf us too.

Grandfather:
Antonio

Photographs taken before the war

Grandmother:
Maria Antonia

Father Returns

One morning before midday we had a wonderful big surprise. A miracle that we had so much wished and prayed for appeared at the door. It was my father. My own and Mother's overwhelming excitement defies description. For a moment we remained as if paralysed. We had regained a part of ourselves that had been so much missed, one essential for our very survival. The knowledge that he was alive and well and our mutual love filled our minds and every bit of space in our home. We rejoiced in the excitement of our reunion – ecstatic moments when no words or actions were necessary, just tears and embraces.

Father sat on a chair in the middle of our big kitchen. I stood on his left side, my right hand holding on to the top bar of his chair. I was happy, I was proud, I felt important. He was dressed in civilian clothing, unshaven and tired, but there was a sense of joy about him, and joy within me and especially Mother, who talked and talked while preparing lunch and moving around the kitchen as if she was dancing, because we had something very special to celebrate.

The news of his return sped round like a burst of sunlight. So many people came to see him, relatives, friends, neighbours and acquaintances, all asking how he managed to get home. He said that he was in the north of Italy but the situation became so bad that his regiment was given the order to disband; everyone was to look after themselves and try to return to their families. He had been travelling for eight days, avoiding areas that were occupied by the German army, getting lifts from one town to another and at each place gathering information from the local people about the routes that were thought to be safe, sometimes across mountains.

Many times he had to travel in the opposite direction to home, and it had been hard to work out how to reach home safely. With Father back it seemed that all our troubles were over, but little did we know what the future was going to bring.

There was no respite for Father, as from the day of his return he took full charge and started to hide more of our possessions in various ways. I was always with him, including when he dug a huge hole in the vineyard and filled it with many things, such as our best saucepans and cutlery, but Father's chief concern was to hide foodstuffs, like bottled tomato puree, a huge demijohn full of dried beans, sausages preserved in jars, bottles of olive oil and other preserves; he then placed wooden boards on the top, put back some of the earth and carefully replaced the slabs of earth with grass growing on the top. Finally, he pressed it down to bring it to the same level as the rest. The huge pile of earth he had excavated was taken to the bottom of the vineyard and scattered over a large area. With Father back I felt that Mother and I were free of all responsibilities, including those concerning Mother's parents, which Father now dealt with.

Surprise Raids

Although the Germans hadn't yet occupied our town, they would suddenly appear and take goods from our houses as well as chickens, sheep, cows and pigs for their food and, above all, men, whom they marched away at gunpoint.

A good warning system existed within the community so that when the Germans were coming the men would disappear into hiding in the fields, hills or mountains around us. Father would usually go up the narrow lane opposite our house leading to the fields and vineyards and lie down in the ditches, which were there for drainage in the winter but at this time of year were still dry. Plants, shrubs and grass grew quite high along the sides of these ditches, so they made good hiding places. When the search was over and it was thought that the Germans had left the town, I would go to tell Father and he would come home.

I knew that it was dangerous to call him from afar in case some of the soldiers were still around. Usually he saw me and would then come towards me. One evening it was getting dark before we felt they had gone. I went to get Father but he didn't see me come this time, so I went up the hill a little and then walked along one of the watercourses where I thought he might be because the wild shrubs and grass either side of it were quite high and dense. I kept looking through the shrubs and soon saw him two or three metres ahead lying face down. Then I accidentally kicked a small stone making a little noise and Father jumped up, looking very scared. I think he had fallen asleep and momentarily didn't know what was happening and I felt sorry that I had scared him. We walked back together but before we reached the road I always went ahead to make sure that there was nothing suspicious going on, then I would beckon him to come. We ate our supper and sat around the fire. It was good to be together as a family, but there was always that underlying insecurity and fear that the day had filled us with which prevented our hearts from fully rejoicing in our togetherness. The sound of footsteps, the bark of a dog, even the voice of a neighbour or relative calling, aroused immediate suspicion and uneasiness in us. It was impossible to forget our fear and allow our minds and bodies to relax and be happy.

The fear that they would come and take Father away was constant. Each step that he took I would see him looking and thinking where he could escape to if they suddenly arrived. One afternoon Father appeared carrying a very long, thick pole that he placed at the back of our house at an angle, resting on the window-sill of his bedroom on the first floor. Then he practised getting on the pole from his room, adjusting it a few times until he found the best way to quickly get on to the window-sill, mount the pole and slide down into our kitchen garden. If the Germans unexpectedly came to the front door, this was his escape route. There was much speculation that day that it wouldn't be long before they

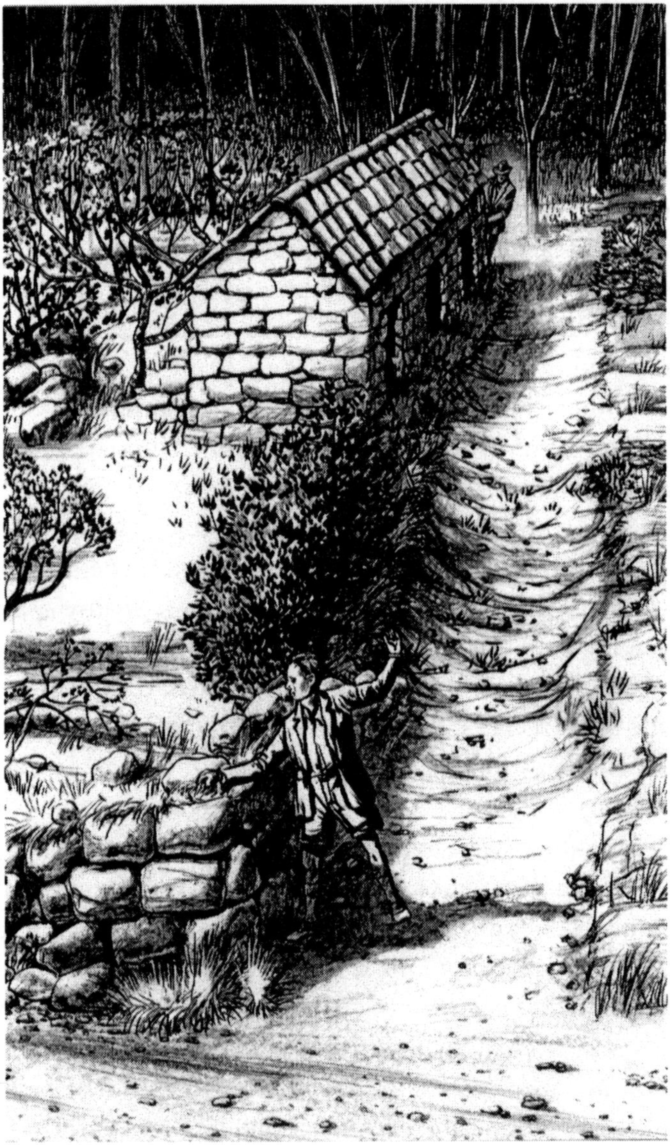

made another raid on our town. Soon, surprise search raids became more and more frequent, entering houses at gunpoint, searching in wardrobes, under beds, in stables and barns and scouring the land around the houses, all part of a blitz attack to prevent the men from escaping. We then learned that we were forbidden to own or listen to the radio and that there would be severe punishment if caught. It was also rumoured that they would soon start making night raids for men. This made Father decide to go and hide in the mountains as other men had done.

Father's and Mother's parents were landowners as well as owning sections of mountain. The part of the mountain owned by Mother's parents also had grazing land with stables and housing for the shepherds. The woodland was periodically sold to makers of charcoal, a commodity much used in certain types of stoves for cooking and for grilling. Charcoal was also used in specially designed copper pans to warm rooms in the winter. I recall Grandfather sealing deals with the charcoal makers when he sold the wood to them just by shaking hands.

So Father went to stay in the shepherds' stone-built rooms on the mountains, sleeping there at night and coming down during the day. Arriving at the foot of the mountain he would look for people working the land or approach the nearest house to ask if it was safe for him to come home. If it was thought to be safe, he would walk home across the fields, avoiding the road or open spaces. Everyone was on the lookout and any significant information about what the Germans were up to, or had done or were suspected of doing, was passed on continually. The first thing Father did when he got home was to make sure that the pole at the rear of his bedroom window was firmly in place. He continued to hide our possessions as well as those of Mother's parents, provided logs for the fire and attended to other domestic matters. With each return to the mountain he would fill his rucksack with foodstuffs to store there – potatoes, dried beans, olive oil and other preserves.

Journey to the Mountain

After a few days of Father journeying to and from the mountain, I very much wanted to go with him to the place I'd heard spoken about over many years. I begged him to take me. "Only for one day," he told me. "You will get very tired going up and coming down. I can't leave you there, I must bring you back the next day." "Sei sicuro che ci vuoi venire?" (Are you sure that you want to come?) "You will get very tired." "Si, si, si" (Yes, yes, yes) "I want to come." He then said "Sei contento?" (Are you happy?) "Si, si, si, sono molto contento" (Yes, yes, yes, I am very happy). "If all goes well, I will take you tomorrow. Today I will take more blankets, it's very cold there during the night," Father said. Mother looked at me, ruffled my hair and said, "Fai attenzione (Be careful) and do what Father tells you all the time otherwise you will get hurt, it's dangerous there." I felt that Mother was pleased to see me happy but not pleased that I was going. I waited anxiously for Father to return the next day, listening attentively to what people were saying in the hope that nothing bad would happen to prevent him coming home. I was very happy about my adventure and it seemed too long to wait for the next day to arrive, but finally it did. Father returned, dealt with the usual matters and early in the afternoon packed his rucksack.

I too had my small rucksack with some bread, cheese and fruit to eat on the way. Father gave me a walking stick he had prepared and said, "It will help you on the way up and when we come down tomorrow."

The moment of departure had come, both of us with rucksacks on our backs and holding our walking sticks. As I kissed Mother goodbye, she said, "Remember to be careful where you walk and do what Father tells you." She came out on the roadside with my brother and followed us with her eyes until we reached the corner of the road, when we waved to each other.

I felt important. My heart was beating at twice its usual rate with excitement. After a while we left the road and walked down a lane with very high hedges on either side. Before we reached the foot of the mountain we had to cross a narrow shallow river by a long slender tree trunk cut flat to walk on. Father then said, "Now you must be careful. Look a little ahead while you're crossing, not down at your feet."

Almost a hundred metres after we crossed the river we began to climb the mountain. I felt confident, determined and proud to be participating in the same task as Father, with my rucksack and walking stick. Father led the way and I followed. He kept turning round and looking at me, telling me where to walk or not to walk and to be careful. The route up to the mountain was a narrow, rough, stony track curving continually upwards.

When we reached a small plateau, clear of trees and woods with many rocks sticking out of the ground, Father found two low stones with a flattish surface on which we sat. Father said "Sei stanco?" (Are you tired?) and I said "No, sto bene" (No, I'm fine), but I certainly welcomed the rest. Father told me that the plateau was known as Frate Giacomo (Brother Jacob), as many years ago a reclusive monk called Frate Giacomo had lived in a cave on the face of the mountain. This cave never got the sun, and Frate Giacomo was often seen by shepherds and charcoal carriers on the plateau drying small amounts of produce he had been given in the sun to preserve it for the winter. He told me that about a thousand years before many monks lived in the cave, which was now called 'The Old Trinity'. Father pointed out where the cave was, in a deep recess in the mountain next to a massive ridge of rock protruding from the green and brown leaves of the dense woodland. The rock looked like a big ship in the middle of the sea.

It was nice to sit and rest, but Father looked at me and said "Vogliamo andare?" (Shall we go?) " Are you all right?" "Yes," I replied. He took my rucksack and put it on me, strapped on his own rucksack and off we went, beginning a much steeper part of our journey.

The mule and donkey track we followed was a continuous trail that spiralled up and up and up. It was all very steep climbing over bumpy rocks with hundreds of loose stones. It was impossible to take my eyes off the track otherwise I would have fallen – and I didn't want Father to regret having taken me with him. I now really understood and appreciated the importance of the walking stick for supporting and balancing myself. In places the track narrowed and went near the edge of the cliffs, and I could see the deep valley below. It was scary, but whenever there was a hazardous area to negotiate Father stopped, saying, "Fai attenzione qui" (Be careful here), watching every step I took until I had got past that point. Now and again he would say, "Are you tired, do you want to rest?" I always said "No", but my legs were feeling very tired. It was a relief when Father said, "We'll soon reach the peak, then we'll rest and have something to eat."

At long, long last we reached the peak, where nature had provided some large, solid rocks which over the centuries had formed a resting place for the many travellers on their way to different parts of the mountain – lumberjacks, shepherds, charcoal makers, cattle owners and wood carriers. We ate in the silence of the mountain, resting as my exhausted body had craved, hearing only the soft sounds of my breath; my eyes, however, were absorbed by the amazing panorama, views I could never have imagined, views of the world in which I lived that were overwhelming from this perspective. The huge, powerful mountains we faced with their scattered towns and hamlets looked so different and much closer, and the view of our town below so fascinating, large and colourful, an infinite geometric design that completely absorbed me.

Such an expanse of green fields and meadows, brown areas of ploughed earth and golden fields shining in the summer sun, all surrounded by green hedges marking the different owners. Scattered groups of houses, clusters of oak trees, the mirror-like water reservoir of the flour mills, the bell tower of our church. The gravel-covered roads that lined the town like veins looked so white against the mass of brown and green. Father's voice broke into my trance as he pointed out where our home was. I wondered what Mother and my brother were doing, I felt so far away from them now. Then Father asked "Vogliamo andare?" (Shall we go?). "Si," I replied. "We have to walk into the mountain next," said Father. "It won't be so difficult now, we have finished climbing."

There we were, Father in front and me following, walking on the undulating mule and donkey track, with many more uphill stretches than flat terrain. Tall trees and dense woods enclosed the path, their leaves just beginning to mellow into soft golden autumn colours. In some places the branches formed a canopy over the track, making it look like a tunnel to the mysterious place I had heard so much about. It was desolate, soundless, the only sign of life the noise made by our shoes over the loose stones, sliding and scraping against rocks. It felt as if we were the only two people left on earth. Our conversation now consisted of me saying, "E ancora lontano?" (Is it very far?) and Father replying, "Are you tired, do you want to rest?" I always answered the same, "No, I feel fine." Now and again Father had to wait for me as the gap between us widened but then, at long, long last, I heard him say the eagerly awaited words, "Siamo arrivati" (We have arrived). We left the track, passed under some huge chestnut trees, up a rocky mound and there on a rocky slope were two small groups of low stone-built rooms, each with its own door, their rooftops covered with terracotta tiles, dark with age, some sagging, some mossy and all with heavy stones on the corners to prevent the wind from lifting and blowing them away. All bore witness to the constant struggle against the mountain winds, rain and snow they had been subjected to over many generations. In front of the room Father and I entered was a communal well with a stone wall around it.

I popped my head inside the other shepherds' rooms. All so small, crude, no windows, just stone walls, no ceilings, just wooden rafters supporting the tiles. On the vertical supporting beams in the centre hung jackets, ropes and copper pots. The walls and rafters were darkened by the smoke from the fire in a corner of the room; there was no chimney. Everything so primitive, no one to be seen, no sounds to be heard. It seemed as if life there had ended long, long ago. Father found me wandering about and said, "Come, I'll prepare supper before it gets dark, stay with me and don't go near the well." We went back into our small, dark room, built against a huge rock and with three sides built of stones. The only light came from the open doorway. Straw and blankets on the floor where we were to sleep occupied most of one side and on the opposite side, in the corner away from the door, stood a small table with a bucket of water, a small jug to drink out of and a terracotta candle-holder with hardly enough candle to last us through our supper. Next to the table was a small chair with a wicker seat that looked as if it had seen many lives pass through. These were the only contents of our room. They left us very little space to move around.

Father took his jacket off and hung it on one of the nails at the back of the door, where he had also hung his hat. He coiled the rope he had used to draw the bucket of water from the well, hung it on the metal tube driven into the wall above the table and began to empty the foods from his rucksack into the baskets by the table.

Alone on the Mountain

It was then that Vincenzo appeared at the door. He greeted Father and looked at me in surprise. "Hey," he said, "What are you doing here, do you want to be a shepherd?" "No," I replied, "I'm going home tomorrow." Vincenzo was our next-door neighbour in the town. He was the same age as Father and they were great friends. I liked Vincenzo very much, as at home he used to let me go on his tractor and I would pretend to be driving it. He was there for exactly the same reason as Father. His place was next door, on higher ground, and he insisted we should go and eat and stay with him, which we did.

Well, Vincenzo's place was very different from ours. It had a separate kitchen, better walls, a proper fireplace with a chimney, a table, two chairs and a cupboard. It was getting dark, the mountain air was becoming colder and Vincenzo lit a huge fire in the kitchen fireplace. It was comforting to sit and rest there. I heard the shepherds returning with their flocks, but my body was feeling the effects of the day's strenuous exercise, so I stayed by the fire while Vincenzo and Father prepared supper together. One of the dishes was peppers, cooked over the charcoal fire and prepared with olive oil and garlic. I heard them talking over and over again about how much they liked the taste of garlic with the peppers and how good it was for one's health. For light there was a small lantern, moved constantly as it only gave a ghost of a light, but the huge flames from the fire gave a pleasant warm glow to the room and illuminated Father's and Vincenzo's faces as they worked in harmony together. We ate our supper sitting around the fire. They prepared a bed in the kitchen for me next to the brightly burning fire and I took off my shoes and got into the bed fully clothed. The hard journey and warmth of the fire made me sleep very soundly.

The next morning when I awoke it was so calm and silent the air seemed empty of everything until I heard two shepherds speaking outside. One of them said, "Dove porti le pecore oggi?" (Where are you taking the sheep today?) The other answered, "Dopo la valle" (Beyond the valley) and went on to say, "but you don't know what happened in the town last night." Then as they walked away I heard, "No, why? Why?" Their voices carried in the air so clearly that they seemed the only sound in the whole world. Then I heard the bleat of a sheep, then another, then another, each bleat separate and different, as if they were all learning to play the trumpet. Next I heard a shepherd abruptly mumbling to the sheep as he drove them out of the stable to the pasture. This I had to see. I got up quickly and stood by the door watching the sheep and goats passing as the shepherd steered them, gently tapping on their backs with his long walking stick. The morning air was very cold, so I went back inside where Father was lighting the fire to make breakfast. He asked if I had slept well, how my legs were feeling and if I felt up to making the journey back home later in the morning. I said yes, but my legs felt stiff. Father, Vincenzo and I were enjoying our breakfast when a man walked in and said, "Buon giorno (Good morning), be careful if you are returning to the town. Last night the Germans began to occupy our homes." Father and Vincenzo's faces were full of dismay and for a time they remained speechless, just staring at one another. Then Father said, "Why are we shocked? We knew it was coming."

Father decided that it was better if I remained there for that day and they would try to go back to see what was happening and bring more food up. He hurriedly told a man who was staying there that I would be alone and asked if he would look after me. "Don't worry," the man answered. Father left my lunch and water to drink on the small table, begging me to be careful, not to go near the well and not to go far from the rooms as I would get lost. He asked me to collect dry bits of wood from under the trees to start the fire when he returned.

The sun was bright and warm and it must have been about ten o'clock when Father and Vincenzo left, the empty rucksacks on their backs, and Father told me again, "Be careful, I'll be back before it gets dark." I went back to our room to have a drink of water and sat on the chair for a while, feeling confused and unsure of what was happening. A while later I heard footsteps advancing, so I stood up. It was the man whom Father had asked to look after me. "Are you all right?" he said. "Yes," I replied. Then he told me he was worried about what might be happening to his family, so he too would try to go back home. He said, "Don't be frightened.

Nothing will happen to you. Don't go away from here. Your father will be back later," and walked away. I immediately went to gather bits of dry wood and twigs for the fire from under the trees, wanting to impress my father and Vincenzo when they returned. I knew that the twigs and bigger pieces from the oak trees were best. After having gathered a good amount, making a heap in front of Vincenzo's place, I sorted it into two neat piles, thin twigs to start the fire with and chunkier pieces. It didn't look a lot now to impress them so I gathered some more then went and sat on a stone on the rocky mound in front of the rooms, from where I had a good view of the surrounding area and distant mountains, enjoying the warmth of the sun and the fresh, minty scent of the mountain vegetation. I felt lonely, bored and a little frightened, being in such a strange place with no one to see or speak to. It was very, very quiet and still. Sometimes I heard the muted bark of a sheepdog or the sound of a shepherd coming from the distant mountain, then all went quiet again. I felt lost in a soundless world, wishing that Father would come back sooner than before dark as he had promised and bitterly regretting having come to the mountain. Only the sun was there to comfort me. I went on sitting on the large stone, facing the sun, waiting and waiting for the day to go by, all alone and in complete silence.

I thought of my mother and brother and wondered what they were doing. The sun on my face made me feel sleepy. Time seemed to have stood still. Then I heard the faint, gentle sound of a bell, then again, so I stood up and listened more attentively. Yes, it was a sweet ring in that silent world and seemed to be getting nearer and nearer, ding ding, ding ding, ding ding, over and over again. I fixed my eyes on the brow of the hill from where the sound was coming and waited, hearing it get nearer and nearer. Then all at once, from among the woods and rocks, appeared the head of a donkey wearing a collar around its neck with a tiny bell hanging on it. Each time the donkey took a stride and nodded its head, the bell rang. Following the donkey were two shepherds. I knew them both and went towards them, pleased to see them. "Berto cosa fai?" (Berto what are you doing?) they said. I replied, "Aspetto che ritorna mio padre" (I am waiting for my father to return). I stayed by their side, looking on as they prepared their lunch. One began to peel potatoes. I followed the one who went to draw a bucket of water from the well for the donkey and stroked its head, which it liked. It seemed docile, had calm eyes and I thought we had become friends. I asked the shepherd why the donkey wore a bell. He answered, "The donkey wanders away to graze in the woodland and the bell around its neck helps us to find it."

The fire to cook their meal was lit in a niche in the wall outside their room. It was black with soot. A strong metal chain hung in the centre with a movable metal hook on which to hang the bucket-like copper pot above the fire. They too had thin dry twigs and bigger pieces of wood, but their fire was started by lighting a few handfuls of crisp, dry leaves.

Now and then the flames were encouraged by gently blowing air on the fire through a long metal tube. Seeing them cutting big slices of bread from a round loaf made me hungry, so I went to eat the lunch Father had left me. I soon went back to the shepherds, hoping to spend more time in their company, but to my disappointment they were about to go back to their sheep with the donkey. Again I was all alone in that soundless forsaken wilderness, void of everything I knew. I tried to amuse myself by playing with stones and twigs, making a stable and pen for my imaginary sheep, but the day seemed to drag on and on and on. I wondered what Father was doing and what would happen if he and Vincenzo were captured and decided that I would ask one of the shepherds to take me home. I went back and sat in Vincenzo's kitchen. It was cold there without a fire and my arms and legs had goose-pimples. Feeling restless, I went back on top of the rocky mound. The sun was still there. It was boring just sitting and it wasn't yet time for Father to return, so I walked around for a while just looking, but there was nothing really to look at, it was all rocks and woods and a few very old, sad stables that only made me feel melancholy.

Now there was an old man in one of the rooms, but I couldn't see him properly as it was dark in the room and sunny where I was. He was repairing something and saw me but didn't say anything. I felt I shouldn't be there so I went back to the mound, but the sun had gone by now and I felt really cold. I walked along the path in the direction Father would come from, but the tall trees and high hedges either side made it very gloomy and I was frightened of getting lost, so I returned to the mound.

It was beginning to get dark, and so cold without the

sun. My legs and knees were all goose-pimples and I shivered continually. I wished I had long trousers like grown-up men. I knew it was getting late because the shepherds were coming back with their sheep. I even saw the donkey with the bell coming back, but I wasn't interested in him any more. All I wanted was Father to return, so I stood on a big high rock stretching myself so I could see further along the path from where he and Vincenzo would come.

I waited and waited, feeling cold, lost and sad. I listened for the sound of footsteps over the stones, but all I could hear was my nervous breath. I kept looking in the gaps below the high hedge along the path hoping and hoping to see them coming. It was then, in the subdued glow of the evening light and total silence, that the empty air brought me the wonderful sound of the fine two-tone whistle Father always gave to call or announce himself to me and my brother. This time it was the most exciting sound I could ever have wished for. I could only see two full sacks moving above the hedge and I ran to meet them, forgetting the day's misery, my mind and body both rejoicing. As I approached them I saw their heads bent stiffly to one side as each balanced a heavy sack on their shoulders as well as carrying full rucksacks. Their faces were anxious and weary. Father handed me his walking stick, touched my head and said, "Stai bene?" (Are you all right?) in a breathless voice expressing total exhaustion. I walked behind him, Vincenzo following, without another word being spoken as we went the few hundred metres to the rock mound then into Vincenzo's kitchen. They put their heavy loads on the floor, then Father sat on a chair and leant forward, his forearms resting on his knees, head bent down.

Vincenzo sat resting his elbows on the table holding his face between his hands. Both were breathing heavily as if they had just finished a race. After a few moments they looked at each other, just staring, communicating nothing, seeming dazed and unable to speak. A shepherd walked in saying, "Hey, buona sera" (Hey, good evening) "you are back." They both straightened their slumped bodies, Vincenzo saying "E scuro" (It's dark) as he picked up the oil lamp to light it.

Father put his hand on my shoulder and said, "Hai fame?" (Are you hungry?) "We have brought food already cooked and we'll eat soon." Vincenzo said to Father, "I'll light the fire, you put the food on the table." The shepherd asked, "Che succede?" (What's happening?) and Father replied, "It's better you don't know." "E cosi male?" (Is it that bad?) asked the shepherd. Father's answer was: "We hide the food we have worked for as if we've stolen it. We have to leave our families and hide as if we are criminals." Vincenzo then said: "We are no longer owners of our homes, nor of our possessions. My wife has to bring my little girl to the foot of the mountain for me to see her. Is this living? Is it human?"

The shepherd, hearing about their difficult day and sadness of mind, started to leave, saying, "Let's hope it will all soon be over, ci vediamo domani" (We will see each other tomorrow). "Buona notte" (Goodnight). I was disappointed that the shepherd went because with him present there would have been more conversation, it might have been more cheerful. Soon we had a huge fire and a table full of food. We ate sitting around the fire in total silence except for the sparkling and crackling of the burning wood I had gathered, reminding me of my day's misery, while the glowing flames lit up the two exhausted and dispirited faces.

Lost

Father told me I would have to remain on the mountain. "It's easier for Mother," he said. "We'll go back when the Germans have gone." I answered, "Yes", but I was so disappointed because I felt very sad being there all on my own, with no one to speak or listen to. When I did see others they were older people and they spoke to one another as if I wasn't present. I wished I knew how many more days I had to stay there.

I had now been living on the mountain for quite a number of days. Father and I ate and slept in our small dark room. We cooked against the wall outside the room, where the branches of a huge tree gave some protection against the rain. It was my job to keep the fire going, but sometimes the strong winds made it difficult to control the flames and Father had to come to deal with it so the fire wouldn't go out. I very much regretted having come to this boring, God-forsaken place, but I couldn't ask Father to take me back home as he always looked so tired and stressed. When men who were staying in other parts of the mountain came to see Father and Vincenzo, all I heard them talk about was the danger we were all in and how aggressive, arrogant and cruel the German soldiers were. I sensed the fear in everyone, which also saddened me.

It was just another monotonous day when Father left for the town. He hoped to be able to go home undetected as there was so much Mother couldn't do on her own, also he wanted to give her moral support. This time I was left in the care of Vincenzo, who had decided not to go that day. As always, before Father left he told me not to go away from the shelters and that he would be back before dark. His last words were: "and be careful".

Soon after lunch that day, Vincenzo said that he was going to cut and split some tree trunks for firewood and left carrying a huge hatchet with a long handle, an equally big sledgehammer, a big bottle of water and two metal wedges to help split the tree trunks. The wedges were tied each end of a short piece of rope. He placed the centre of the rope at the back of his neck with the two metal wedges balanced either side of his chest; all this told me that he was going to be away for the whole afternoon. I felt disappointed that Vincenzo was not going to be around and I would be left alone again.

Shortly afterwards, I saw a shepherd. I went over to him and he told me that he was going to return some goats he had been looking after to the owner, who was in another part of the mountain. He said I could go with him but it was a long way and he wouldn't be back until the evening, when it was getting dark. "You'd better come with me," he insisted, "otherwise you'll be all on your own." I felt uneasy about going in case Father returned before me, so I said no. He then told me that if I went part of the way, there were hazelnut trees and still a lot of nuts on the ground which I could collect, fill my pockets and come back, so I agreed. We set off with the goats, which he guided with a long walking stick through a narrow path down a valley towards another mountain, and eventually reached the hazelnut trees. I don't remember if we found any hazelnuts, but what I do remember is him telling me how to get back, where to turn right and where left along the path we had just taken.

I started making my way back slowly, but after walking for some time I realised that by now I should have reached the place where we were staying. I also became aware that the path was not the same one I had walked along an hour or so before. It was more overgrown, and the woods on either side were closing into each other so I had to hold branches aside in order to get through. I turned back to where the path was joined by another, clearer and wider, but I still didn't remember having been there before. I was worried I might get lost so I began to run, keeping my eyes on the path because of the rocks sticking out of the ground and the crevices, loose stones and slippery earth. I ran round one bend after another, sometimes up, sometimes down, until I came to a less densely wooded part where there was more light, looked around and realised I was near the bottom of a valley. The hill in the direction I felt I should go was mostly rock, and I thought that if I climbed to the top I would be able to see the roofs of our shelters and make my way towards them. I was becoming frightened now. I climbed as quickly as I could, struggling through rocks, thorns, shrubs and slippery ground, all the time thinking that when I managed to reach the top I would see the shelter roofs, but when I did, I found myself facing another, much higher hill with a deep and densely wooded valley below me. I was panting now and so frightened that I began to cry. I just stood there sobbing, feeling completely lost and confused, until I remembered that Vincenzo was somewhere among the mountains cutting the tree trunks. I called his name as loudly as I could, elongating the sound, "Vincenzooo! Vincenzooo!", then listened for a response. It was as silent as could be except for the thump, thump, thump of my heart and my heavy breathing, which were interfering with my listening. I turned in all directions, calling and calling Vincenzo so loudly that my throat began to hurt and I couldn't shout any more. I stood there dazed, feeling lost and very frightened, then the sound of a single distant whistle penetrated my senses. I responded by hoarsely calling Vincenzo's name.

I listened and heard the whistle a second time. I called Vincenzo again, and when I heard the whistle a third time I realised it was the whistle of a bird. Angrily I shouted back, "Stai zitto tu!" (Be quiet, you!). The whistle had brought me out of my daze, though, giving me momentary hope, and I began to think what I could do in my horrible situation. Seeing that the hill opposite was even higher, I imagined that if I climbed to the top I would be able to see the roof tops, but first I had to go down into the deep valley. Crying bitterly I started to descend, battling my way downhill over stones that rolled noisily, often stopping to decide the best way. The concentration needed for this difficult and dangerous descent made me stop crying, but when I reached the bottom of the valley there was no sun. The dense woods blotted out the light so much that I thought it was getting dark, and the fear that I would still be lost when it became completely dark returned and made me start to cry again.

Slowly I began to climb the very high hill, convincing myself that from there I would see the roof tops of our shelters. I wanted to stop crying but I couldn't, and the more I climbed the steeper it became. Then I found myself by a very steep ravine that I couldn't climb and had to make my way out sideways. Now I could see near the top where the sun was still shining, and although that relieved some of my fears the climb was becoming impossible. I was exhausted and kept falling, scratching my legs and arms, having to squeeze through barriers of shrubs and thorns. Often I found myself face to face with high rocks or obstructed by rocks and woods so that I had to go some way down again and attempt my climb from another direction.

I came to an enclosure that had a massive rock and high earth bank to one side with dense woodland on the top. There was a big hole in a corner leading to the next level, probably a passage used by foxes, which I tried to crawl up, it but it was so steep and the earth so powdery that I kept sliding back. Despairing, I started to cry so hard that I couldn't see for tears. I kept wiping my eyes with my hands but they were sticky with earth and perspiration and dirt got in one eye. My tears soon cleaned the eye, but they still blinded me. I sat on a stone sobbing hysterically and when next I wiped my eyes I used my forearms so as not to get dirt in them. After resting for a while I made further attempts at crawling up the fox tunnel. Persistence got me through in the end,

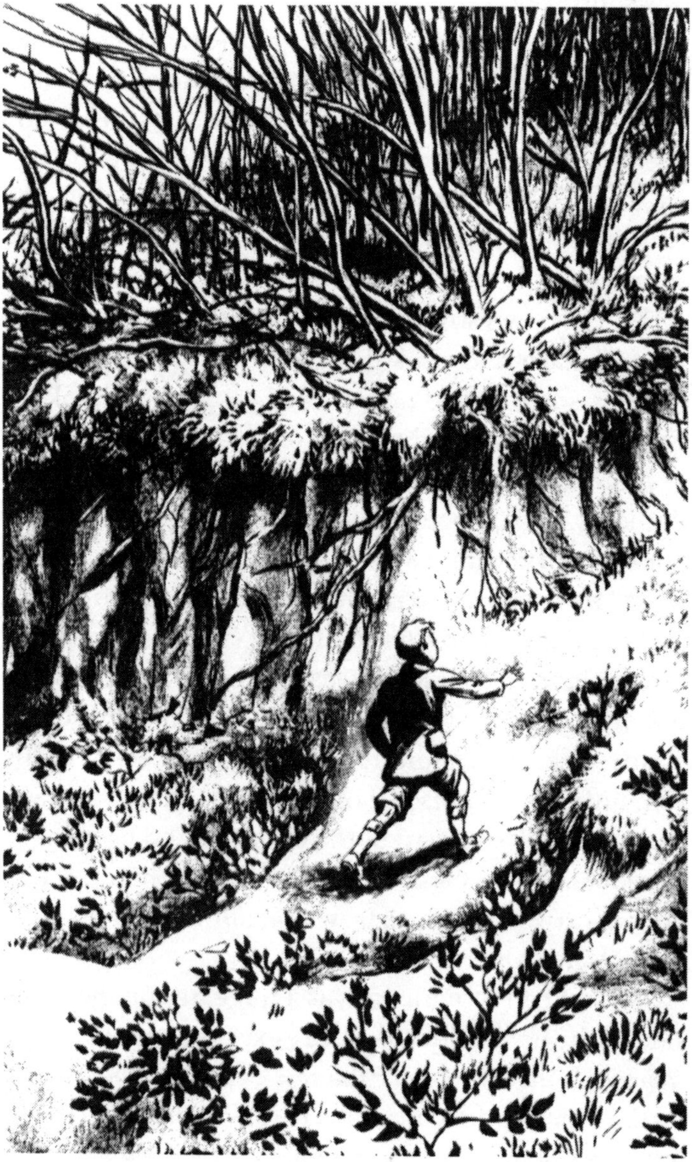

but it seemed to have taken such a long time to climb this short way.

I could see now that I was near the top, so I pushed on until I found myself on the crest of the hill, but after all that turmoil, exhausted, fearful, panting and sobbing, my heart thumping, all I saw before me was an expanse of rocks and dense woodland, still and empty of life. I used every bit of energy left in me to squeeze out a call to Vincenzo, only to hear back the echo of my own strained voice. After a few calls I gave up and started to walk downwards in a state of total despair, sobbing and taking deep gasps that shook the upper part of my body. I kept on walking until I came to a donkey track, where I noticed the shoe marks of donkeys and sheep's droppings. This revived my hopes, but I couldn't stop the gasping, which began to worry me. I started to run along this undulating track, turning one corner after another. Whenever I stopped I felt pain in my ankles, knees and hip joints, but what disturbed me most was that I still couldn't control the sudden gasps shaking my body. And then I saw something I recognised, something that told me I was heading towards a part of the mountain I'd been taken to some days earlier, where a shepherd called Fortunato was living. He was from our town and I knew him well.

What I had recognised was a huge tree on the lower side of the track with a partially exposed root like a big tree trunk that went over the track and into the ground on the higher side of the hill, creating a steep step that I had to raise my leg to step over. On I went as fast as I could, stopping now and then to look at the changing landscape for a clue as to where the shelters and Fortunato might be.

I was at the bottom of a valley when I saw on the brow of a hill some stone shelters and a thatched stable where I hoped I would find Fortunato. I turned into the track leading to the shelters, stopped and called Fortunato's name as loudly as I could, then listened for a response. The response – so sudden that it made me jump – was the bleat of many sheep that I couldn't see but which were only about two metres away over the high edge of the track. I think my sudden shout in their soundless world had scared them too. I called again, but again only the sheep replied.

I continued to walk up the track, and when next I raised my head there stood Fortunato and another shepherd in front of the thatched stable, both wearing caps. They looked stunned, unable to believe my sudden appearance. As I approached I saw them looking at one another, adjusting their caps, moving their feet, their faces expressing total bewilderment. My distress was so obvious that they spontaneously exclaimed "Berto! Cosa fai qui?" (Berto! What are you doing here?). Speaking hurriedly and nervously, I told them I had been lost all afternoon and asked if they would take me back very quickly. They asked me which direction I had come from, and when I told them they suggested I should go back the same way, stay on the track and eventually I would arrive where I was staying. I begged them to take me back as I was so frightened of getting lost again. They agreed, but first they had to regroup the sheep otherwise some of them could get separated from the flock.

I asked them to hurry so I would be back before Father, also not to tell anyone so Father wouldn't find out as he was always telling me not to move away from the shelters, and they promised they wouldn't. On the way back I wanted them to walk fast or run with me, so I kept a little in front, turning back to look at them to show my anxiety and concern to return before Father, but it didn't work. They just walked calmly on, chatting, unaware of my day's ordeal, which had left me feeling so insecure. Eventually they told me that the shelters weren't very far now and I could continue on my own. Again I begged them to take me all the way, stressing how frightened I was of getting lost again, and they agreed, telling me to stop rubbing my eyes as they were very red. I wasn't aware that I was rubbing my eyes; what was worrying me more was that the deep gasps that made the upper part of my body tremble were coming back. Unable to control them, I wanted them to go away before I saw Father. Finally we reached the shelters and the shepherds went back. I entered the dismal dark room that Father and I lived in, found he hadn't returned yet and sat on our chair. I was so relieved to be back safely, but I felt disorientated and couldn't believe it was really true.

After a while I went outside the door. There was no more sun, it was beginning to get dark, and I was still gasping and shaking. I felt restless and went back into the room and sat down, then went outside again to see how dark it was. I wanted it to be really dark so Father wouldn't notice my red eyes or the grazes on my arms and legs that I kept pulling my socks up to hide. I went back into the room, really dark by now, and waited for Father to return.

After a while, I heard Father's two-tone whistle announcing his return. He entered the room, put down the sack he was carrying on his shoulder, took his rucksack off and in an exhausted voice said, "Are you all right? I have brought the food already cooked, in a while we will eat." I was so pleased to see him but I didn't want him to see me, so I stayed away from the meagre light of the candle. We ate and went to sleep close to each other on the straw.

The next morning I was awakened by Father calling me in a loud voice, "Berto, Berto, svegliati" (Wake up), "it's late, I've been calling you for some time, aren't you well?" I replied, "I am well", but I felt so sleepy and dazed I could hardly think where I was. He said, "Vincenzo and I are going to try to go home again today and bring more goods here. We're leaving now." I lifted my head. The door was slightly open to give the room some light, and I could see Father's worried face. Then he said, "Get up, eat what I've prepared for you. Your lunch is on a separate plate. It's in the big plate with the lid on it, and be careful, do you understand?"

As he opened the door fully to leave, I could see by the strong daylight that it was late. I heard Vincenzo's voice saying, "Sei pronto adesso?" (Are you ready now?) "Andiamo" (Let's go). Father replied, "I'm coming, I'm coming", but didn't move from the doorway. I kept my head raised to reassure him I was all right, but I could hardly make sense of what was going on, my body felt heavy and my head as if it had been battered. Father remained by the door staring at me, but I was in the dark corner of the room so he couldn't see me properly. He looked confused and uncertain. Again he said, "But aren't you feeling well?" I replied, "I am well, I am well." "Che ti fa male?" (What's hurting you?) he asked. "Niente, niente" (Nothing, nothing) I replied. "If you need anything," he said gently, "ask the others around here. Vincenzo's father has arrived this morning, go to him, they all know I'm not here, have you understood? And be careful." I heard Vincenzo's voice again calling to Father, "Hey, let's go, it's getting late" and the sound of their boots on the stony ground as they moved away. Remembering the turmoil of the previous day, I could have stayed curled up in my corner of the room for ever and ever so the memory would go away.

I remember being awakened again by the strong voice of a man. It was Vincenzo's father. "Hey, aren't you feeling well? It's past midday. You couldn't do this if your father was here, get up." I started to get up without saying anything, trying to show I was sorry and ashamed. He went out, saying, "If you need anything, come to see me", leaving the door fully open. I sat on our only chair and had something to eat, but I wasn't hungry, it was just something to do. I still felt sleepy, dazed and heavy. I would have liked to have gone back to sleep, but I was afraid Vincenzo's father would come back and tell me off. As I became more aware, I was pleased Father wasn't there, I felt that by the time he returned I would have overcome my fear and the tight feeling on the skin of my face. I didn't want Father to find out about my ordeal of the previous day, which would have added to his enormous problems and worries.

Feeling restless, I went out and walked around the shelters to see who was about. There was a man called Antonio with his son repairing a small thatched roof and I saw Vincenzo's father and two other men I didn't know.

They all looked worried and preoccupied. Once I had seen them I just walked away, not wanting to be seen or to talk. I kept going to sit in our room for a few minutes then went out again, over and over again. I felt so lonely, but I didn't want to speak to anyone, not that day. It wasn't until the evening that I began to feel better. I appreciated being safe and became increasingly aware that I was all right and was not going to let it happen again. So I went to my favourite place, the rocky mound in front of Vincenzo's rooms. It was still sunny there and I had a good view around me with some flat space if I wanted to play with my pretend sheep's stable and pen and my imaginary sheep, but I just sat there, comforted by the warmth of the sun on my face. It was from there too that I always awaited Father's return and now I was waiting for him again.

Time seemed to go more slowly than a snail. I waited and waited, but by now I was used to waiting and since my horrid experience of the day before, nothing, but nothing, would worry me very much. I wanted to see Father so much now and to be close to him and look at his face, because the night before I hadn't looked at him.

I had kept myself out of his sight, away from the light of the candle so he wouldn't see my face.

As the long hours passed, I realised that I was feeling calmer, more at ease and not in the state of despair and guilt of the night before. I was eager to be with Father now I felt like this. I wanted to support him to make up for not looking at him the night before and to feel less guilty about keeping my terrible secret from him. It wouldn't have happened had I obeyed his constant request each time he left to be careful and not to move away from the shelters. I knew that it wasn't time yet for him to return as it was still quite light and I had accepted it was always beginning to get dark when Father returned. I just sat on my usual stone feeling aware and grateful that I was safe; this time even the silence felt good.

As I rested sleepily in that silent world where all was still and lifeless, I was surprised by the unmistakable sound of Father's whistle. I ran to meet him. He was heavily loaded and looked exhausted. Vincenzo was the same, following a few steps behind. It was still light, so Father and I would be together for a longer time before we went to sleep. In our room Father placed his heavy load on the floor and sat on our chair. I just stood by him, listening to his heavy breathing. For a moment or two my mind went back to the horror of the previous day and I felt bad that I was keeping this secret from Father. He soon stood up, drank some water from our terracotta jug and said, "Are you hungry?" "Yes," I replied as he added, "Soon we will eat. In a minute I will light the fire."

Father was very capable, methodical and quick when

he had to do something and was like that when he cooked our meals. He lit the fire between the two huge stones that leant against the wall outside our room with a space between them. The copper pot rested on the stones.

It was my job to keep an even fire under the copper pot. Often I had to call on Father for his help, as the strong winds would almost put the fire out. This time I gave the fire all my attention and Father didn't have to see to it even once. It made me happy for us to be working together. He had brought beans and tomato sauce already cooked, so we boiled pasta then added the beans and tomato sauce to it. It was still light and we sat next to each other on the tree trunk outside our room eating huge plates of pasta e faggioli. I began to regain some confidence as I tried to forget the terrifying ordeal of the day before.

Bad News from the Town

Each day someone from the mountain would make an attempt to go to or near the town. If not from our group, there were others staying in other parts of the mountain who would try to go, so we were well informed on what was happening on a daily basis, such as: had the troops changed, was there a greater number of soldiers than before, had they been searching for men that day, where was the huge amount of ammunition that had arrived being stored, whose houses had been taken over, the demands made on women and older men to wash clothes, cook, clean stables where soldiers kept their horses, provide wood for their fires and perform other domestic chores. This news usually reached us towards the end of each day. It was what everyone waited for and was all-important, since people longed for a glimpse of hope, some change for the better in the awful situation that was preventing everyone from living their lives as they wanted and were used to. Days and weeks passed, and people spoke of little else but the war, always with the hope that soon the Allies' soldiers would come and free us from this tyranny. It was this thought that gave everyone the strength to endure, to suffer and struggle against the unacceptable, hoping that soon the catastrophe would be over. That was what people yearned for and believed, but the activities that continued to take place did not offer much hope.

Father and Vincenzo returned one evening with news that a new battalion had come to the town, taking over more houses, confiscating goods, behaving even more aggressively and with such arrogance that people were becoming afraid and beginning to leave their houses. The few who had or could get any form of shelter came to the mountain. Anyone who had relatives in Rome or any region thought to be safer went there. Others just abandoned their homes to search for places that weren't occupied by the German army. My father's parents, two brothers and two sisters went to the part of the mountain where I had met the shepherd Fortunato. Mother's parents also left their home, but as Grandfather wasn't in good health, Father decided they should only go about a quarter of the way up the mountain to stay where there was a chapel called La Trinita (The Trinity). Mother accompanied them to the foot of the mountain where Father was waiting to take them up to the chapel. Father had to make many journeys to carry blankets, pots and provisions for them. He found a stable with some hay near the chapel and carried the hay to them so they wouldn't have to sleep on the bare stone floor. The town became almost void of people, except for a few old men and courageous women like Mother who could not just abandon their homes and all their valued possessions that could not be hidden. They were also depended on to supply provisions, things like potatoes, cornflour, dried beans, smoked sausages, salted hams and other preserves, which were hidden in various places. They met together at night to make bread, a very important food for us all, in some isolated farmhouse.

Danger on the Mountain

People also came to take refuge where we were from Atina, the next town to ours. Within a few days about forty people arrived. All had their own fearful story to tell and looked as lost as I had felt in my first few days there, struggling to carry their possessions in suitcases, bags, sacks and boxes, as well as blankets and provisions. Although their town was near ours, they spoke with a different accent. Some were housed in stables, others constructed shacks by cutting thin tree trunks and branches to make the basic structure then using any other type of material they could carry, like canvas, boards and thin sheets of metal. The shacks protected them from the rain but only partly from the wind. The quiet, lonely place was now full of people for me to see and listen to. The women from Atina gathered around the well, where someone would draw buckets of water for them to fill their containers, telling them not to waste water. The women moaned how cold and uncomfortable they had been that night; others said they didn't sleep at all. The mountain air was now very cold from sunset to sunrise. They would speak of all the comforts they had at home, how their big kitchen stove warmed the whole house, but I couldn't understand why they spoke of something they couldn't have now. Each time someone returned from having been to their town, people gathered around wanting to know what was happening there and whether they had seen a certain relative or neighbour, was it still possible to buy food, how safe was it to go back? Each stable or shack was full to the very last bit of space with sleeping arrangements, provisions, cases of clothing and people's valuables. It was also the kitchen, although cooking had to be done outside in the open.

During the day people could only gather outside, always looking for a sunny spot to try to keep warm. When I sensed that the men were speaking about important matters concerning the war I always tried to listen. I became aware that as I approached them they changed the subject, so I began to stay within listening distance pretending to play. If I suspected that they were aware of my listening, I would quietly start to sing, then listen a little more followed by another quiet song. I could never properly hear what was being said except that I knew it was bad because I used to hear the words "sono crudele" (they are cruel), "assassini" (assassins), "uccisi" (killed).

Apart from cutting and carrying wood for the fire to cook and warm themselves, the men from Atina had nothing to do. Their pastime was playing card games. One day, nearing lunchtime, I was sitting on my rock mound enjoying the warmth of the sun. About two hundred metres from me, on lower ground, were about twelve to fifteen young men, some sitting and some lying on the grass, all playing card games in three groups. Now and again I would turn and look at them, particularly when there was an argument or a burst of laughter, as their voices carried clearly and loudly in the quiet empty space. Otherwise all was very peaceful. As I sat in the silence and calmness, comforted by the warmth of the sun, which sent me almost into a trance, I was suddenly shocked back to reality. I heard one of the card players shout "Tedeschi!" (Germans!), jumped up to look and saw all the card players taking off fast and, like a flock of frightened birds, scattering and disappearing into the woodland, leaving all the cards spread on the grass. At the same time I saw two German soldiers with pistols in their hands running after them. I quickly ran into Vincenzo's kitchen, where he and Father were preparing lunch. As I was hurriedly telling them what was happening, we heard two shots.

Father bent forward to face me, placed his hands on my shoulders and speaking very quickly and nervously, said, "You go where the women are, go where the women are and stay with them. Do you understand?" "Si, si," I replied. Like lightning both disappeared. I felt frightened and confused, and thinking that I might meet the soldiers as I went out of the door, I remained inside the kitchen with the door closed and my heart pounding, waiting and listening in anticipation of the noise of the German soldiers' footsteps over the rocky ground. I wanted to go where the women were but I didn't have the courage to leave the room. After about half an hour I casually went out to my rock mound, pretending to get a few pieces of firewood. While bent forward picking up bits of wood, I had a good look around. All seemed to be quiet, so I went to the edge of the valley and quietly called Father. After a few minutes Father and Vincenzo

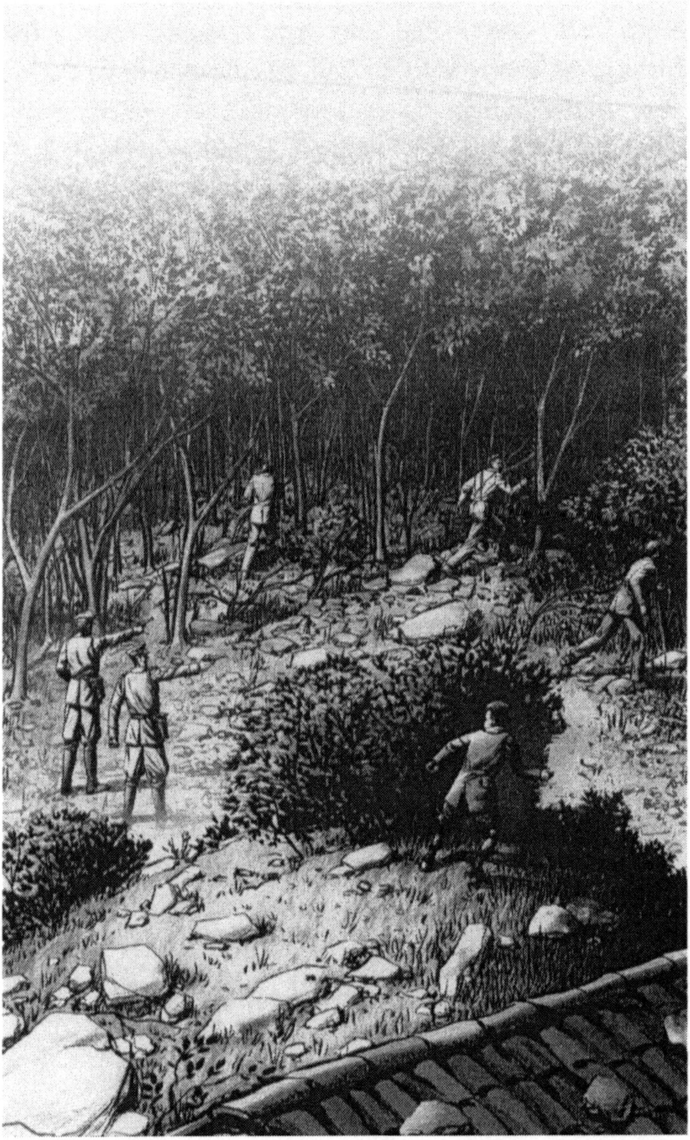

cautiously appeared from behind some trees and I told them I thought the Germans had gone. They urged me to go back, saying that they would return soon. I felt Father was annoyed that I had taken a chance in calling them as the soldiers could have still been around, and I returned to Vincenzo's kitchen. About half an hour later Father and Vincenzo came back, first Father and a few minutes later Vincenzo, and we had lunch while watch was being kept. Now, the men knew that it was no longer safe to feel free even on the mountain.

The Invisible Hand

Father continued to go to the foot of the mountain at prearranged days and times, when Mother would be waiting with provisions for him to take to her parents, now staying in the chapel. He then went back, loaded himself with goods for us and returned to where we were staying. On his arrival, if he hadn't seen me, he would make his distinctive whistle and I would immediately go to him and stay by his side in our room while he sat on our chair and rested, regaining his breath after the exhausting climb with his heavy load. Usually he drank a jug of water. For a minute or two his face looked tired, pensive and distant. His first words to me were always the same: "Are you all right? Are you hungry? Soon I will cook and we will eat." Even if I was hungry I would say "No" so as not to worry him. He would hand me a fruit or something, saying, "Mother has sent you this, she is missing you and will see you soon when the Germans have gone". Then all at once he would stand up and quickly unpack, draw a bucket of water from the well, light the fire between the stones outside our room and cook something Mother had prepared. All this had to be done before dark and I always played my part in trying to keep the fire going.

One evening while we were having our meal, Father told me that the next day he would go and fetch my six-year-old brother Enio so Mother would be freer to provide our needs and protect what we had at home. I understood why my brother had to come up as it was now well known that the soldiers had become more threatening. I did hear Father say that if the Allied Forces didn't come soon our town would become a battleground because of the large number of soldiers and big guns installed there.

It was usually dark after our meal so we went to sleep next to each other on the straw on the floor with blankets over us. In no time Father fell into a heavy sleep and all I could hear was the sound of his exhausted breathing. The next morning, after breakfast, Father left to collect my brother at the foot of the mountain where Mother would hand him over. He told me he would not be late coming back that day.

I wasn't as bored or lonely now as I used to be because there were a lot of people around, but that afternoon I did spend much of the time on the mound looking over the path, waiting for Father and my brother to appear. It was still light and sunny when I heard the sound of Father's whistle. At first I didn't think he had brought my brother as I could only catch glimpses of his legs as he passed along the path, but the moment he stepped into the open, not so heavily loaded, carrying only the rucksack on his back, I knew that he had brought my brother, who soon appeared a little way behind. I was very pleased to see him. "Mum and I have always fed your rabbit," he said. His face looked tired and lost as he glanced around the place. Well, I was an expert on the area surrounding the shelters now, so I took him round showing how much I knew. Since he was only six years old, I felt responsible for looking after him in this strange and difficult environment. There were three of us now sleeping on the floor of our small dark room. I did wish that Mother would come there too.

The next morning I was busy telling people who my brother was. Then I showed him the stables and told him where he shouldn't go because it was dangerous. The morning passed very quickly. In the afternoon Father said that we were going to cut some wood for the fire. The three of us set off and had to walk for about ten minutes to reach the place where we got the firewood. On the way we came across a sloping strip of terrain, clear of woods with grass cropped close by sheep and white rocks sticking out of the ground. Some of the rocks were nearly as high as I was. I felt happy because Father hadn't gone away that day and my brother was with us. I started going down the slope a little faster, pretending I was driving a tractor around the rocks, making a tractor noise and pretending to be steering. The sloping ground continued into a small piece of cultivated land overgrown with some tallish plants that had not been reaped. They had dried during the hot summer months and were lying flat on the ground. Walking on the dried bed of plants was fun because it was bouncy, as if I were walking on a soft cushion, so I started going a little faster, raising one leg high and then the other, jumping and bouncing along the field. Then all at once I distinctly felt a man's right hand pressing on my chest, immediately stopping me – I say right hand because I could feel each finger and thumb. It was a strong hand, as if someone was standing in front of me holding me back, but as there was no one there I turned my head expecting to see someone behind me, but all I could see were my father and brother peacefully walking along quite a way back. I turned my head to the front again, but there was no one to be seen, then glanced around the field and saw that the woodland was too far away for anyone to run and hide there so quickly. A slight noise made me look at my feet and I saw I had disturbed the earth near the opening of a well level with the ground and it was going gluck, gluck, gluck as it hit the water in the well. My next footstep would have taken me right in the well. The thought of what would have happened had I not been stopped sent a wave of shock through my whole body. For a few seconds my legs felt paralysed and I saw the goose-pimples on my arms as my body trembled. It took all the courage I could muster to take one step backwards, turn and go back to my father and my brother. I walked quietly behind them and stayed close to my father for the rest of that day.

Father had to go and meet Mother the following morning for provisions, more blankets and other possessions to carry back and prevent them being taken. After breakfast he prepared our lunch and before he went begged me to be careful and look after my brother. "Take care," he said again, "don't leave Enio alone, not even for a minute, he doesn't know his way around this place, he could get lost or hurt himself. Don't go away from the shelters and if you need anything, go to Vincenzo. Promise me that you'll be careful." "Yes, yes," I answered sincerely, still in the grip of the fear I had experienced the day before. To look after my brother was easy, he just followed me everywhere I went, stopped when I stopped, sat when I sat, even drank water from the jug when I did. It was only his third day there and it was still very strange to him. He was very quiet, especially as Mother and Father were not with us, I suppose. After we had eaten the lunch Father had prepared for us he curled up on the bed of straw on the floor and fell asleep. He was probably tired because of following me around. I sat on our chair watching him for a while, then started going in and out of the room. Each time I heard a voice I went to see who it was, but soon returned to sit on our chair. There was not much to look at in our room, just the chair I sat on, the small table with the bucket of water on top, the water jug, the terracotta candle-holder and candle and the coiled rope hanging on the wall. Our provisions were piled up under and beside the table. It was very boring, especially as the room was so dark. Each time I went out I faced the well, which was only a few metres from our room and, although it had a high strong stone wall around its opening, was a horrible reminder of my experience the day before.

Sitting in the gloomy room waiting for my brother to wake up I felt distressed, restless and insecure thinking of the despair my father would have suffered had the invisible hand not stopped me. I felt guilty because he was always telling me to be careful, not to run and to look where I put my feet, and I never obeyed him. I also felt guilty because now I was keeping two secrets from him, the first when I got lost and now the horrifying incident of the well. I couldn't burden Father with my horrible experiences, it would have made him suffer too much.

The bark of a dog woke my brother. It was getting cold and we went out of the room to my rock mound and sat facing the weak winter sun. Enio asked, "When will Father come back?" "Tonight," I answered. "When will we eat?" "Tonight," I answered. "When will the sheep come back?" "Tonight," I answered. The day seemed endless. The sun was my clock – I wanted to see it hide behind the higher mountains because Father always returned before dark. Then unexpectedly, Father returned much earlier than usual. He didn't announce himself with his usual whistle this time, he just appeared on the mound and must have seen our lost, cold and miserable faces. He put on a great act pretending to be happy. "Hey, how are you, are you cold?" he exclaimed. "I am going to light a big fire and we will all warm up. Mother has sent you some cake and a very nice meal. Come and help me make the fire. As soon as the war has finished we are going to have a very big feast. Come and see what Mother has sent you." We returned to our room and he gave us a piece of cake each. We waited until the fire was lit, warmed ourselves up and soon after had our meal. Then came the best part of the day, both of us sleeping either side of Father.

Moving On

As time passed there were no signs that the war would end soon, nor that the Allied soldiers were getting any closer to liberating us from the enemy. The winter was making itself known, particularly from sunset to sunrise, when the mountain air was bitterly cold. Mother's parents, who were staying in the chapel, were alone. Grandmother was afraid to be in such an isolated place with no one else around and wanted to come up to the mountain where we and many others were staying. The fact that the chapel was at the very peak of a high hill that formed part of the mountain meant they had a good view of the town and with Grandfather's binoculars they could see the German cavalry. Viewing their troop movements and gun positions made it more painful and frightening for them, so it was decided they would come to stay where we were. It was impossible for all of us to live in the tiny room in which Father, my brother and I were staying and there was no other space within the complex of shelters for them, so Father arranged that they would take over our room and the three of us would go and stay with his parents, two brothers and two sisters in another part of the mountain. He carried most of our possessions there and the next day fetched Mother's parents' stores and blankets, making two journeys. On the third journey he arrived just before dark with Mother's parents, both looking lost, tired and very sad. Grandmother greeted my brother and me, saying, "Berto, Enio, how are you both, are you well? Don't be afraid, this will soon be over." Grandfather took us either side of his arms and just held us close to him. Little else was said at that moment as Grandmother became concerned about how we would all fit in to sleep on the floor of our room and preoccupied that we two boys needed to be fed. Father soon saw to everything.

At home, Mother's parents' pretty house was across the road from us, set on a large piece of land with a kitchen garden, fruit trees and a vineyard. There I kept my pet rabbit. Grandmother too had a pet, which used to follow her around the land like a little dog or stay by her side when she sat in the sun at the rear of the house knitting or sewing. It was a real friend. There seemed to be an understanding and affection between them and they were inseparable.

Unusual as it was, it was certainly a true pet in the fullest sense of the word. Grandmother's pet was a chicken. When Grandmother arrived up the mountain that evening she was carrying a bundle of clothing in her arms and to my surprise up from the bundle popped the tiny head of her pet chicken, looking around with beady eyes, briskly turning its head right and left and up and down as if to say, "Where am I now? This place isn't as nice as the chapel" – where they had stayed for the last two weeks.

The next morning, after Father had settled my grandparents and shown Grandfather how to draw water from the well, he assured them he would return frequently to provide them with food and cut wood for their fire. We were then ready to go. I was pleased to be leaving the place where I had been so lonely and experienced so much fear. I was looking forward to the new location, because as well as Father's parents, his two brothers, one about twenty-one and the other about twenty-seven, and his two sisters, thirteen and fifteen, were also there. At home their house was less than two hundred metres from ours and I used to see them frequently and we had lots of fun together. I was certainly pleased and happy to be going to stay with them. Outside the room we said goodbye to our grandparents while Father put the rucksacks on our backs and handed us each a walking stick he had prepared, took up his own rucksack with the remainder of our food, raised the bundle of all our blankets on his shoulder and we started to leave. Grandfather and Grandmother stood by the doorway saying, "Goodbye and be careful on your way, we will see you soon, don't be frightened, this will soon be over." Before turning the corner we stopped and waved.

We took our time walking along the undulating mule and donkey track, treading carefully over the loose stones and bumpy rocks as the track wound round and round the bottom of the valleys among the mountains. Although Father said it wasn't too far, we did stop for a rest. It was well before lunchtime when we neared our new home, turning onto a steep narrow track leading to the top of a small hill. Through the trees, now devoid of foliage, I could see the small stone-built rooms with tiled roofs and next to them, at the end of the path, what with its low doorway could only have been a small stone stable for sheep with a thatched roof. We were seen by Father's sisters, Civita and Teresa, who, exclaiming "Berto and Enio are coming!", rushed to meet us, followed by our grandparents. We hugged and hugged each other, they relieved us of what we carried and we were all happy. As we walked the last fifty metres or so towards the sheep stable, Grandmother kept looking at me and caressing my face, saying, "My beautiful child, how are you? Are you well? Don't be afraid, it's better now we're all together." My aunts Civita and Teresa walked in front of us either side of my brother holding his hands, their chattering echoing in the vast empty space of the valley. As we reached the top my father's two brothers, Uncle Domenico and Uncle Benedetto, appeared from the opposite direction carrying firewood on their shoulders. They immediately threw the bundles on the ground to come and hug my brother and me.

The thatched sheep stable was where my grandparents, two uncles and two aunts were living and where we also were to stay. As we entered the stable only my brother and I could walk straight through the low doorway. Father and Grandfather removed their hats and had to walk with their heads bowed so as not to hit them on the rough tree poles forming the ceiling. A primitive, gloomy picture it certainly was, even for the previous occupants, the sheep, I thought. It measured about five metres by four metres at the very most. There were no windows and the only light came from the low doorway. A tree trunk, wedged at the base with large pointed stones protruding above the ground, was sunk in the centre to support the ceiling. The uneven floor was part rock and part earth, trodden down and hardened. Along the crude stone wall facing the door was a low platform constructed of thin tree poles with straw and blankets to sleep on. The left-side wall, where only a meagre amount of daylight penetrated, was a mass of grey rock. The small floor area on the left housed baskets and sacks holding all kinds of foodstuffs and an improvised small table with two buckets of water and a ladle to drink out of. Copper pots lay on the earthen floor, shining on the inside and soot black on the outside. The fire to cook and warm us was housed between two stones placed against the blackened wall on the right of the doorway. A large sheet of metal was fixed to the poles that formed the ceiling above the fire area to prevent the place catching fire. The pleasure I had felt in seeing my grandparents, uncles and aunts almost vanished at the thought of our being reduced to living in such a ramshackle and squalid place. It was so degrading, so humiliating and so sad. There was hardly any space for nine of us to move around. We all had our lunch holding our plates and sitting on a low bench, milking stools and wooden boxes. Grandfather and Grandmother sat on the only two chairs there. I felt safer being with so many beloved members of our family, but at the same time disorientated and confused in such a confined space with so many people after my virtually solitary life in the last place.

After we had lunch, Father, my brother and I went out and walked a few steps up the rock that also formed the left wall of the stable. There was a cleared area in front of the stone-built rooms where many of our relatives and neighbours from the town were living. I knew them all, and they greeted us and made a fuss of me and my brother. Then along came my best friend Bruno. His house in the town was only about fifty metres from us. We went to school together, but he was in a higher class as he was a year older than me. After school we got together whenever we could. Bruno and I stayed close to each other for a long time as we watched and listened to Father, his parents and the other people speaking about the war. Later Bruno showed me the stables at the back under the rooms where sheep and cows returned every night, then, as it got dark and the mountain air bitterly cold, people automatically retired to their shelters. We too went into our stable, where Grandmother had prepared supper, and we all ate by the light and warmth of the fire. When Grandmother and my two aunts had finished washing the pots and plates in a bucket outside the stable, Grandfather placed the ancient rustic door in the low doorway. The door was made of vertical planks of wood held together by two horizontal pieces nailed near the top and bottom and another nailed diagonally, and it still had a piece of iron hanging on the exterior as it was meant to be secured from the outside after the sheep had entered the stable. Now it was held in position from the inside with a pole jammed into the stones on either side. It just stopped some of the wind coming in. Firewood was obviously plentiful and a good supply was brought in for the night. The nine of us sat close together forming a half circle around the fire. It was very comforting.

At home in the town, after supper Grandmother always insisted that before a member of the family went out they had to recite the rosary together. I tried to avoid going there at that time. This she still did, especially now that she had the family captive, so we all had to respond to the prayers as she moved her finger over the rosary beads. Grandmother was well known for going on and on with her prayers. At times I thought she prayed to saints that didn't exist as she mentioned names I had never heard of. Then we had to pray for all the souls of the departed relatives. When we heard Grandmother say, "Pray for all the departed souls of the world" I thought that was the end, yet Grandmother always managed to come up with a few other names of saints or souls to pray for. What a relief when she finished! Everyone quickly made the sign of the cross to signify the end in case Grandmother thought of some other names to pray for. Now we were all ready to chat or one of my uncles would say something funny or speak in a different accent to make us laugh. It felt good and cosy being all together around the fire, but I did wish that Mother was there too, instead of having to hear how frightening it was for her to try to protect our possessions, how the German soldiers shouted and just seized things they wanted, and how careful she had to be in taking goods to the foot of the mountain unnoticed for Father to collect. I felt sad for her.

We had to sit very close to each other to fit around the fire. The huge fire made us thirsty and when someone got up to drink they had to bring a ladle of water to anyone who asked, making sure it wasn't spilt on the ground as the earth would become muddy. The oil lamp hanging on the tree trunk in the centre wasn't used as it consumed olive oil and the flames of the fire gave light all around. We all went to bed at the same time, just took our shoes off and slept next to each other, so close that it was difficult to turn. The big fire continued burning as the flickering flames lit up the various areas of uninspiring rustic stone and grey rock wall and the flaking poles of the low ceiling, which also formed the floor under the thatched roof where hay was stored.

When I awoke in the mornings it felt good to be in the company of my grandparents, uncles and aunts. Father and Grandfather were up first, had relit the fire and were discussing the plans for the day ahead, including going down the mountain for provisions and saying how cautious they would have to be. It was the men's responsibility to provide the food, cut and carry wood for the fire, repair leaky roofs and other heavy jobs. The women were always occupied preparing the next meal under the most difficult conditions. Grandmother, with the help of my two aunts, seemed to be occupied most of the time preparing and cooking with copper pots resting on the two parallel stones with the fire underneath. There was no proper table to prepare the food and only a limited amount of water, as the water in the well was diminishing fast with so many people now using it. The doorway had to be kept open for daylight so they struggled to keep an even fire under the utensils as the wind blew the flames and smoke to one side or another while preventing bits of straw or pieces of dry bark from the ceiling poles from getting into the food. Despite all the difficulties, inconveniences and lack of basics, however, they invariably produced a good substantial meal. We always ate as a family unit with a hearty appetite enhanced by the mountain air. The days usually followed the same pattern. The adults gathered outside, went to a sunny spot to keep warm if there was any sun and discussed our situation, what could be done as a group for the common good and how long we could survive with the food reserve each family had. As most people were farmers, they spoke of what they should be doing on their land at that time of the year, voicing their anger and frustration, their faces worried as they shrugged their shoulders, nodded their heads and gestured with their hands. The only communication from the outside world was when a person returned from meeting someone at the foot of the mountain for provisions or had taken the risk of going to their home undetected. Regardless of what the last person had said only hours before, people never failed to gather quickly around the one who had just returned, wanting to know what they had to say, hoping there might be some change for the better, but invariably the news was only about the continual aggression towards the people, the seizure of goods, farmers losing barns full of hay taken by the Germans to feed their horses, hidden goods being discovered. Question after question was asked but could not be answered, nor was any ground for hope apparent. The gathering then broke up as, thoughtful and dismayed, everyone returned to their shelter.

Home for a Day

One evening, Father returned from collecting the provisions Mother handed to him at the foot of the mountain. It was still daylight, but the cold air made everyone gather inside the stable, so we were very much in each other's way. Father gave me and my brother a cake each that Mother had made while baking bread. I knew that the cakes were made with flour, sugar and eggs; the outside was crispy, the inside soft with a lemony flavour. Father said that Mother had been able to buy a good amount of pasta and salt, which was a scarce commodity. The more important news was that the day before a large number of soldiers had moved out of our town. Grandmother exclaimed, "Tonight we'll pray that they'll all go, so we can return to our homes." I noticed Father looking at me more than once, as if he wanted to tell me something. He soon did. "Mother hasn't seen you for a long time, she would like it if you went to see her. How do you feel about going down and coming back the next day? I'll take you, of course." I could hardly believe what Father had said. The thought of being away for a whole day from the boredom and misery of our existence was bliss. I felt as excited as when we used to go to a feast. "Tomorrow, we'll go tomorrow," I said. Father replied, "We'll go tomorrow if the weather is good." I immediately asked

Grandfather and my uncles, "Is the weather going to be good tomorrow? Is the sky going to be clear tomorrow? It's not going to rain tomorrow, is it?" I wanted the night to pass quickly and the morning to come soon, so I could go on my exciting journey home and see Mother. I was even pleased when Grandmother said it was time to say the rosary, because that meant it was getting towards the time we all went to sleep on the straw-covered platform.

When I woke up the next morning my first words to Father, who was sitting near me at the foot of our sleeping platform, were, "Are we going? Are you going to take me to see Mother now?" He answered, "Yes, but let's wait for the sun to warm up a little." Grandmother prepared the usual bowl of milk with chunks of bread for my brother and me earlier than usual and we ate it sitting by the fire. Father kept talking to my brother so that he wouldn't be too upset about not coming with us, saying, "The journey is too tiring for you. Your mother hasn't seen Berto for a very long time. You stayed with Mother when Berto was here with me. Do you remember?" My brother accepted it was just me who would go and see Mother and soon we were on our way. Father led the way with the empty rucksack on his back and I followed using the walking stick he had provided. He kept on telling me to be careful. "It's more dangerous going down the mountain than coming up," he told me. He always stopped when we came to places where the track narrowed with steep drops. "Be careful here. Be careful here," he would say as he stopped to watch where I placed my feet. But I was used to dealing with the dangers of the mountain now. He didn't really have to tell me, I thought. We continued down and down the steep, slippery, stony track winding into the crumbling rocky surface. When the panorama of the town appeared I didn't stop to look because of my anxiety to reach home quickly and having to concentrate on where to place my next footstep.

Before reaching the foot of the mountain we left the track and made our way into the dense woodland, the secret place where Father and Mother met. To our surprise, Mother wasn't there. She had sent her friend Assunta to collect me, who also brought provisions for Father to take back. Assunta was younger than mother; I knew her well. Father filled the rucksack and arranged the time he would be there the next day to collect me. He told me, "Be good. Do everything Mother tells you and don't leave her side. Do you understand – don't leave Mother's side." The three of us went back to the track, where Father again told Assunta the time he would be there the next day. His last words were, "Be careful, all of you." He turned and started to walk up the track, the full rucksack on his back. Assunta and I walked the short distance to the foot of the mountain. We crossed the river by the long flat tree trunk, went along the lane with the high hedges and soon came into the open road that would take us home.

It was a sunny day, but the air was cold. I was now on home ground and felt excited being in the happy surroundings that were part of my life. Assunta kept speaking to me. She sounded happy. She asked, "Are you pleased you will soon be with your mother?" "Yes,"

I answered. She said, "I know your mother is very happy you've come to see her. Are you feeling tired after coming down from the mountain?" "No," I replied. My eyes were busy looking at the near and distant places that were familiar to me. Some distance away I saw a few soldiers coming out of a group of houses. We passed a cluster of huge oak trees by the roadside hiding a big gun and stacks and stacks of shells, each encased in its own crate. I kept turning to look, but Assunta walked along quickly. Two soldiers wearing helmets were coming towards us. Assunta took hold of my hand and crossed over to the other side of the road. After the soldiers had passed I asked Assunta, "Are they going where the big gun is? Are they the ones who fire at the aeroplanes?" She replied in a subdued voice, "I don't know." Then I saw a group of soldiers on horseback coming towards us. I exclaimed, "Look, look, Assunta, look at the big horses!" I felt Assunta's body stiffen as she squeezed my hand tightly and pulled me over to walk on the grass verge. She murmured, "Don't be frightened, they won't say anything to us." As they went by, Assunta pulled me closer and busied herself looking into my face saying, "In a while we'll be with your mother, she's going to be so happy. Are you hungry?" "Yes," I replied. I had never seen such big horses. The soldiers looked very high up, their backs straight. They wore leather boots up to their knees and their faces looked straight ahead under the peaked caps. When they had passed, Assunta gave a long sigh and said, "You see, I told you they wouldn't say anything to us."

When we arrived home Mother opened her arms and

launched herself at me saying, "My beautiful Berto!", holding me in her arms for a long time. I saw Assunta looking at us smiling as if she was savouring Mother's joy. Mother said she was cooking a special meal for me, and Assunta returned to her house. After being indoors with Mother for a while I wanted to go out and look around the place, but Mother said, "No, stay inside, stay by me. It's better if not too many soldiers see you. They might start asking questions like 'Where is your Father? We haven't seen you before. Where are you staying?' Stay by me, in a little while we'll eat." After our meal, I asked Mother again if I could go to see the hut where I used to keep my rabbit. But Mother again said, "No, be good now. There is an officer in Grandmother's house; he isn't very nice. Stay by me, I haven't seen you for such a long time." Seeing her concern, I remained by her side.

Some time later a loud voice drew me to the door. A soldier was angrily shouting from our neighbour's balcony to another soldier who was on the roadside with a horse on a rein. It seemed as if the one with the horse was being severely told off, because he only spoke a few short sentences in return in a low voice as if he was frightened. Mother pulled me back and closed the door saying, "Don't let him see you." I asked, "Why is he shouting? He looks angry." Mother replied, "The one on the balcony is an officer and the one with the horse is an ordinary soldier. Perhaps he wasn't treating the horse properly. Officers are proud of their horses." "How do you know he's an officer?" I asked. "Officers have special signs on their uniforms and wear peaked caps and leather boots up to their knees," said Mother.

"Ordinary soldiers wear helmets and shorter boots."

Sudden loud clattering sounds quickly brought me to the door again, but this time I only opened it a little so Mother wouldn't get annoyed. Four-wheeled carts passed, all loaded very high and covered with canvas and each pulled by two huge horses. Motorbikes with sidecars sped by then all went quiet. I knew that if I only opened the door slightly and looked through the gap Mother wouldn't tell me off, so whenever I heard a sound I went to the door and watched. When I heard the thump thump, thump thump, of boots I rushed there and waited, hearing the sound getting nearer and nearer until a large group of soldiers appeared marching towards the piazza. They all carried huge rucksacks on their backs and rifles on their shoulders, and the faces under the helmets looked straight ahead. For the rest of the day I stayed inside with Mother.

When it was dark, Mother picked up a parcel she had prepared and we went quietly to Assunta's house, only two minutes away from ours, and Assunta hid the parcel. We returned home with Assunta, who slept in our home to keep Mother company. On our way back, Mother told me not to speak and to walk quietly so we wouldn't be heard by the officer who was staying in the house next door. However, as we were about to reach our front door the officer came out, walked towards me and asked what my name was, saying "Nome". He ruffled my hair and continued to speak in German, which we didn't understand. Mother told me to say "Good evening", which I did, and he indicated to Mother to go inside and switch the light on. Mother murmured to Assunta to pretend they didn't understand and he took the keys from her hand, opened the door, switched the light on, took a cup and asked us to wait. He returned, handing the cup to me full of some kind of soup. Mother told me to say thank you, as she also did, pretending to be very pleased. After he went I tasted the soup, but I didn't like it as it was very salty so we threw it away, but Mother said if I saw the officer the next morning to thank him again and tell him I liked it very much.

The next day it had been arranged that at a particular time after lunch I would be taken to the foot of the mountain, where Father would be waiting. During the morning Mother made sure I had a good wash and changed my clothes. She prepared a parcel of clothing for my brother and again said she would cook a very nice meal for me before I left. I felt bored and frustrated having to stay inside and not being able to look around the place where I had lived all my life. Without Mother noticing, and not being fully aware of her fear that the soldiers might decide to question me, I casually walked out and wandered around. I saw a soldier taking something from our neighbour's property and called the lady and told her what he was doing, thinking I was performing a good deed. She immediately came out and started arguing with the soldier while I stood by her side. The soldier shouted back arrogantly and the noise brought out Mother, who soon learnt from our neighbour that I had told her what the soldier was doing. While the argument raged, Mother called me back and told me off, saying to our neighbour she now feared the soldier would take revenge on her because I had reported him. Her face was red, she frowned as she spoke and I could see the deep fear in her eyes. Then she took hold of my hand and pulled me inside. I felt really sad that Mother was so frightened and it was all my fault. We ate our lunch in total silence.

I don't know why, but it was Assunta who came to take me back to Father. Mother gave me a very long hug as if she didn't want me to go and kept looking at my face. She told me not to be frightened and that soon all our suffering would be over. I could see she was trying not to cry. She looked sad that I was leaving, but I also sensed her relief that I was going back. Assunta took hold of my hand and said to Mother, "I'll see you in a while."

Assunta and I started to walk and I kept turning round because Mother remained there looking after us. Before turning into the road on our right we stopped. Mother and I waved and waved until Assunta put her hand on my shoulder and said, "Let's go now, your father is waiting." I turned and walked away, feeling sad and guilty.

Keeping Watch

The Germans had become aware that men were hiding in various parts of the mountain because, although they rarely captured any during their raids, they saw the jackets, hats and boots that the women hadn't been able to hide quickly enough. Their raids became more frequent and more aggressive.

Father and other men made a shelter higher up the densely wooded, very steep part of the mountain where they could escape to hide in bad weather. There was no path to this place so it was difficult to find them and they kept the location secret for safety's sake. If we were interrogated by the German soldiers, my brother and I were to say that Father had been taken by them weeks ago, some women were to say the same about their husbands and some were to say that their husbands had been killed in the war.

On rainy days when the men could not do anything, it was safer for them to go to their hideout and stay there. They returned to eat while constant watch was kept. When I was told to go on the lookout, although I was only a few metres from the stable I was frightened in case the German soldiers came – or that I might not see them coming. I felt tense, constantly watching the gaps in the woods along the track from the town on the hill opposite and the track at the bottom of the valley. At the

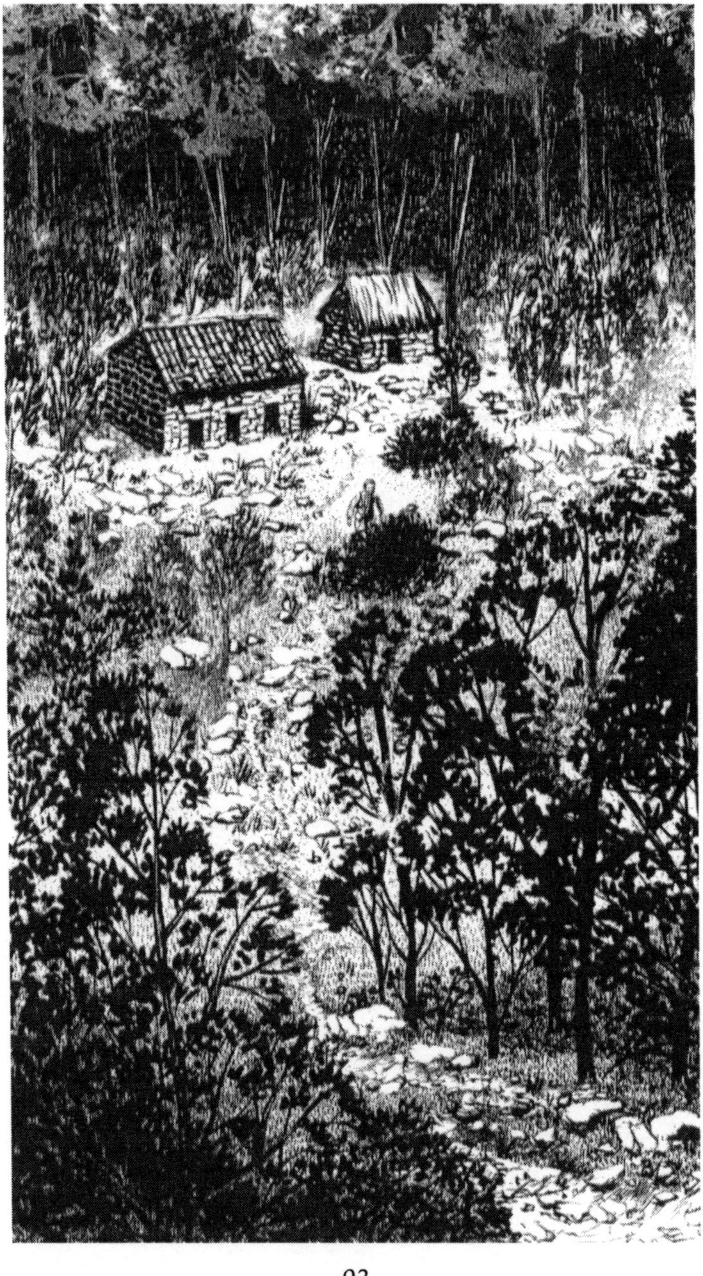

same time I listened attentively for the sound of their boots on the stony track. It was a tremendous relief when I was called back and someone else had to go on watch.

The winter weather worsened, with strong winds and heavy rainfall. The whole area became very muddy including the floor just inside the stable, as the wind drove the rain into the open doorway. The earth inside was sticky underfoot. The wind also drove the rain into the old thatched roof and it filtered into the stable; pots were placed on the floor to collect the drips. Father arranged that on the next clear day as many men as possible would help to dismantle and re-thatch the roof, using the same straw and any other material available, such as pieces of board, metal, canvas, anything that would prevent the rain coming into the stable.

A few days later, it was nearly midday when the sky looked clear of clouds. Father, my two uncles and another two or three men prepared themselves to work on the roof. It all had to be done before dark, in the hope that it wouldn't rain and above all that the German soldiers wouldn't come that day. Lunch was eaten very quickly and the men began to work on the roof at great speed. I stood watching them, each preoccupied with his task. It was very quiet. Then Father, who was at the very top of the pitched roof, suddenly exclaimed, "Guarda che cosa stiamo facendo" (Look what we are doing) "exposing ourselves on this roof. If the Germans come they can see us from far off. We don't stand a chance of escaping." He came down from the roof and called his sister Civita, who was thirteen years old, and me too. He told us to go to the top of the hill opposite and keep watch on the track from the town. If we saw the Germans coming or heard their voices or the sound of boots, we should shout a password, "Noi ce ne andiamo giù" (We are going down), and start to go down for a while so as not to arouse suspicion.

Civita and I were both frightened and said we didn't want to go. Father explained that because we were young, the Germans wouldn't suspect we were there on watch for them and that there was no need to be frightened. Civita said that there were other young people who could go. Father calmly replied, "I can't order other people's children and the roof we are repairing is for our benefit, so you will have to go, and there is nothing to be frightened about."

Reluctantly we set off down to the bottom of the valley and then climbed the diagonal track across the hill. The further we went, the greater our fear. When we reached the top we were directly opposite the men working on the roof, but much higher up. They looked like ants carrying bits of bread over a grey stone.

Civita stopped and said that she wasn't going any further. It felt safer to stay in view of the men. When Father saw that we had stopped, he and my uncles kept making hand signals to us to go further ahead. They didn't want to shout in case the Germans were patrolling on the mountain and they would be heard, as voices on the mountain carry a long, long way. So we did go further. The track wound around a lot and the woods on either side almost formed a canopy, making it quite dark in some places as we passed through. Many times we walked back to where we could see if the men had finished, but when they saw us they angrily signalled for us to go forward. We stopped at a point where we could see the track below and sat on rocks opposite each other on either side of the narrow track. We were surrounded by tall trees, the place was gloomy and the air was cold. All was still and silent, increasing our fear, while we turned our heads, fixed our eyes on the next bend of the track and kept our ears alert. Now and again we looked at each other for a moment or two, but we soon turned our heads back to the track and continued our watch.

Civita looked really scared as she twisted and twisted and twisted the handkerchief she was holding. The only conversation I recall with Civita as we looked at each other was I said: "Your face is white." She replied: "You should see how white your face is." I think she was offended by my remark and I felt sorry I had said this. We were both petrified. I imagined that at any moment we would see the armed soldiers appearing round the bend of the track below us. Every time a small branch fell from a tree or we heard the slight sound of a fox moving my heart sank into the ground and Civita jumped, still twisting her handkerchief. Even the gentle sound of birds among the crisp dry leaves made us jump. It began to get dark. We were numbed by cold and fear and we went back to the point where we could see the men, still working on the roof. Father signalled for us to go back and we went down the hill as fast as we could, Civita in front, our eyes fixed on the ground to see where to place our feet, not turning our heads or looking at each other once. It had been a long and fearful day for Civita and me.

The next morning I woke up feeling cold air on my face. The door of the stable had been removed for the daylight to enter. Father and his two brothers were up and had lit the fire. The rest of us remained lying on the straw-covered platform with blankets and coats covering us. Father and his brothers were discussing the usual matters of the day ahead such as: should someone be on watch all the time, the amount of food we had, who would go and cut wood for the fire, was a shepherd going to kill a sheep and the meat be shared among the families? What caught my attention most was hearing Father say, "As soon as the sun has warmed the air a little we had better finish securing the straw on the roof – the three of us will do it in less than two hours." I immediately concluded that Civita and I would be told to go on watch again, but since we hadn't seen any Germans the day before and the work would take less than two hours, I didn't worry too much.

After we were all up and had had some food, everyone tried to crowd around the fire, because the morning mountain air was always very cold. Father's brother Uncle Benedetto took hold of the water bucket and rope to go to the well for water, but Father said to him, "Leave that now, it's better if we finish the work on the roof, otherwise if we get a blast of wind it can ruin all the work we did yesterday." Then Father turned to Civita and me and said, "Now you two, go where you went yesterday and keep your eyes and ears open, especially your ears, and if you hear German voices or the sound of boots walking over the stones, shout 'We are going down', do you understand?" Civita immediately responded, "Why can't someone else go this time? Berto and I went for a long time yesterday, it was very cold and frightening." Father repeated what he'd said the day before: "I told you yesterday not to be frightened; if the Germans come they won't suspect that you are there on watch because you are young, also I can't order other people's children to go. Don't be frightened. See if you can find a sunny spot and you'll keep warm."

Soon after, Civita and I were reluctantly on our way, heads down, looking where to put our feet. When we reached the top of the hill opposite the stable, we stopped looking at Father and his brothers working on the thatched roof. Civita and I chatted, saying we would look for a sunny spot even if we had to come off the track. After a minute or so Father saw that we had stopped and signalled to us to quickly go further along the track. We began obediently to walk along the cold track, now engulfed by the tall woods. We had only walked for about two minutes, looking for a sunny spot, when Civita turned towards me looking scared, placed her hands on my shoulders and shouted very loudly, "I told you we are going down! We're going down!" At the same time a soldier sprang from round the bend a few metres in front of us shouting "Alt! Alt!", aiming his rifle at us, while another soldier came out of the woods on our right. We immediately put our arms up in the air. Civita spoke very fast, telling them that we had to go down the mountain for bread and I didn't want to go. For a moment they just stared at us as they spoke to one another. The eyes under the helmets were more frightening than the barrels of their rifles pointing at us.

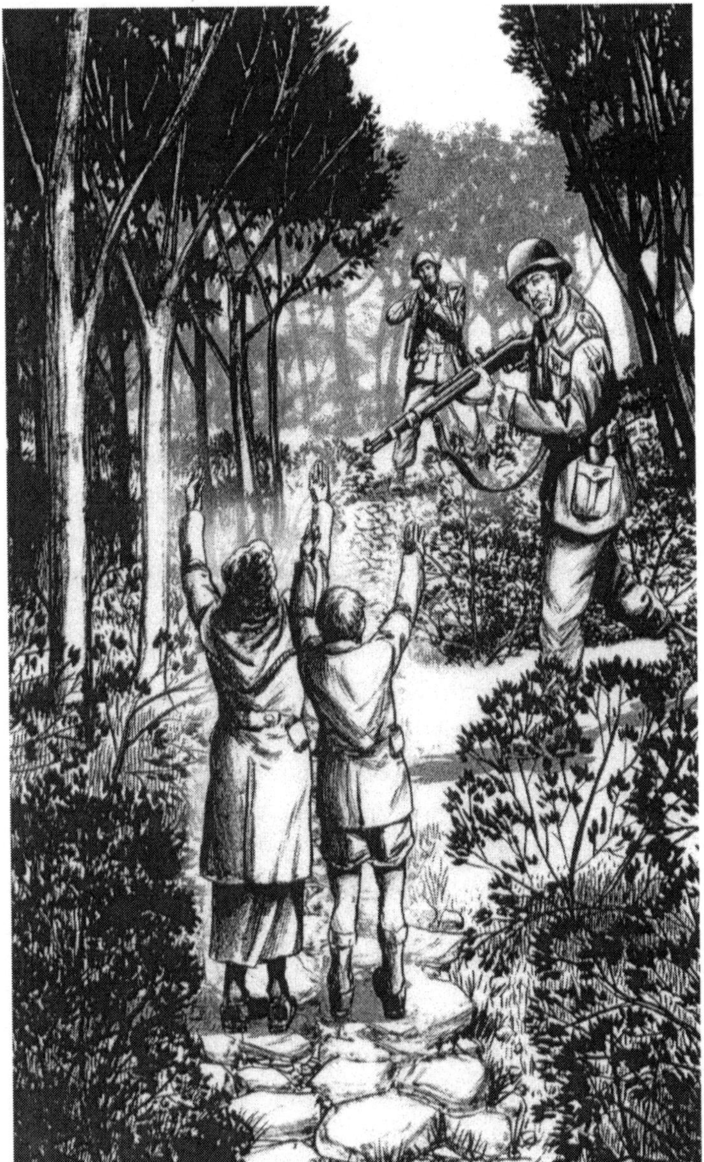

Civita and I just stood side by side, our bodies pressed against one another. The tension probably lasted for two minutes, but it was a very, very long two minutes. Then the soldier in front of us said something and nodded that we could continue on our journey. As we took the few steps forward we had to pass very close to him – that was really scary!

We continued to walk, speechless, trembling, our hearts pounding. I was breathing hard as if I'd been running. The narrow track with stones and huge rocks didn't allow us to walk side by side and I always followed Civita. When we felt we had distanced ourselves sufficiently we stopped and began to talk. Civita said that a slight noise had made her look and she had seen the soldier in the woods first. Our big worry now was that when the soldiers passed us to return down the mountain and saw we hadn't actually gone down for bread, they would be suspicious and start asking a lot of questions. If we tried to go back, we might meet them on the way. The thought of seeing them again was so frightening that we decided to leave the track, hide among the dense woodland and wait until we heard them pass. We rushed upwards, careful not to disturb any stones that might make a noise, and came to a ditch in which we hid. It was gloomy and cold in the woods. We couldn't sit as the earth and moss on the rock was damp, so we stood facing each other in silence, except for when we shifted our feet to relieve the tedium and the sound of our breathing. Even when Civita yawned she made sure that hardly any sound emerged from her mouth. It was so cold, and I felt the dampness of the ditch penetrate my whole body. We both gently breathed on our hands and now and then we looked into each other's eyes, but not a word passed our lips. The utter emptiness seemed to be waiting to be filled, perhaps by the frightening sound of their voices or boots crashing against the rocky track. The silence too was frightening.

We began to whisper to one another. "Shall we go?" Civita said. "What are we going to say if we meet them?" I replied. Civita just shrugged and we remained motionless and speechless, numb with cold to the point of stupor. It seemed time had literally stood still for us.

Then the silent world was broken by whispers from somewhere among the woods, calling, "Berto, Civita, where are you? The Germans have gone, where are you?" It was Father's voice. We both quietly answered, "We are here", as if it was a crime to speak. Neither of us moved, waiting until Father found us before we came out of the ditch. When Father saw us he closed his eyes and shook his head, looking very sad. We came out and Father said, "Don't be frightened, this will end", put his hand on my shoulder and squeezed me against his body. We walked back to the stable, Father leading the way, without talking. Back in the stable Civita and I drank a lot of water and had our lunch. I heard then that the soldiers had interrogated Grandmother for a long time, wanting to know where the men were, then took the track leading out of the mountain to the town of Atina. Father said to Civita and me, "You saved us from being captured." Civita answered, "I am never going to go on watch again." "Nor me!" I added.

Fighters and Bombers

Once we were all up in the morning we were very much in each other's way in the confined space of the small primitive stable. Sitting near the fire was made unpleasant by the cold air and wind coming in through the open doorway and then Grandmother had to do the cooking and I would be in the way. The obvious thing was for me to go outside and put up with the cold and wind. My brother always followed me. The valley below was a sea of thick grey-white mist, which slowly dispersed when the sun began to appear. The sun didn't last long because the high mountain on the south side kept it away from us. It was high on the north side too, rocky with sparse clusters of thin woods and shrubs and some pasture in between. A track led diagonally across and through the mountain top towards the descent for the town. We were thus on a small hillside within a valley engulfed by the mountains. The place was dull, cold and damp.

I would go in front of the stone-built shelters, where I might see my friend Bruno or someone would come out to get firewood from the big heap. If one of the men went to get water from the well, at the bottom of the valley, I would go with them, but never too near the well as there was no wall around the mouth, only a few flat stones for the men to stand on while drawing buckets of water. I stood a little behind watching as they slowly lowered the bucket into the well, keeping the rope at the centre of the opening then giving it a sharp pull to one side to tilt the bucket in the water then haul it to the surface, keeping their bodies straight and their feet firmly planted on the ground.

By now I had seen hundreds and hundreds of English and American warplanes flying overhead, on their way to machine gun or bomb German targets somewhere beyond our area. It seemed we were directly under their flight path. We heard their sound before we saw them coming. Bruno and I waited for them to appear, counted them and soon recognised if they were fighters or bombers. The fighters were smaller, flew faster and made a high-pitched sound. They appeared impeccably organised, not a centimetre difference in their spacing. In lines of three and groups of nine or twelve, one group appeared, then another, then another, until the whole squadron had gone by, numbering thirty, forty, sixty – we even counted eighty sometimes. The bombers were much bigger planes, more powerful, and they made a roaring sound like a slow, deep, mournful chant, sinister, mind-blowing and very frightening. They were an amazing spectacle against the vast, clear sky as they flew calmly past in perfect formation just above us, among hundreds and hundreds of puffs of smoke from the exploding shells from the German guns below, knowing the shells couldn't quite reach them. The marvellous formation remained undisturbed, their height and calm speed unaltered. When the whole squadron had passed, taking the intense sound with

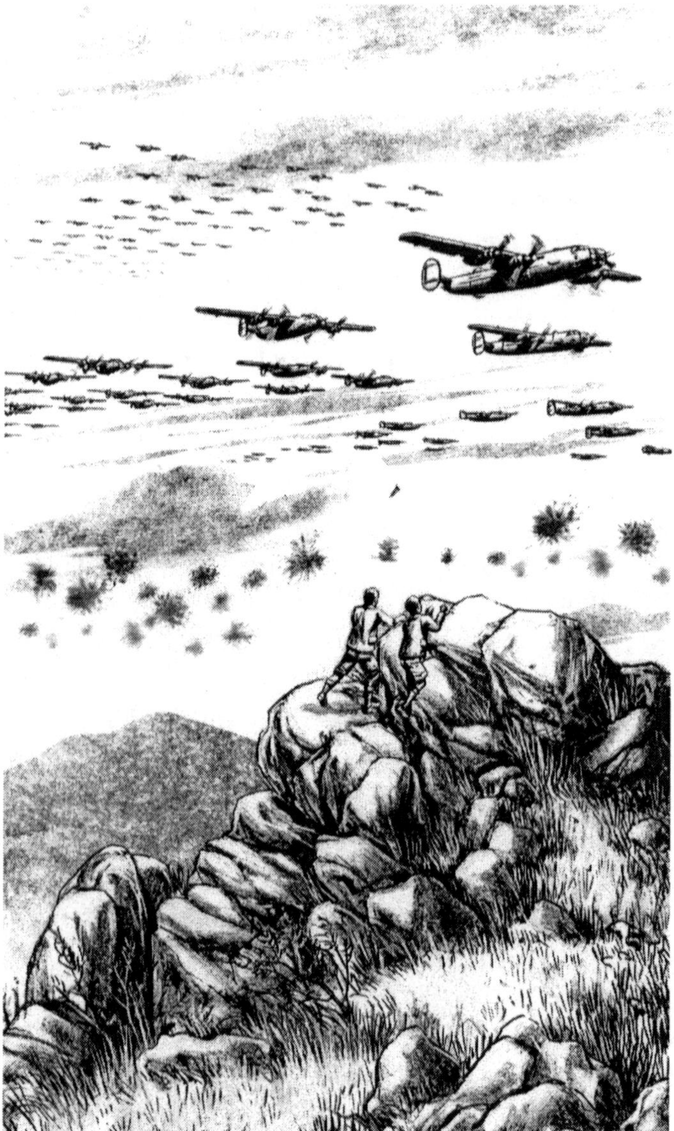

them as they disappeared into the distant horizon, the explosions in the sky stopped too and we were returned to our lost, primitive, silent world. The breathtaking, overwhelming episode left me disorientated, mesmerised, dazed and amazed, for I could hardly understand what the conflict was all about, but then I would be brought back to reality and our predicament by the gentle bleating of a sheep sounding in the empty air.

Bruno and I waited for the sound of the aeroplanes to return so we could count them again and see if any were missing, but each time we lost count as they were no longer in the same perfect formation. Ten might appear, then three, then one, then maybe twenty, scattered about the sky, which was again filled with the pounding of exploding shells. It seemed they had done their job and were now flying home fast, away from the horrifying hostilities.

The Fighters Attack

Father was as busy as ever. He continued meeting Mother at the foot of the mountain to be given provisions for us and for Mother's parents at the other part of the mountain, where he made frequent trips to supply their needs and provide reassurance. Being the oldest of his family, he took the lead in decision-making and other matters. Whenever any other family needed help, Father offered his own without hesitation. His trips home were made when troop movements were taking place and only a skeleton force remained to man the anti-aircraft guns. These were rare opportunities, advantages that had to be seized immediately as a new influx of soldiers would re-occupy the town within a day or so.

On one of the occasions when Father went home, moments before he was due to leave German soldiers came in search of men. While Mother tried to argue with them by the door saying there was no one else there, Father managed to escape by sliding down the pole from the first-floor bedroom window at the rear of the house into our kitchen garden.

When Father was on the mountain he always kept my brother and me with him, including when he went to cut wood for the fire, which was consumed in very large amounts. One day, he told me and my brother that he was going to cut firewood in a certain place and would take us somewhere further away, from where we could see our town and our home. Living in such a dismal place with nothing to do, this was exciting. Off we went at an easy pace, walking along the rocky track and the mountain top, going up, going down, turning right and turning left until we reached a point where all at once, like a burst of sunshine, the town came into view.

We saw several groups of houses, the church, the green border surrounding the fields, the white gravel roads against the green background, such a variety of geometric designs, attractive and fascinating – and that was where Mother was. I wondered what she was doing and felt sad that she was so far away and all alone. I looked and looked, filled with melancholy and nostalgia, feasting my eyes on the only place I had ever known, the place that was such a big part of my life, where I had grown up to be who I was, the place where I had received so much love and happiness, now brutally taken from me.

While pointing out places to my brother, saying, "Look, that's the flour mill with the big water reservoir, that's Via Roma where we used to go on Sundays", we were distracted by the sound of aeroplanes, which began to appear from the western horizon in superb formation. We soon recognised them as fighters and wondered where they were going, visualising as always the heroic pilots in them, admiring their skill and wishing them success.

The fighters were flying just above the mountain top, three in line, in groups of nine, coming directly towards us, their powerful deep roaring filling the air. Where we stood was an exposed area on the crest of the mountain, with a steep, deep fall below. As the first group approached, one of the fighters detached itself and came directly towards where we were. Flying almost parallel to us, it tilted a little to inspect us and momentarily I saw the outline of the head and face of the pilot. It terrified me, because what I saw bore no resemblance to the face of a person. Was the pilot wearing his oxygen mask? Was he wearing goggles over his headgear? I don't know. I don't remember. What I do remember is that the brief glance shocked me to the core and really frightened me.

Then suddenly the first group arrived above us, the powerful, penetrating sound shattering our minds and bodies, leaving us stunned, unable to think or act, as if our minds and bodies were paralysed.

Seemingly only a stretch of my arm away, one by one the fighters tilted, revealing their metal undersides, launched themselves down, down, down, then swept into attack, machine-gunning their targets over the town, each plane making an ever increasing screaming, screeching howl. It was deafening. It was hell. Then all at once the German guns opened fire, filling the sky before us with explosions and puffs of smoke. Father immediately took us by the shoulders and made us lie down. I could see his worried face and mouth shouting, but I couldn't hear what he was saying. We lay face down, the smell of grass making my nose tickle so I had to keep my head up. As each group arrived in front of us, they tilted and launched down, tilted and launched down, again and again. There didn't seem a metre difference in their spacing nor a moment's difference in their timing as each plunged into the deep downward dive. The noise of that screaming howl never seemed to stop, terrorising every cell in my body.

When the sound of the last fighter began to fade we got up, seeing the last few still flying over the town and the others scattered high in the sky at the far end of the mountains opposite. Stunned by the noise and fear, disorientated, just able to hear my breathing and my heart pounding, I was aware of Father trying to reassure us that the aeroplanes were now going away. We watched the fighters going towards the west, from where they had come, now hearing only the intermittent sound of the German cannons still firing at them, then, as we watched, in just a few seconds the fighters had regrouped and were returning towards us. Immediately the German guns opened another massive attack. Father said quickly, "Lie down, lie down", and within seconds they were back at exactly the same place for a second attack. Again we endured the horrific noise and terror, waiting and waiting for the last one to dive, but were saddened to see one aeroplane pouring out a huge trail of black smoke. We saw the pilot jump out and waited anxiously for his parachute to open, which it never did. The body hurtled down in the centre of the town a few metres from Via Roma and the plane crashed about half a kilometre away in front of the flour mill, exploding into a ball of fire and black smoke. All the other planes were now scattered high in the sky, disappearing over the horizon as their sound diminished.

Father looked at us. He said, " We must go back. I want to go down to the town to see if Mother is all right." We walked back to our shelter as quickly as we could, the terrifying incident still with me.

At the same time I felt very sad for the pilot, who had obviously died. I kept thinking of his family waiting for him for supper that evening, visualising them sitting around the table with an empty chair. I wondered how they would ever know what had happened. I knew now that the impressive and fascinating silhouettes in the sky, which we welcomed because they came to liberate us from the relentless tyranny, were ferocious machines and we should avoid being in their way.

We returned to our shelter breathless and still terrified. I could sense Father's anxiety as he told us that it would be too late for him to return to the mountain that night and he would sleep in some barn. He assured us he would be with us the next morning before we woke up, which he was, telling us that Mother was all right.

Soldiers on a Sunday Afternoon

It was Sunday after lunch. All the men had gone to their hiding place as it was safer for them to be away from where we were in case the Germans suddenly came and captured them. My grandparents, my brother and I were the only people in the stable. Grandmother took my brother's hand, saying "Come with me, both of you", and we went across to one of the stone-built rooms where two of our old aunts were sheltering. The sky was overcast, it was drizzling and the air felt very damp, making me feel even colder. Grandfather wasn't feeling well but he came also, carrying the only two chairs we had.

The room was small, oblong, about five metres long and three metres wide, with a narrow window in the wall opposite the door, allowing a dull light into part of the room. Aunt Benedetta sat on the only chair there, Grandfather placed the two chairs he had brought against the wall and Grandmother and our other aunt sat there, and Grandfather, my brother and I sat on folded blankets on the floor. Apart from the three chairs, the only other piece of furniture in the room was a chest of drawers near the window.

The reason for going there was to pray together as it was Sunday, when normally we would all have gone to church. Grandmother, the rosary beads in her hand, started reciting the prayers to which we all responded, otherwise the place was soundless except for the gentle, almost hypnotic tick, tick, tick, tick of the rainwater from the roof dripping outside the small window. There was no fire in this room. I felt cold, and the gloomy room coupled with the intermittent sorrowful sighs gave me a feeling of isolation, but I also understood why the three women needed to express their anguish.

Grandmother was only halfway through the recital of the rosary when suddenly, bang, the door slammed against the stone wall, filling us with terror as an armed German soldier leapt into the room pointing a machine gun at us, followed by another, both shouting. They indicated that we had to stand in line against the wall, which we quickly did, as they stared at us with vicious eyes just visible under the rim of their helmets. The room was so narrow that the barrels of their guns were within touching distance of us. One continued to point his machine gun at us, waving it from side to side, keeping his finger on the trigger and aiming at each of us in turn. The other soldier began to search among some clothing, then grabbed a sack full of goods and emptied it on the floor. We knew that they were looking for articles of gold and other valuables. Then he went over to the chest of drawers, the machine gun under his right arm, finger on the trigger, looking at us now and again while with his left hand he pulled everything from each drawer onto the floor. Out of one of the drawers out came a whole cheese, the usual round shape, which rolled along the floor, curving slightly until it reached Aunt Benedetta, slipped under her long dress then stopped. It was too

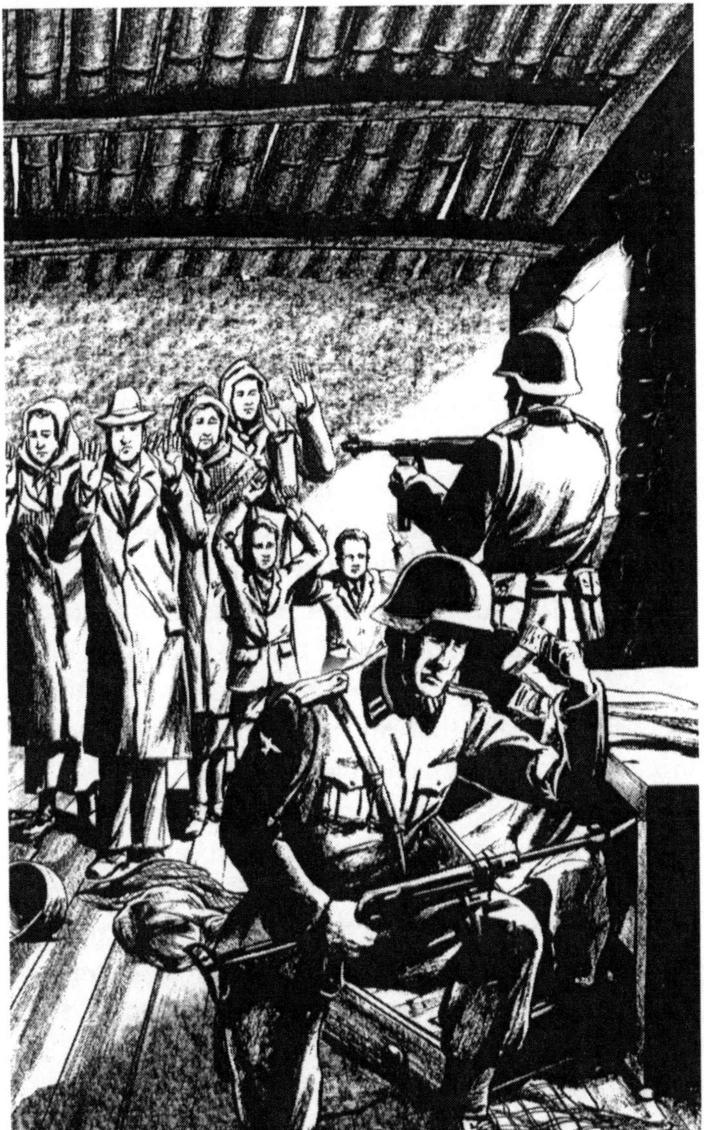

horrible to look at their faces so I stared at the machine guns and saw that the barrels were perforated towards the end; although they were much thinner and shorter, they reminded me of the vertical fume exhaust pipe on the bonnet of the tractor, which was also perforated towards the end.

The soldier then kicked the contents of the drawers all over the floor, still looking, but there was nothing of interest there for them. Muttering to each other they walked backwards, still pointing their machine guns at us, until they were out of the door. Grandfather's first words were, "Where has the cheese gone?" My brother answered, "Look under Aunt Benedetta's skirt." Grandmother and my two aunts began to tremble in despair, saying, "Oh Madonna, what's happening to us? What have we done, what have we done to deserve this?" as they moved around restless and confused. Grandfather called some other women to comfort them, spirits were brought out and strong coffee was made. Grandfather said that my face looked pale and my brother and I were given water to drink.

We went back to our stable in a state of terror. Apart from being so frightened, I was very, very disillusioned with the soldiers, not because I hadn't encountered them before or wasn't aware of their brutality, but because their faces looked young and in my mind I compared them with the young men I knew who were so kind and benevolent towards me and everyone else. I could not understand why they should have been so hostile.

Soon after, Father and the other men returned from their hiding place and I was eager to tell them what had happened. Father said they had watched the soldiers coming and when they left, but were powerless to do anything because they were armed and it was better they didn't see that there were men about. It was a horrible Sunday afternoon; the fear, and more so the hurt, stayed with me for days and days.

Preparing for the Worst

So much was happening in the nearby towns and villages occupied by the German army that people were becoming more and more frightened. I felt the atmosphere of deadly concern, suspicion and fear in the men around me, and when I approached men in conversation I often sensed that they changed the subject. I noticed too that when the women asked, "Are you speaking of something bad?" the answer was always the same, "Non è niente, non è niente" (It's nothing, it's nothing). This indicated to me that something very bad was going on but I couldn't find out what it was. What I did manage to learn from the snatches of conversations I overheard was that the Germans who had taken our homes, our food and men at every opportunity were now committing atrocities unimaginable to ordinary innocent people in the small towns and villages they occupied. I couldn't really find out what was happening, nor did the men let the women around me know.

It was not until after the war when we returned to our homes that I began to hear people speak about some of the atrocities. Often when people refused to obey orders they were shot. In a place near our town a man who protested when they were taking his cow was shot dead. In another farmhouse, where the whole family was present, they went to the stables to take their cows, and when the woman owner began to protest she was shot, then another member of the family, a man; both died immediately. They took the cows away and left the family with the two bodies on the ground. In another town not far from ours, they suspected a man of cutting one of their telephone wires just because he was passing that way. The man was hung on a tree with a notice saying this was an example and the family forbidden to take the body down for some days. Afterwards, it was found that the wire had been trodden on by one of their horse's shoes. As time went by I heard more and more of these horrible stories, whole families put in a room and machine-gunned, a mother with a child in her arms begging them not to harm them both shot in front of others, a man suspected of having or listening to a radio shot and thrown into a well in front of his family. Sadly, as an adult, I learned that the stories I had heard as a child, and many, many worse ones, were recorded facts. My father, like the other men, must have been aware of these inhuman acts, which spurred him to further action for our greater protection.

Father, his two brothers and a cousin went away for hours and hours, taking with them shovels, picks, an axe and a sledgehammer. About three days later he told the whole family that we had to go to a secret place where they had made a shelter to see if we could all fit inside. It had been prepared in case it was suspected that the Germans were coming to take us away, when we could all go and hide there. It was also felt, especially if they had to suddenly retreat, that the soldiers might comb the mountain areas as a final act of revenge and shoot us. The secret hiding place was intended to serve for a few hours until such a critical situation had passed. So, my grandparents, two uncles, two aunts, Grandfather's brother and his family of four, Father, my brother and I, thirteen people in all, set off to see if we could fit inside the new hiding place. Father led the way and we followed in single file, the only way one could get from one place to another through the difficult mountain terrain. A lot of chatting went on along the way. I followed Father and when I glanced back every head was looking down at the ground, where to take the next step to avoid falling – a lesson I had learnt from my early days on the mountain and from which I still bear a scar. In fact, the whole of the mountain was steep, rocky and dangerous; even the donkeys always kept their heads turned towards the ground, carefully looking where to place their next hoof. Donkeys are not stupid.

We travelled quite a way along the track, first down the valley, then up the north hill, and soon arrived in uncharted terrain, which was very awkward to get through. Father kept warning everyone when to be extra careful, especially when traversing sloping places which offered only a precarious foothold while holding onto shrubs or branches. Each time we encountered these difficult places Father stopped, turned and said, "Fate attenzione qui" (Be careful here). The woods were so dense we often had to crouch for two or three metres in order to get through. Some parts were full of thorns that caused difficulty for Grandmother and Grandfather's brother's wife with their ankle-length flowing dresses;

many times we had to stop so they could disengage the bottom of their dresses from the thorns while they cursed the war and appealed to the saint, saying, "Perchè questo, Santo Antonio?" (Why this, Saint Anthony?) "We didn't deserve this punishment, when will it end and we can go back to our homes?"

After struggling through for some time, Father stopped, waited until everyone was close in line, and said, "We will soon pass by the shelter, see if you can tell where it is." Shortly afterwards he stopped again, looking rather pleased with himself, and said, "Allora" (Well then), "you have all passed in front of it and haven't noticed anything, let's go back." A few metres back, in what looked like an undisturbed area, surrounded by woods, shrubs and thorns, Father removed some small evergreen trees and revealed our hiding place.

The opening was just big enough for one person to get through, then it widened inside and was high enough for the tallest person to stand. The cavity went into the mountain. The roof was supported by a number of tree poles placed close together; a decorated kitchen table oilcloth between the poles prevented the earth and rain coming through. The sides and back were just earth and rock and the opening was on the side and not on the top, so it could better be described as a big, deep grave.

After scrutinising it, we went in one by one. Father was last. He replaced the trees in front of the opening and wriggled in, pulling the last shrub towards him to fully hide the opening. He said, "Andiamo" (Come on), "get closer, there has to be room for three more, my wife and her parents." We all shuffled our feet, pressing ourselves more tightly together.

It was very dark standing crammed together. An immediate commotion started up: "It's so dark, we won't last long in here", "For how long do we have to hide in here?", "I don't want to die in here." Grandfather's brother's wife, who was quite a large woman, said, "There is no air here at the back, I can hardly breathe, if I have to stay here for too long I will faint." Grandmother said, "Madonna, che male abbiamo fatto?" (Madonna, what harm have we done?) "What sin have we committed to deserve this?" Then one by one we all came out. Father took little notice of the moaning. He replaced the evergreen trees in front of the opening and pointed out the top of the shelter, which looked undisturbed, with the slabs of earth with weeds replaced and stones covered with moss so it looked natural. I think Father felt good about the shelter; he said: "Non avete paura" (Don't be afraid), "they will never find us here." He then showed us where the excavated earth and stones had been carried, all covered with old tree branches with leaves spread on top. No trace or suspicion of our hiding place was evident. Such was the extent of our fear – a fear that sadly became a reality.

Peppino the 'Traitor'

The German army's need for able-bodied men to carry artillery guns and ammunition to the mountain areas and dig trenches near the battlefront was as important to them as the houses and food they stole from us. Therefore, to prevent being captured, vigilance was of paramount importance, even in our hiding places among the mountains. The approach of an unknown person, a different sound or a different human voice put everyone on alert. Anything different and even the sheep stopped grazing and stared, dumbfounded. At night it was felt to be safe, as the climb to the dark, densely forested mountain was very difficult, dangerous and it was easy to get lost. I knew this only too well. A warning system existed from one group to another, so when the raids for men came they had already disappeared to the more difficult and remote parts.

The soldiers used to suddenly appear with their loud blustering voices, in a language that no one could understand, aggressively pushing their way into every nook and cranny, always holding their machine guns in the firing position, fingers on the trigger. It made our hearts thump.

I used to hear the men talking about a man called Peppino who spoke German and who fraternised with the soldiers and became their interpreter. When they spoke about Peppino it was always quietly, as if it was a secret. One day when I asked, "Who is Peppino?" I was answered quickly and abruptly, "Non è nessuno" (He is no one), "You don't know him", "He is not from our town" and I was told off for asking. Obviously they didn't want me to know what they were saying, nor who Peppino was.

Living in such a confined space where conversations were only about the war and more so about our survival, little by little I did learn that the man called Peppino was paid by the Germans to take them to places where men could be found, even up to the mountains. I remember the first time Peppino came with the soldiers to where we were. It was a cold, dry day with a cloudy sky. All was calm. Soon after lunch a boy was spotted hurrying along the track at the bottom of the valley, coming towards our place. Within moments men and women gathered together, looking at each other apprehensively and saying, "Lo sai chi è?" (Do you know who he is?), "Do you recognise him?", "I wonder why he is in such a hurry?" From a distance no one recognised who the boy was, but the fact that he was walking fast made them anxious. Normally people walked slowly and carefully among the loose stones and sharp bumpy rocks as it was easy to fall and hurt oneself. Everyone was waiting anxiously for the boy to get nearer so as to find out who he was and why he was coming to our place. As he came nearer he still wasn't recognised because, hurrying up the hill, he naturally kept his head down, looking to see where to place his next footstep. When he was a few metres from us he lifted his head and looked at the reception awaiting him. One of the men, who recognised him, exclaimed, "Benito, perchè vieni qui?" (Benito, what are you doing here?), but he didn't answer, continuing to walk the last few steps towards us. He looked about fifteen years old, his dishevelled hair tumbled over his forehead and face, and he was perspiring and panting deeply. He began to speak in a hurried, anxious voice: "The men must hide quickly. I Tedeschi vengono per loro." (The Germans are coming for them) "Presto. They will be here soon. I should have been here long ago. I couldn't find this place. Tell me how to get to the next place. I'm thirsty, do you have any water? Be quick, be quick, I mustn't be seen by the Germans, they will recognise me." Grandmother went to fetch the bucket with the water and a ladle and the boy drank several ladles of water then was taken hastily to the next place.

The men disappeared like a flock of frightened sparrows, while the women tried to hide anything indicating that there were men living with us, jackets, boots, trousers, etc. Grandmother even hid some dinner plates to show there were only a few of us living in the stable. Then she pulled her headscarf off and ruffled her hair to look older and abandoned. After everything had been seen to, they tried to act as normally as possible, pretending they were cooking, mending clothes or just handling a saucepan, but no one, no one, uttered a word, just waiting for the soldiers, not knowing what to expect. Interrogation at gunpoint perhaps, as a group or alone; whatever, a good act had to be put on. We were just waiting, with fear brooding in the very air we breathed. Grandfather was unwell; he lay on the sleeping platform with blankets on top of him. Now and then someone would pretend to go and fetch a log or other pieces of firewood, while casting furtive glances towards the track to see if the soldiers were approaching, so as to prepare ourselves mentally and physically to face the enemy, to look as if we were surprised by their sudden appearance. The whole place had become still and silent, only tense faces and fearful eyes saying so much. The suspense and atmosphere were really scary. I knew I must stay quiet, ask nothing. If I did, I would certainly be told off. I could see Grandmother's lips moving slightly as she prayed in silence to the saints for their help.

Unexpectedly, without anyone having been seen coming up the track, a strong, loud voice was heard in the gloom outside the shelters: "Buon giorno" (Good day), the customary greeting, but this time it carried a sinister overtone which seemed to fill the whole valley with fear. Slowly everyone came out looking surprised, almost idiotic, as if they had just woken up, and gathered in front of the soldiers, saying, "Bon giorno, buon giorno", and there was Peppino with the armed soldiers. He had brought them not via the track but through the dense woodland so we couldn't see them coming. Peppino lost no time in questioning the women, with a superior air and in loud, arrogant tones: "Dove sono i vostri uomini? vostri mariti?" (Where are your men, your husbands?). The women answered together, their faces sorrowful, and with lamentations, looking partly at Peppino and partly at the solders: "My husband was killed in the war", "My husband was taken by the German soldiers weeks ago and hasn't returned", "My husband too was taken away"," I am a widow", "We have children to feed and no men to help us". Peppino continued to question them aggressively, with piercing eyes: "Where are your brothers? Your older sons?" They answered: "My brother works in Rome", "I have no brothers", "I have two sons, they haven't returned from the war". Their answers sounded more like a chant than spoken words, as they shrugged their shoulders, rubbed their heads or crossed their arms over their chest, putting on sad, pathetic faces.

After some minutes of interrogation, Peppino turned to the soldiers with a friendly expression, speaking calmly in German for a minute or so. I could tell by his face and hand gestures that he was saying he believed what the women had said. After a short discussion they walked away without speaking or looking at us, just leaving the many trembling bodies behind.

I felt hurt that they left without a glance or a word of sympathy for us, so cold and insensitive to our situation. I also felt very angry towards Peppino. I recognised him, he was from our town, known by everyone, someone I used to see walking the streets with other people. On Sundays he used to chat with groups of men in the piazza in front of the church. Now, how could he do such a thing? This time my hatred was not so much for the German soldiers, more so for Peppino the traitor, who was paid to betray us.

The women were such good actresses that they convinced Peppino and the soldiers and they didn't search anywhere, just left for the next place. As ever, making and drinking coffee was the sedative after the ordeal. The women talked and talked like a lot of frightened hens: "How fortunate they've gone", "Sant'Antonio che paura" (Saint Anthony, what a fright), "We were so lucky they didn't search anywhere", "I hid my husband's clothes and boots in the woods", "I hid things under the pile of firewood", "What a fright, what a fright. I can still feel my heart pounding", all voicing their hatred for the German soldiers, not mentioning the traitor Peppino. They were all still in shock and I dared not say anything, knowing that if I spoke I would be told off.

Later, when all had calmed down, the men cautiously returned and I heard them speaking of Benito, the boy who came to warn us. Then I learned that the boy had been sent by Peppino, that he was Peppino's son, and I felt guilty about my unjust hate for Peppino. Then I thought he was an excellent actor too, and more courageous than the actresses.

The Calf

Up to now we had eaten good, basic, substantial meals, but the reserve of potatoes, dried beans, jars of preserved tomatoes, smoked sausages, salted hams and olive oil began to diminish. The Germans had taken all the cows, sheep and chickens from farms around the town and now they began to come to the mountain for them. The first time I saw German soldiers taking a cow on the mountain I was with Grandfather, who was speaking with a man who owned a small herd of cows, about twelve or so. They were his living, his property and his pride. The cows were peacefully grazing within sight on the hill opposite us. The man noticed that they had become disturbed, moving quickly among the woods and shrubs, and as we looked we saw two German soldiers, one with a machine gun pointing at a young cow, the other trying to put a rope around its neck. The cow was resisting being taken as it went forwards and backwards amidst the rest of the herd, who were all becoming agitated. I was hoping the cows would attack them, but alas, much to my disappointment, they didn't, as cows are so calm and peaceful. Eventually the soldiers managed to isolate it, put a rope around its neck and with some difficulty pulled it along and went away. The owner didn't say a word to us or make a sound. He glanced at Grandfather with a stricken face, shook his head a few times and walked away towards his herd, looking down as if he were in mourning.

From that day, the owners of sheep and cows sold them at a low price. Each time one was slaughtered the meat was sold to the various groups of people hiding in different parts of the mountain. The amount Father bought each time for the whole family was put in pots or wrapped in sacks and kept outside the stable under a pile of firewood with stones on the top to prevent sheepdogs and foxes getting to it; the cold weather preserved it for several days. Our meals now contained much more meat than potatoes or other vegetables and the food wasn't so good any more. I forced the meat down first then enjoyed the potatoes, beans or bread.

The first slaughter I watched was of a beautiful calf. It was brought to the cleared area in front of the stone rooms.

Men gathered around to assist and waited for the expert to come to kill the calf, which was held with a rope around its neck. It stayed still – I think it was frightened with so many men around. I stood in front of it looking at its beautiful face and wanting to hug it so much. I felt very sad about what the men were going to do and couldn't make up my mind whether to go or stay and watch. The slaughterman arrived, a very short man wearing a cap, baggy trousers and a jacket much too big for him. He carried a small bundle under his arm. He began to speak to the men about the war as he unwrapped the bundle he was carrying, spreading it over a pile of firewood and revealing several shiny knives of different sizes. He continued to speak to the men as if he had come there just for the chat, never mentioning once what he was going to do. I thought he wasn't going to do the job right away so I stayed.

The man went on chatting while taking off his jacket and rolling up his shirt sleeves. He then picked one long pointed knife, which he placed in his left hand and a short pointed one in his right hand. Still talking, he casually approached the front of the calf, raised his right arm holding the short pointed knife as high as he could and came down with a mighty force on the calf's head. The calf immediately collapsed; the knife was left in the head. The man then quickly transferred the long pointed knife from his left hand to his right and went for the throat. The men assisting hadn't done anything like this before and they looked apprehensive, nervous and confused about what to do. They told me off for being there, so I walked away. I was sad for the beautiful calf but I was pleased that I stayed and saw that the calf didn't suffer too much.

A Different View

It was a day with a bright clear sky and a gentle breeze. Father told my brother and me that we were going to cut wood for the fire near the place where we would have a good view of our town. "Don't be frightened," he said. "Today the aeroplanes won't come like they did the last time. You can stop and look as long as you like." Happily we walked quite a distance to a place where Father began to cut into a cluster of thin tall trees and from where we could only see the northern mountains across the town, but Father promised that after he had cut an amount of wood we would go to the part where we had a full view. My brother and I stood on a clear patch of a few square metres where the wood had already been cut. It was a very steep slope, rocky and moss-covered, otherwise we were completely surrounded by tall, slender trees. It was cold. We watched Father find a firm position for his feet, then he raised the long-handled axe, his arms extended high above his shoulders, and with a mighty force brought it down at an angle, hitting the base of the tree. He repeated the action until the tree fell to the ground, every now and then turning to look at us to make sure we were a safe distance from the chippings flying in the air. It was very quiet except for the simultaneous distinct sounds of Father's heavy breathing as he brought the axe down and the solid knock each time the axe hit the tree trunk that echoed in the empty space around us.

After some time Father stopped, wiped the perspiration from his brow and took his jacket off, saying, "Are you feeling cold?" "Yes," we both replied, to which he said, "In a while we'll go, the walk will warm you up." He picked up the axe to start cutting again when we heard the sound of aeroplanes. Father said, "Don't be frightened, they are a long way from us this time." The sound came from the eastern end of the town, not the west, from where we normally saw them coming. The deep growling sound told us they were bombers and soon they began to appear in groups, in their usual perfect formation. In our minds we welcomed them since they were trying to oust the enemy from our homes, but at the same time we feared being injured, nor did we want our homes destroyed. The view of them from the mountain top was always an amazing sight that compelled our attention and it had become a habit to look and count them until they were out of sight. As they came closer to the centre of the town the deep growling, mournful sound increased, which was scary, but we didn't feel threatened because they were flying in the wrong direction. When they reached the centre of the town, all at once the German guns opened fire, relentlessly filling the sky with hundreds and hundreds of explosions below and in front of the aeroplanes' flight path. The noise of the aeroplanes and the exploding shells was horrifying. The bombers continued without altering their course, speed or height, displaying their usual gallant magnificence. Suddenly, they began to release the bombs, which from where we were standing looked like big dark bottles. In the first few seconds I counted eleven raining down on our town. When Father realised what was happening, he shouted, "They are coming our way. Get down, get down, keep your head down!" as he rushed towards us and flung himself down next to my brother. We lay face down as the bombs exploded, the noise in the sky just above us so powerful it seemed as if two huge metal castles were crashing against each other, intense, savagely brutal sounds that terrified me. In between the sounds I heard Father repeating, "Keep your head down, keep your head down!"

A bomb exploded somewhere on the mountain – I heard the shrapnel hitting the stones around us ping, ping, ping and the ground with a fast whooshing sound. I had counted eleven bombs but there were many, many more, it seemed they were never going to stop. I lifted my head slightly once and saw Father's arm extended, his hand covering my brother's head. I felt hurt that he wasn't covering mine too, but a second look made me realise he was too far away to reach me. When the bombs stopped exploding and the roar of the aeroplanes diminished, the guns stopped firing. Father shouted from his prone position, "Are you both all right?" "Yes," I shouted back. It was all over, but the three of us remained lying face down; the terror and shock had been too great for us to get up straight away. I felt devastated and couldn't hear properly, only feel my heart pounding.

We slowly got up. I felt stunned as if I had just awakened from a heavy sleep. Father looked at us, his face anguished, his eyes stunned. All he said was, "Let's get away from here", as if the place was evil. He picked up his jacket and axe and we followed him as quickly as we could, not a word being spoken, just lifting our legs over the rocks and bumpy ground. Father kept looking back to see how we were doing. I looked back once and saw clouds of smoke in the sky above the town. All we wanted to do was distance ourselves from the place where we had been so traumatised. Father took such long strides that it seemed at times he had forgotten we were following and trying to keep up, then he would stop and turn, waiting and looking at us. His face looked so agitated, frowning and full of fear, and though he didn't say, I knew why. I wouldn't mention it either, because it was too frightening to contemplate, but I was worried too, because Mother was where all the bombs had exploded. We met three or four young men from the shelters hurrying to the point where they could see the town, all looking anxious. They stopped and one asked Father, "Did you see where the bombs exploded?" Without stopping, Father replied, "No, but I'm going down as soon as I've taken the boys back."

Back at the shelters, inside the stable, Father took his empty rucksack and hat. Grandmother had anticipated Father's action and handed him some food wrapped in a linen serviette, saying, "Eat something on the way otherwise you'll fall ill, what would we do then?" He turned to me and my brother and said, "I will be back tomorrow morning before you wake up." He was back very early the next morning and told us Mother was all right, but spoke of the utter devastation the bombardment had caused.

Pastimes

The winter weather had taken a turn for the worse, with bitter cold days, torrential rain and blustering, howling winds. Dampness penetrated the body and it was impossible to feel warm or comfortable. Outside, the ground became very muddy with puddles of water everywhere. Inside the stable, it was tacky underfoot. Although a big fire was kept going all the time, it never warmed the place up as the wind came through the open doorway and the stone wall. If I sat by the fire I was often in the way; cooking for lunch and supper took a long time and then someone would return from getting provisions or cutting wood and had to dry their jackets, trousers and socks, so there wasn't space for me. There wasn't even space to stand without getting in someone's way and people became irritable over the smallest thing.

We didn't go into each other's shelters because every place was the same, straw and blankets on the floor, pots, baskets with foodstuffs, a fire with no chimney in a corner, so many dispirited people just standing around, trying to keep warm. Each family felt immensely humiliated to be in such a situation. If it wasn't raining, discussions were held outside the shelters. When the weather was dry and not too windy I would go outside with my brother and we would somehow amuse ourselves playing with sticks or stones until we felt too cold to remain in the open air. There wasn't anything else to play with or to do. My brother was only six years old and most of the time he stayed with our young aunts, who treated him like a little boy. He was much more placid than I was and I don't think he was fully aware of our misery and plight.

I was active all the time. I now think that my biggest problem was my sensitivity to the situation and to other people's feelings; little escaped my attention. I felt compassion and with it came concern and a feeling of responsibility, that I had to be of help. I tried to be helpful by bringing firewood inside, and although I was frightened and protested, I did go on watch many times. I was always asking how Mother was, and when they discussed something I eagerly offered my opinion, which I am now sure made me an absolute nuisance. I was obedient and never, never complained. There was nothing more I could do in that dangerous, uncontrollable situation where even men of experience were unable to help. Pray, maybe; that I did.

We received only bad news at this time but the adults didn't want me to hear it, so I learned to listen without their noticing, by acting uninterested, pretending I was playing, or quietly singing. Since most of the communication was conducted outside, I tried to listen while pretending to get some firewood then returning to tidy the pile up. The few snatches of conversation I heard told me the core of the problems, which only served to make me unhappy and which I couldn't share with anyone because I wasn't supposed to know. I also worried about Mother, who was holding on in the town trying to protect the contents of our home and that of her parents, as were some other women and older men.

Some of the conversation I overheard indicated that the soldiers were getting more and more aggressive and cruel. I heard that Mother was courageous and tried to be clever by not showing any resentment towards the soldiers. Mother's parents' house was now occupied by an Austrian officer who behaved more reasonably towards her. She washed his clothes, which helped her to remain unsuspected and therefore able to continue to take provisions to the foot of the mountain where Father would be waiting to collect them. Then another officer went to our home with three soldiers and told Mother to get out, saying he needed the place to house his soldiers. Mother then went to sleep in a barn with other women at night, but she continued to return to our home during the day in the hope that if she was around they wouldn't take all our possessions away. The great hope always was that any day now the Allied soldiers would arrive and liberate us from the tyranny, misery and fear. Only hope gave everyone the strength to battle on in silence day after day. There was no other way but to wait.

I remember nothing, absolutely nothing, of what was for me the most wonderful day of the year, Christmas Day, with its infinite beauty, excitement, fraternity and love. Where did it go to this time? I only remember hearing that Mother's parents' house had been taken over by a new officer, who was arrogant and aggressive. When Mother wanted to take two of the terracotta pots with the large foliage from the balcony to help decorate the church for Christmas Day mass, she politely asked permission and told the officer why she wanted them. He allowed this, but waited at the foot of the stairs with two armed soldiers to make sure she took nothing else.

I heard too that the soldiers liked our town very much. They found comfortable homes and, what was more, being mostly a farming community, the houses were full of the summer's harvest, including large vats of good wines, which couldn't be hidden. Some soldiers, instead of calling the town by its proper name, 'Villa Latina', called it 'Villa D'Oro' (Villa of Gold.) They also said to Mother that after they had won the war, officers would take charge of Italy's cities and solders would be given charge of towns like ours. Mother was told that our house and everything in it was now theirs, and a soldier took a deckchair of ours and gave it to her, saying, "This is a present for you", just to make his point. They meant to stay. They installed themselves in our homes, arrogantly confiscating our goods, displaying their supremacy. Reason, understanding, justice and compassion were completely disregarded.

We continued to endure the misery on the dismal wet cold mountain, living in what had been built as shelters for sheep, and very poor ones at that. My escape from the unremittingly depressing situation was my great and enduring passion for the wonderful, mesmerising sounds of music. My earliest, clearest memories are of listening to music and singing. Now, in this life of squalor, the agonising day-to-day struggle, to hear music or someone singing was as impossible as having an intelligent conversation with a donkey or sheep.

At times when I wasn't feeling afraid, I found it difficult to suppress my desire to sing. If I could sit by the fire I went into my own private world and would very quietly sing or hum my favourite songs, one after another. It pleased me to do that very much, but soon I would be told to be quiet, so I stayed quiet for a while but then I would start to sing again without realising it, only becoming aware that I was singing when I was told off once more, this time more sharply. There were times when I hummed my songs very, very quietly, then an inner sense told me that if I didn't stop I would be told off, so to prove it was right I continued humming and within a few seconds was indeed told to be quiet. If it wasn't raining or too windy, I would go outside and sing quietly, but soon I would hear a loud voice saying "Stai zitto" (Be quiet). My attempts to escape and snatch a few moments of peace, tranquillity or pleasure were invariably denied me, but I never felt hurt by the telling off. I knew only too well how tragic the situation was and felt I was wrong to indulge my desire to sing, but couldn't help myself. The wonder and beauty of music were always there, flowing in my veins and uplifting my heart.

Days passed and the weather continued cold and damp in the misty valley. Grandfather's health became worse. He didn't get up any more and he coughed and coughed; it was so sad to hear his sounds of pain and discomfort. With no possibility of a doctor's help, Grandmother and everyone else were very worried about his state of health. I seemed to be in everybody's way inside the stable. Every time I went near the fire I had to move while a large and a small saucepan were arranged on the fire to cook lunch or supper, for ten of us now as Father's cousin also came to sleep in the stable. Terracotta bricks had to be continually warmed by the fire then wrapped in a piece of cloth and placed under the blankets near Grandfather to keep him warm. Everyone looked gloomy and bad-tempered, in the depths of misery, so I often went out in the hope of seeing my friend Bruno, whose company I always enjoyed.

One morning it was drizzling, but avoiding the muddy ground I walked the few metres to Bruno's shelter stepping on large stones sticking out of the ground. I was seen by Bruno's mother, who said, "Come in, why are you getting wet?" Inside the small room were seven members of Bruno's family; overcrowded it certainly was, but not as much as our place. Bruno's mother told me, "Warm yourself by the fire or you'll catch a cold." I did warm myself and it was good to have a change of scenery, Bruno's family were always so very, very nice. Soon Bruno said, "Vogliamo andare fuori?" (Shall we go out?).

Outside it was still drizzling so we went under an oak tree, but the wind blew the rain on to us and we were getting wet, so we went to shelter in a stable where the sheep were out grazing. In the stable were two old men sitting on three-legged milking stools, peacefully chatting and smoking their pipes. The smell of the tobacco smoke was pleasant as it took some of the stench of the stable away. Bruno and I sat on the opposite side where the low manger stood, just watching the pipe smokers. We found the scene quite amusing. As one spoke the other listened, slowly smoking his pipe at the side of his mouth and every few seconds, keeping the pipe in the same position, opening the other corner of his mouth and puffing out little white clouds of smoke. Then a short pause and he slowly took the pipe out of his mouth to speak while the other went through the same procedure, except that in his case the little white clouds were released from the centre of his mouth. They went on doing this alternately, with Bruno and I chuckling at the scene, until eventually they went out. Bruno and I laughed and laughed, watching each other imitating the pipe smokers by puffing out at the centre and side of our mouths. We were so fascinated by the amusing scene and the pleasant smell of tobacco that Bruno said, "Shall we smoke a pipe too?" "We haven't got a pipe," I answered. Bruno moved away, saying, "Come with me, I know what to do."

Nearby was an oak tree with the biggest acorns I had ever seen. We searched among the leaves under the tree for the largest, and back in the stable Bruno produced his pen-knife, cut off the top quarter of the acorns, scooped out the inside, then made a small hole near the bottom. We found a shrub which had branches with a soft centre from which Bruno took two very thin straight twigs, cleaned the insides with a piece of wire, cut them to size, pushed them in the hole at the base of the acorn and there we were, each with a pipe. For tobacco we crushed dried oak leaves and packed our pipes. Bruno cautiously went to get a lit piece of firewood and we both began to puff our pipes, imitating the way the two old men smoked. We tried hard to get the little white clouds out of the corner of our mouths, our eyes strained as we puffed away, coughing and coughing, but couldn't quite achieve the desired effect. However, we did feel good about our secret. We hid the pipes between the spaces in the stone wall inside the stable and planned to return for our smoke the next day. We knew that if we were found out we would both get a good telling off, so feeling guilty but putting on an innocent look, we returned to our shelters, feeling like two grown-up men of the world. The smoking left an unpleasant, bitter taste on the tongue and in the mouth; it was so unpleasant, remaining for the rest of the day, that after two or three days we decided to give up smoking.

The Priest: January 1944

One morning at about eleven o'clock – it was cold but there was a gentle winter sun – we had a surprise visit from our parish priest. A chair was provided for him to sit on facing the sun in the cleared area in front of the shelters. His name was Don Pasquale. He was dressed the way we had always seen him, with the long black robe and very wide-rimmed domed hat. This time he was also wearing a black overcoat and a black scarf around his neck. Everyone gathered around him as greetings were exchanged, then he asked after the people who weren't present. When he heard that Grandfather was ill, he immediately went to him inside our stable, while everyone stayed outside. I think he heard Grandfather's confession. In the meantime coffee was prepared for when he returned to the chair and once again he was surrounded by everyone present, mostly women and youngsters like myself. Everyone was hoping that he might have some good news about the war ending. The priest was the saintly man who baptised and married people, and more so he was the saintly man whom we used to listen to every Sunday preaching the gospel loudly from the altar of our church and speaking of the wrong people do, but he also seemed to have the answers to resolving what was unjust. The words of the saintly man were believed; they gave reassurance and guidance for a better life on earth and in heaven. Now, was the saintly man going to give good news regarding the war? Was he going to give reassurance and guidance, as he gave each Sunday from the altar? That was what people craved. Questions upon questions were asked. The priest had hardly finished answering one question before another was put: "Don Pasquale, when do you think the war will end?", "Don Pasquale, do you think the Allied Forces will get the Germans out of our houses soon?", "Don Pasquale, the Germans have made us leave our homes, they won't make us leave here as well, will they?"

"What do you think?" "Where do we go?" The questions never seemed to stop, all hoping to receive favourable replies, but the answers from the priest were always the same: "Maybe, let's hope, perhaps, God willing." When he had the opportunity to say what he had come there to say, only then did we hear the priest's true opinion. He said something like this: "I have come to see you all to say goodbye. I am going to leave the town. The aggression and tension are bad now but I see it becoming much worse. The war will continue. The Germans have established themselves so strongly, with so much armour, in our town and all the surrounding areas, guns are positioned everywhere, it will be difficult to get them out. I think the battle will continue for a long time and it will be even more ferocious than we have already seen." These words filled the minds of everyone around him with clouds of melancholy, more fear, more insecurity; he was believed now as he was believed when he gave his sermons at the altar. He shook hands with everyone, saying, "Let's hope that we will see each other again soon," and went, leaving his flock with their minds in a deeper wilderness than the mountain where we stayed.

Capture

A day or so later, Father received a message from Mother saying that she couldn't remain to protect our home for much longer. Matters had become much worse. Would he make one last attempt to get home to see what more could be hidden and what needed to be taken away to the mountain, then she too would leave and come to the hideout.

The next day Father managed to get home and achieved quite a lot, in particular filling one of the rooms with our better and more important possessions. He then sealed off the doorway with blocks and placed a large wardrobe in front to hide it. Afterwards, he got together what he was going to bring up the mountain, while Mother kept watch. If any German soldier came towards our home Father would escape by sliding down the pole from his bedroom into our kitchen garden. The pole had already saved Father from being captured once before.

It was on this particular day that I started to feel ill. I had a sore chest, which felt as if something was burning inside it, and I hoped that Father would come back soon so I could tell him. As time went on, my chest became more painful, so I told Grandmother how I felt. Her answer was, "Don't worry, it's nothing, it will get better." I knew she was worried about Grandfather's state of health, so I felt I couldn't approach her again. My only hope was that Father would return earlier than his usual time, then perhaps he could do something. Anxiously, I waited and waited for him, looking at the track on the opposite hill and wishing and wishing that he would appear. It was getting dark and Father always returned before dark. I sat by the fire, thinking any noise or footstep was him, but each time it was a big disappointment.

Some time later we heard firm footsteps coming up the track. Grandmother rushed out and I followed, hoping it was Father, but instead it was my friend Bruno's brother Pasquale returning from the town, carrying a rucksack and a full sack on his shoulders. "Have you seen my son Crescenzo?" Grandmother asked. Pasquale answered, "Err, yes err, I don't think he's returning tonight, I don't know." Pasquale's answer was confusing, as if Father wasn't returning he would have sent a definite clear message. The way Pasquale answered made me suspect that something wasn't right. I stayed outside and, hiding behind a huge heap of firewood, saw Pasquale speaking to two brothers, Domenico and Giustino, but I was too far away to hear what he was saying. It was almost dark now. The three stood facing each other and I could see how engrossed they were in what was being said. I picked up a twig and squatting down, my back turned towards them, I lightly drew a small square on the ground, pretending it was a house. Because of the darkness I could hardly see what I was doing. Remaining squatted, I quietly moved backwards towards the men, drawing two parallel lines, pretending it was a path to the house, until I could hear what Pasquale was saying. I kept the twig pointing to the ground to continue drawing in case I was noticed, and listened while Pasquale described how he managed to hide when the soldiers approached his house and that they had caught between twenty and thirty men. Then came the shock when he said: "They caught Crescenzo [Father] as he was sliding down the pole at the rear of his home. His wife pleaded with the soldiers not to take him, then pleaded with the officer who was staying at her parents' house, but it was all in vain. They marched him away at gunpoint and Lisetta (Mother) was left by the roadside crying." They began to move away, Pasquale saying, "Don't let his mother know."

For a moment I remained where I was, feeling as if my body was a heavy piece of metal, then I rose from my squatting position and slowly walked back to the stable, desolate and loaded with a sorrow I couldn't share because I wasn't supposed to know anything. Also, it would have been such a dreadful shock for Grandmother, and more so for Grandfather who was so ill. As I entered the stable my brother was sitting by the fire in our usual corner away from the door. He looked at me and asked, "When is Father coming back?" I replied that I didn't know. My chest was still sore and I said to Grandmother that I wasn't hungry and was going to sleep. I covered my head with the blankets, wishing that my chest wasn't so sore, and kept on thinking of Father being led away at gunpoint, having to carry heavy guns and ammunition up to the battlefront with the armed soldiers behind him. I thought of Mother, left crying by the roadside. Tears came to my eyes. I wanted to cry, but I managed to hold it back because no one had to know what had happened to Father. I heard my uncles talking while they were having supper, justifying Father's non-return, saying that he had to do so many things as everything had to be abandoned, and that it was safer to carry goods through the field to the foot of the mountain at night. They started to say the rosary, which was the nightly ritual, and when they recited the prayers collectively I cried under the blankets and took gasps of air because their sound obliterated my crying. I fell asleep and when I woke up my chest felt a little better, but I immediately thought of Father. I wished that it wasn't true. I wished that I hadn't woken up.

It must have been quite early the same evening because the fire was still alight. I watched the flickering flames sending flashes of light to different parts of the flaking poles forming the low rustic ceiling. I wanted to sit up and watch the fire, but I couldn't because we were packed so close together. Everyone was in bed and I raised my head to look. We were all in line, one by one, my two aunts on my left, my brother on my right and the others lying next to each other on the platform made of tree trunks which served as a long bed for the ten of us. Everyone seemed to be in such a deep sleep, making different sounds as they breathed with now and then the occasional murmur, otherwise it was very quiet. Then I heard the howl of a fox followed by the shriek of a crow. It sounded frightening out there, so I put my head under the blankets again. I kept on waking up throughout the night, thinking of Father. I felt so lost, so helpless, it was such a heavy burden on my mind, such a long, long, sorrowful night.

I woke up again to the sound of people speaking. Firstly I saw that the door was off the doorway and the cold air was hitting my face. It was very early. There was hardly any dawn light so it was very dark inside the stable. I just saw Uncle Benedetto lighting the fire and Uncle Domenico coming in with a bundle of firewood. Then I lifted my head up and sitting at the foot of the platform next to my brother was Father, who moved over to me, touched my head and said, "Are you all right?" Then he took my hand and held it tightly, just looking at me. I pretended that I knew nothing. The unbelievable surprise, the shock, my amazement, were such that I remained speechless and so stunned that I hardly showed any reaction, but something very heavy within me suddenly went away. My mind and inner body were rejoicing to the full. Everyone was awake while Father continued telling the frightening story of how he and Vincenzo's father had escaped from the soldiers guarding them and spent the whole night walking through mountains and crossing a river in the dark. Soon after crossing the river they found themselves within a few metres of where the Germans were positioned with an anti-aircraft gun; the reason they didn't walk into them was because the soldiers were all talking inside their tent. They quietly moved away and re-crossed the river. It was a long, frightening story. Father said that before he came up he went to the barn where Mother was sleeping to tell her that he was safe and that he would go and fetch her the following day. It had been a very long and painful night, but all was right now.

Mother's Story

As I have said, Mother and a few other courageous women persisted in remaining in the town among the German soldiers both to protect their homes and possessions and to secretly take foodstuffs to the foot of the mountain for their men to bring up to the hideouts. They also informed the men when there was a reduction in the number of soldiers in the town and it might be less dangerous for them to cautiously return home and take away heavier goods. I also mentioned that there were three soldiers living in our home, so at night Mother went to sleep in a barn with other women but returned home every morning in the hope that her presence would prevent soldiers confiscating everything from our and her parents' home across the road. When I asked Mother what it was that finally made her decide to abandon everything and come up to the mountain hideout, she gave me the following account.

From time to time Mother had minor confrontations with the soldiers, protesting when they arrogantly broke into our home taking whatever they wanted, although they just said it was all theirs now, taking no notice of what she said. The actual Italian words they used were "Noi padroni" (We owners) "Tutto nostro" (All ours). When the three soldiers who were staying in our home came back from duty, the first thing they did was remove their helmets and place them on top of the sideboard in the kitchen, then took off their belts, which held their revolvers, and hung them on the coat stand. The belts remained there while they washed, ate, slept and so on. One day the three were about to go back on duty. They were all ready in their uniforms with helmets on and went to the coat stand to take their belts. One belt had the revolver missing. Suddenly the three turned on Mother like an enraged pack of dogs, pushing her against the wall, shouting and demanding where she had hidden the revolver. Mother, shocked at the sudden attack, nervously answered that she had not touched the revolver, but they were convinced she had stolen it.

She was kept against the wall surrounded by the three, all shouting questions at the same time. Then one took his revolver and pointed it at her face, fiercely demanding that she tell him where she had hidden the missing revolver. Fear made Mother shout back over and over again that she had never touched anything of theirs, telling them to think where else they could have put it when they came back. The one whose revolver was missing went into the room where he slept while the other two furiously continued their interrogation, keeping the revolver pointed at her face, saying, "Who have you given the revolver to? Who else comes here? You know where it is, tell me now."

Mother told me she was absolutely terrified. Then a minute or so later the one who had gone into his bedroom came out holding his revolver. Each apologised profusely, asking Mother to forgive them as they were very tired and to lose their arms was an extremely serious matter.

Mother said that being alone, surrounded by the three men, particularly with their helmets on, it didn't seem to her that they were the same people. Their shouting and wild looks terrified her. Afterwards, horrible thoughts entered her mind about what they might have done had the revolver not been found. The next day the three moved away, but Mother couldn't forget how easy it was to become innocently involved in a situation which could have had severe consequences.

Mother went on to tell me of another incident that took place two days later. At the rear of her parents' house there was a large, substantial store-room, which contained much of the overspill of the house, table, chairs, beds and other household goods. Mother had hidden things of value among these. She saw an officer and a soldier inspecting the outside walls of this room and went inside, thinking she might stop them looking by telling them that the two casks that normally held wine were empty, as the wine had been taken by previous soldiers. Once inside the room the officer spoke to his soldier, who turned to Mother and told her to empty the room completely as it was needed to carry out some tests with gas or something, she didn't quite understand what. Her immediate thought was "I am not going to help you to kill us", so she answered, "Non lo posso fare, e troppo pesante per me" (I can't do it, it is too heavy for me). The soldier said, "Devi fare" (You have to do it), but Mother replied that she wasn't in good health and couldn't. The soldier said he had seen her carrying things and washing clothes, so "Fare tutto immediatamente" (Do everything immediately). "It's too heavy, I can't do it," Mother replied, directing her answer to the officer hoping he would overrule the soldier, but the officer didn't reply, only continued to observe the situation. The soldier, shouting in German and staring hard at her, then made a sign with his hand, passing it across his throat. This frightened Mother and made her walk away. For the rest of that day and night she couldn't rest thinking of the horrid look on the soldier's face as he stared at her, making the cruel gesture across his throat which could only have meant she would be killed. All this made her reflect more deeply on a matter that was a permanent fear in her and that would have brought catastrophic consequences if the Germans were to have found out. Since the Germans had taken full control of our town hall they were able to check on all matters concerning our town, particularly the number of men, their professions and political allegiance. That was where information on each person was held, including the records of people's date and place of birth. Mother told me, "My body trembled with fear in case they found out that I was born and educated in Scotland and spoke fluent English."

These two serious incidents, together with the threat to kill her and the thought that they might find out she was a British subject, instilled a deep fear in her that her situation was a very dangerous one. She felt terrified that at any moment they were going to appear and take her away, or something worse. That was why she sent the message to Father to go and get her, fear for her life having now vanquished her courage.

Mother went on to tell me about the last day Father went home, the day he was captured. While waiting for him she saw a small metal object on the window-sill. She tried to see if it unscrewed, which it didn't. There was another part which wouldn't come away either. She didn't want to use force in case it broke, so left the article where it was. When Father arrived that day he immediately told her not to touch it as it was a hand grenade and had she used force it would have exploded in her hands. A second grenade – I will explain later how it was discovered – was buried among the ashes in the kitchen stove, just below the grill where the charcoal burned. Mother didn't use the stove that day because she was so distressed by Father having been captured. Obviously, the soldier meant to carry out what he had signified with his hand.

The day Mother left she had arranged to meet Father at the foot of the mountain in the late morning. She said, "I left the barn where I slept and plucked up the courage to make one last visit home to say goodbye. While inside I prayed and said to the saints, it's up to you now. I made the sign of the cross, shedding tears, and quietly walked away. I was alone, carrying a bundle of clothing under my arm, on the way to meet your Father. I was afraid, fearing that I had pushed my luck too far. When I saw soldiers I walked slower, but I felt my heart beating faster with anxiety to get away, feeling that at any moment I was going to be confronted, or hear their voices calling me. I felt sad, guilty and a great sense of loss, because after the struggle, the sacrifices and the danger I had put myself in, now I was turning my back on everything. I felt as if I was betraying all that we treasured, but my determination, my courage, had now been overtaken by fear. I was probably the last or one of the last to leave the town. When I saw your Father waiting among the woods at the foot of the mountain, I felt as if a big load had been taken off my body. The climb was tiring, but it was all forgotten when I saw you and Enio. I was no longer sorry I had left."

That was my Mother's story.

Reunion

It was late in the afternoon when my brother and I spotted Mother and Father coming along the track over the hill opposite us. Now being real experts on the mountain terrain, we ran like spring lambs as fast as we could, bouncing from one stone to another down the track. It was at the bottom of the valley near the well where we met. Mother hugged us very tightly for a long time and we shared moments of great joy as she scrutinised our faces and said we looked well. Father looked on for a while then said, "Let's go, you will have lots of time to talk." Together we walked up to the shelters, where Mother was greeted by the relatives, and soon everyone who lived there came to greet her, saying, "You have been very brave, how did you manage to stay there till now? Weren't you afraid?" Mother answered, "All I have done hasn't counted one bit, now it's all left for them to take. Oh yes, I was frightened. I didn't know what might happen to me from one moment to the next; fear has made me leave everything." Much chatting went on until Grandmother called to say that supper was ready. All the people went back to their shelters and we went into the stable and sat around the fire. Grandfather was slowly recovering from his serious illness and was sitting by the fire in his usual place next to the wall nearest to the door with a blanket wrapped around him. Mother sat next to him chatting and sympathising about his ill health. My brother and I always sat next to the wall away from the door and the rest formed a half circle around the fire.

The look and condition of the stable was something we had become used to, but to Mother's eyes it was extraordinary and unbelievable degradation for human beings to live in such a place. She said nothing, but now and again she turned her head to look and then looked again to take in what she could not quite believe. We ate our supper in the usual way, sitting around the fire holding our plates. After Grandmother and my two aunts had washed up the utensils and plates in a bucket outside the stable, a good supply of wood for the night was brought in and the low movable door placed in the doorway and secured with the pole. There were eleven of us now living in the cramped conditions, sitting close to each other around the fire. It was cold, but we always had a big fire. After sitting for some time with the heat of the fire on my face, I felt almost hypnotised by it. I felt content, because we were all together and safe. Some conversation went on and when my brother or I spoke Mother looked at us and listened attentively, with a big smile. Grandmother announced that it was time to say the inevitable rosary. We all made the sign of the cross, then Grandmother would say the first part of the prayer and we all responded saying the rest. Sacred prayers were voiced with profound sincerity in the hope of gaining grace for our desperate needs. The collective voices answered in harmony, making a distinctive melancholic sound, like a chant, within the ancient dark stable, with only the flickering flames lighting up the sorrowful faces forming the tight half circle around the fire. Everyone had their eyes closed, creating an atmosphere of solemnity, as if the Good Lord and the saints were present, listening to us. It was then that I truly saw Mother's face. The stress, the sacrifices, the fear she had endured were clearly etched on her face; it was sunken, exhausted and very sad. I looked at Father, who was sitting next to Mother looking totally lost. The prayers emerged from his lips automatically, he looked so deep in thought while he prayed with his eyes closed. He frowned, raised his eyebrows, shook his head sideways, lowered his head on his hands for a few moments then dropped his hands on his knees and remained bowed, shaking his head sideways again. He seemed lost in desperation. Yes, this was the day that everything was abandoned. Many months of struggle and strife were abandoned too, but then, at least there was hope; now even hope was abandoned.

It was this night, during the recital of the rosary, when I looked at Mother's face objectively and saw Father so distressed, that I sensed the depth of our desolation and desperation. Reduced to owning little more than the clothes we were wearing and with a limited amount of food to sustain us, we had to endure the bitterly cold winter in the squalor of a stable in such depressing conditions, there because of fear for our lives, seeking to avoid the cruelty and bestiality that the soldiers were capable of committing. I was pleased that Mother was now with us, but the fact that she was made me realise that we were now totally cut off from our home and our former way of life. I went to bed feeling very sad and without any hope.

The morning after Mother's arrival, she asked Father if he would take her to see her parents, who were living in the part of the mountain where Father and I had stayed at first. They decided they would go after lunch. That morning, Mother lost no time seeing to me and my brother. With a bucket of water, a towel and soap she launched herself into washing my face, ears, behind my ears, my arms, in fact, she began to spoil our happy reunion with all this. Since I'd left the town my face hadn't known what water was unless it got wet when it rained. After the washing I was presented with a pair of her knickers to put on. I didn't want to wear them, but Mother said they were made of wool and would keep me warm. They were much too big. Good, I thought, I don't have to wear them, but Mother soon produced a long safety pin, gathered the material up and secured them. When I put my trousers on and they didn't show, I felt pleased because no one would know. My brother went through the same procedure while I sat by the fire. Afterwards, Mother looked through the bundle of clothing she had brought up with her, took out two of her cardigans and we had to put them on. Mine had a row of buttons close together at the front. I didn't want to wear the cardigan as it nearly reached my ankles and we looked like two little girls, but Mother insisted, saying that we looked cold and that the cardigans were thick, made of wool and would keep us warm. She told us we had to keep them on. I felt too embarrassed to go out of the stable, but after some time the frustration of being inside made me pluck up courage and I went out. My brother followed me. I felt self-conscious and uneasy and thought that at any moment someone would say that we looked like two little girls. I avoided making eye contact with anyone. Every footstep or voice I heard I waited for some remark to be made about the way we looked. It didn't rain that day and it wasn't too windy so we stayed out quite a long time and were seen by all the people and no one passed any remark. I remember so well how much more relaxed and warm I felt, a comfort that I hadn't experienced for a very, very long time.

Tragedy Strikes

Days passed with no change in the war situation. It was bitterly cold; the winds were felt even inside the stable. Tempers were very high and everyone seemed so irritable. Squadrons upon squadrons of bombers and fighter aeroplanes continued to pass above us. It seemed that the battlefront wasn't too far away now, as the sounds of exploding shells somewhere beyond the mountains became louder and louder. That was good news, because the Allied soldiers would soon reach our town and we could return to our homes. We didn't fear the shells where we were because there were no German soldiers there, although they had begun to take positions with their anti-aircraft guns about a quarter of the way up the mountain. We knew that one of their positions was next to the chapel where mother's parents had stayed.

Several times just one aeroplane came to do a reconnaissance of the German positions. It remained flying over the town for a long time as the guns continually fired at it. The pilot knew the height he had to stay at so the shells wouldn't quite reach him while he flew back and forth, tilting the aeroplane to one side and then the other, just above the hundreds of explosions filling the air with puffs of smoke. It was amusing, almost as if the pilot was teasing the gunner.

The aeroplane also came over the mountain where we were. I thought he was wasting his time as there were no German soldiers there and I wished I could have told him.

A day or so later in the afternoon, Mother and Father went to see if Mother's parents were all right. Later, when it had become almost dark, we had our supper and sat in our usual positions forming the tight half circle around the fire. Mother and Father had yet to return. Grandmother had just started to recite the rosary and we were all responding to the prayers. All at once we were shocked by the loud long screaming, screeching sound of a shell seeming to pass just above the roof of our stable and then we heard the explosion reverberating somewhere within the valleys of the mountain. The ghastly, sinister sound horrified everyone. Moments later another shell passed over us. Grandmother made the sign of the cross and we all did the same as Grandmother called on the names of many saints to protect us from this unexpected danger, but the shelling went on and on. Each sound created so much tension and fear, followed by a momentary sigh of relief when the danger had passed. The fear of a shell exploding on our roof or near us was horrendous, particularly as the roof was thatched so we had no protection whatsoever. After what seemed an eternity the shelling stopped. Soon people came out of their shelters and began to say, "Why this, there are no German soldiers here, no guns, why are they firing at us?" Many speculated as to where the shells had exploded, hoping it wasn't anywhere where people like us had taken refuge. It was cold and so very dark that I only became aware of people's presence when they spoke, everyone voicing their fear of this new threat. The cold air and darkness soon made everyone return to their shelters. I felt frightened and powerless as no one could tell them that it was us they were firing at. There was concern that Mother and Father hadn't returned, as shells had certainly fallen in the direction they had gone, but fortunately it wasn't too long before their footsteps were heard and we saw they were all right. They told us they were halfway back when the shelling started and took cover behind some rocks, but had no idea where the shells might have exploded. We all went to sleep with the fear of another attack that night.

The next morning I woke up to much talk and sad faces as people spoke of the tragedy the shelling had caused. The shells had made a direct hit on the area where my mother's parents and a large number of people from Atina were living. Mother's parents were safe, but many of the people from Atina were killed and others injured. It was thought that the aeroplane that carried out the reconnaissance over the mountain photographed the large number of people moving around in that area and thought it was a German defence force. The tragedy left everyone in mourning and full of fear for days and days. As I heard people saying "Che disgrazia, che disgrazia" (What a tragedy, what a tragedy), it made me feel very sad as I knew the place well. It was where I had first come to the mountain, where I had spent so much time, where I got to know the people from Atina. One of the persons killed was a nurse who for many days treated an injury on my face and hip due to a fall on a sharp rock – I still bear the scar. She was always so kind and gentle to me.

The thought that the next attack might be on our place made everyone fearful. That very morning, Father organised the construction of a strong army-type shelter within a few metres of our stable so we could quickly take cover in case of an attack. Manpower was plentiful. With picks, shovels and sledgehammers they started cutting into the face of a terraced area, excavating earth and rocks to make a long narrow trench, accessible from the side. To make the top strong they cut down an oak tree, two men repeatedly hitting the base of the tree with big, long-handled axes with machine-like coordination. When the tree fell the trunk was cut into lengths and then split with metal wedges. Perspiration poured down the men's anxious faces as they took turns, using all their strength. The thick chunks of oak were wedged across the open top of the trench then a layer of large stones was placed on them for the shrapnel to bounce off. In a few days we had better protection in case the guns started to fire on us.

There were definite signs that the fighting was escalating to a fierce intensity. The adults around me looked desperately worried and confused as they spoke of the atrocities the Germans were committing and the devastation the bombardments were causing. A man passed by me who had tried to go back to his home, looking stressed and unshaven, his head bowed. No sooner had he entered the shelter where his wife and children were living than I heard all of them crying. I learnt later that a member of the family had been killed in one of the bombardments. The squadrons of English and American bombers continually passed just above us, making their deep, mournful, chanting sound. The Germans, who had taken positions with their guns in all the towns and mountains around us, now began to come closer to the parts of the mountain where we were. Two shells from the Allied guns were fired near to our place. Only two shells. Were these just to test the range of fire for a bigger battle later that or the next day? That was what we feared. I remember handling a piece of the exploded shell as it was cooling down. I couldn't get rid of the stink on my hands for days and days.

New Hiding Places

Then a catastrophe descended on everyone. The German command in our zone gave the order that all civilians had to leave, including those hiding on the mountains. Anyone remaining after the given date would be shot. This news was a devastating shock. Everyone gathered outside the shelters in a state of disbelief, some speechless, staring as if frozen. There were those who refused to accept what was being said, asking: "Ma sei sicuro? Ma è proprio vero? Non puo essere" (But are you sure? But is it really true? It can't be). Others, with tears in their eyes, spoke in anguished tones to one another: "What are we going to do? Where do we go? How do we carry what we need? Will the old people and children be able to walk the distance?" Everyone's mind was in turmoil, but the command had to be obeyed, there was no question about that, or what the consequences would be if it was defied. The order meant what it said. Food, which was still hidden in isolated areas in the town, had to be cautiously retrieved: potatoes, dried beans, smoked sausage, flour, olive oil and somehow, many, many loaves of bread baked in some remote farmhouse.

Heavily loaded with blankets and food, families began to leave. Two days before the final date, the only people left in our place were Father's parents, two brothers, two sisters and Father, Mother, my brother and me. Mother's parents, who were some distance from us, were waiting for Father to collect them the next day, the day of our departure. In the confined space of the stable, goods were being packed in rucksacks, sacks and baskets for everyone to carry the next day. In the bedlam of the preparations, Father exclaimed to his father in a sad but firm voice, "Tomorrow you all go, we can't. I can only carry so much. The boys can't carry much. My wife is not a country woman, she isn't used to carrying things. My father-in-law isn't well, he can't carry much, nor can he stand a long journey on foot. My mother-in-law can't carry much either. You go, we will go and hide – I know where. The Allies will be here soon." Father's younger brother, Uncle Benedetto, said, "I will stay and help you." Father went on to say that there was a small stable where a man used to keep two cows. It was among thick woodland with no track to it, and we wouldn't be found there immediately. Father and Uncle Benedetto carried some of our stores to our new hiding place.

The next day, the day before the ultimatum, it was about ten o'clock when Father's parents, brother and two sisters were ready to leave. We said our goodbyes, hugging and kissing and crying. Uncle Domenico gave my brother and me an apple each as he wiped the tears from his eyes. They loaded their rucksacks and sacks and large baskets for Grandmother and my two aunts to carry on their heads and one by one they started to go. Grandfather said to Father that he would head for a place called Sora where he had a cousin and hoped to reach it in two days if all went well; that was where we would find them if we too were forced to leave. Now they had to descend the mountain via the mule and donkey track. We watched them going down the valley and then climbing the diagonal track opposite. As they reached the top of the hill they stopped, turned and waved at us and we waved back. Uncle Domenico and Civita waved with their handkerchiefs and I felt we all wanted the waving to last forever. They turned and one by one disappeared over the crest of the hill.

Father and Uncle Benedetto went to fetch Mother's parents and their stores. Mother, my brother and I were left all alone. We went back into the stable and sat by the fire. The place was empty now and it was scary. The straw was still on the long platform that had served as a bed for eleven of us, the rest of our goods were all ready for the move. We just waited, huddled together in silence. Mother's face looked so sad and abandoned. Many times I went out of the stable to see if Father and the others were coming, but the place was so quiet and desolate now that each time I went quickly back inside because I was scared. At long last they appeared, coming up the track, Father and Uncle Benedetto carrying the stores, Grandfather carrying some blankets under his arm and Grandmother carrying a bundle of clothing in her arms. Among them popped up the head of Grandmother's pet chicken, looking quite chirpy, whereas the faces of Grandfather and Grandmother were full of fear and sadness and desolation.

We all waited for Father to tell us what to do next. He said, "Benedetto and I will go and take some of the goods now. When we return we will take the straw to sleep on and after that we will all go. Remember we won't be able to make the fire during the day because the Germans will see the smoke and find us." Turning to Mother, he then said, "Boil something, let's have something warm. We will eat here and go before it gets dark." On their return the straw was gathered and secured in two large pieces of canvas, then we all ate and Father reassured us that we had sufficient food to last many days but we had to be economical with the bread. "In two or three days," he told us, "the Allied Forces will come and we can go back home."

We were ready to leave with the last of our possessions. My brother and I too had our rucksacks put on our backs. Father said to me, "Don't let me forget the bucket and rope to draw water from the well, that's important." In single file, we started to walk down to the valley. Leaving the place where I had experienced fear, hardship and danger, I felt somehow sad and even more insecure. At least the experiences we had undergone had been in the company of so many other people that I knew, but now we were alone and going into the unknown. All the responsibilities were Father's, and I felt they were mine too. We went up the diagonal track on the hill opposite and when I reached the top I turned and gave the place one last glance. It looked abandoned and I felt sad, as if we had lost something. We continued along the track, crossing the mountain top, and soon plunged into thick woodland, following Father, walking around shrubs and trees, until we reached the ancient tiny stone-built stable with a tiled roof. It was beginning to get dark and we were surrounded by tall trees that stopped the light coming through. We entered the small, dark stable. The straw was spread on the floor for us to sleep on, as one does for animals. The air was so cold we just stood close to each other awaiting Father's instructions as he looked inside the sacks for the blankets. It was almost dark, we couldn't see very much; only a faint light entered near the open doorway. Then Father said, "Put your blankets down, let's go to sleep and keep warm." My brother and I stood side by side waiting to be told where to lie down. Father took some straw from the floor and placed it in the manger, which we could hardly see. "You two will sleep in the manger," he told us. He lifted my brother into it and then me and we lay facing each other. The manger was deep and narrow at the bottom and too short for the two of us to lie in, so Father lifted one of my legs and placed it between my brother's legs. We lay face upward. I couldn't turn and I couldn't see anyone from the depths of the manger, I just heard their voices as they organised themselves on the floor. This was the place where we were to hide for the next two or three days without making a fire during the day or noise of any kind, waiting until the Allied soldiers came, when we could go home.

I don't know how much later, but it was that very night in that desolate place that we were suddenly awakened, terrorised by explosions of heavy shelling all around us. The shells exploded one after another. They were so loud. I heard Mother saying, "Are you all right?" We all started coughing and Father just managed to shout "Put your heads under the blankets, breathe under the blankets", as the debris and dust from the ancient rafters and crumbling roof tiles kept falling on us. The coughing from the dust was terrible and the shrapnel kept hitting the outside walls among the sounds of shrieking foxes and crows and cracking branches tearing away from trees. The horrific explosions went on and on, seeming as if they were never going to end. It was just as difficult to breathe under the blanket because the dust was there too. When the shelling did stop, I heard Father opening the door to let the dust out, but a gush of cold, smelly air from the exploding shells entered and he quickly shut it again. Mother came to look in the manger and asked if we were all right. She stroked my head and helped me and my brother to sit up as Father brought a cup of water for my brother to drink and then me. It was so dark I had to feel for the cup as I couldn't see it. Everyone had a cup of water, and for a few moments no one spoke. All was quiet now, then Father said, "It's a miracle one of the shells didn't directly hit the stable, just a miracle." He continued, "Try to get some sleep, we must leave this place before dawn. We can't stay here, in the middle of a ferocious battle, we will go and hide in the cave, La Trinta Vecchia (The Old Trinity), no shell or bomb can penetrate there. We must leave as soon as we can see the way. We must not be seen by the Germans."

The next morning I was awakened by Father, who lifted my brother and me out of the manger. Everyone was standing with their blankets folded under their arms and the door was open. It was still dark and so cold. I felt so sleepy I just stood there with my eyes closed. Father said, "We will only carry the blankets,

Benedetto and I will carry some food, the rest can remain here. I will come back for it tonight when it's dark." He put the small rucksacks on my brother and me and said, "Let's go, and don't make any noise and be careful where you put your feet." One by one we went out, following Father, who was carrying his rucksack as well as a full sack on his shoulder. Uncle Benedetto carried the same, Mother and Grandfather carried some of the blankets in their arms and Grandmother carried a bundle and her pet.

We soon reached the track and had to travel across the top of the mountain then quite a way down. Dawn was just about to break as we began the descent to where the cave was situated, halfway down the mountain. It was difficult not to make any noise walking over the loose stones and crumbling rocks of the steep track as it zigzagged on the side of the mountain, but Father kept on telling us all to be careful and not to make any noise. Twice we stopped for a very brief rest, especially for Grandfather, who was finding the descent difficult. We couldn't sit down as everywhere was damp so we just stood for a few minutes. I always closed my eyes; I wanted to sleep.

We could see our town as it became lighter but there was no time to gaze. Father was anxious to come off the track as soon as possible. Grandmother asked if we could stop and rest once more and Father replied that we would soon reach the plateau and leave the track; we could have a good rest then. "Madonna aiutaci" (Madonna help us) said Grandmother, and Father said again, "No one is to speak". He spoke quietly but was quite angry because Grandmother had spoken. We reached the plateau, left the track and followed a very narrow path into dense woodland. There we stopped for a rest, but again were unable to sit anywhere as the grass, moss and stones were all wet. We just stood, breathing heavily from exhaustion and fear, no one wanting to speak, until Father said in a quiet, weary voice, "Let's go, it's not a long way now." We followed him along a narrow curving path into the interior of the mountain, going up and down as it wound around steep bends. In some places there was only enough space to put our feet, with deep drops below. Father always stopped, slowly turned with the heavy sack on his shoulder and made sure that we were all aware of where we had to be extra careful. Then, deep inside the mountain, Father stopped, put the sack on the ground and said with satisfaction, "We have arrived, it's there," as he pointed to a massive vein of rock, "That's where it is, inside that rock."

Father, Uncle Benedetto and I came off the path, climbed a few metres of steep stony ground and were about to approach the base of the massive rock when, to our shock and bewilderment, we came face to face with a man coming out of the cave. For a second or two we all remained still, then the man quietly exclaimed Father's name, saying, "Crescenzo, che succeed?" (Crescenzo, what's going on?).

Father, his voice just about audible, said, "Peppino, I thought we were the only people who'd remained behind, is there room in the cave for us?" To which Peppino answered, "Certamente, vieni, vieni dentro" (Certainly, come, come inside). Father and Peppino helped my grandparents and Mother over the steep, rough ground and we all entered the cave. The first thing confronting me as we entered was a horse and a goat. We stood near the entrance where there was a subdued light while Father told Peppino about our traumatic night and how lucky we were to be alive. Peppino said he had been hiding there for some days with his family, who were all sleeping further inside the cave. I too recognised Peppino; he had been the interpreter for the Germans and he said he feared the Germans might find out he'd been deceiving them. He was called by his wife, who wanted to know what was happening, and went further into the cave to his family. I followed him with my eyes but I couldn't see very much; it was like a dark tunnel.

We were so tired and still regaining our breath but there was nowhere to sit. We hadn't eaten anything since the day before. The cold air was so hostile. We finally sat on our packs and on the stones by placing a blanket over them, Grandmother clutching her pet chicken. Grandfather had his elbows on his knees and bent forward holding his head between his hands. Mother's face was white as she rubbed my brother's hands to warm them.

Father and Uncle Benedetto handed each of us a piece of bread and a piece of cheese, which we chewed as we recovered from our ordeal of fear and fatigue. No words were uttered, just an occasional glance at one another to reassure ourselves that we were together and safe; we had no energy for anything else. The only sound came from the horse's hoofs stamping over the rocky surface of the cave; it too had a long, sad face. The cold grey stone tunnel of the cave only gave us a feeling of destitution and loss, as if life held nothing but sorrow. The fear, the exhaustion and the cold had numbed our bodies and minds. I don't think any of us had much will to live left except for Father, who spoke and acted as if he believed that soon we would come through all the suffering. Father broke the silence, saying to Uncle Benedettto, "We will have to see how we can sleep in here." Since Peppino and his family had occupied the inner part of the cave, the space remaining was near the entrance, through which the cold air and wind came in and where the horse and goat stood. We huddled close together in a state of stupor, lost and dismayed, hardly believing we were in this tunnel of solid grey cold rock. My brother was very cold, full of goose-pimples and trembling. Mother kept on rubbing his knees and blowing warm breath on his hands and she told us not to worry as in two or three days we would be back in our home and all our suffering would be over. Still standing, she pressed my brother's face against her body, her arms around him. Grandmother continued to hold her pet chicken in her arms, stroking the feathers and talking to it, saying, "They are even making you suffer, don't you worry, this will pass. Poor little you."

Father took the rest of the blankets out of the sack and handed them to Mother, saying, "Wrap these around yourselves and try to keep warm, we can't make a fire until tonight when it's dark, otherwise the Germans will see the smoke and find us. Benedetto and I will see what we can find to sleep on." With the blankets around us, sitting on our packs and stones, curled up in a tight circle in the gloomy light of the cave, we closed our eyes, heads bent forward, and tried to rest. From time to time I opened my eyes to see what Father and Uncle Benedetto were doing as they went in and out of the cave bringing in stones of all sizes until they had a very big pile. Then they carefully laid them over the uneven ground, adjusting them to make a level platform. I thought the stone platform looked bumpy and hard, and it was very low on the ground.

Father saw us looking so uncomfortable all crouched together, moving, turning, then standing still and sighing, and left what he was doing and said, "Stand up and move your legs, walk up and down a little, but don't go out and don't make any noise." Mother walked a little further into the cave to speak to Peppino's wife and I went with her. It was much darker there, but I soon became used to it. They were all lying on the platform they had made, even Peppino had gone back under the blanket to keep warm. I counted the bumps under the blankets, nine in all, but I couldn't see them properly. I moved away from Mother's side wanting to help Father, but he wouldn't allow me so I just watched them, keeping the blanket wrapped around me. I was often in the way.

When they had finished making the low platform with the stones they went out again and brought in branches of all sizes, which they arranged flat over the stone platform. Then smaller branches were carefully laid on the top in an attempt to achieve an even surface. Finally they spread some blankets over the top and

Father said, "Ecco, adesso potete dormire" (Here you are, now you can go to sleep). We all lay on the improvised bed and tried to rest, but no matter how I tossed and turned there were so many branch ends digging into my body that it was very uncomfortable. Everyone was moving, twisting and turning, but no one complained. We just stayed close together, our heads under the blankets so as not to breathe in the cold air and keep our warm breath under the blanket.

It was around midday when Father again gave us all a piece of bread and some cheese and we ate it sitting on the spiky platform. I really wanted to get up because of all the bits of wood pressing against my body, but Mother and Father kept telling us to stay a while longer, as it was warmer under the blankets than standing. Father collected dry pieces of wood and twigs to light the fire for that night, made a huge pile, then selected the fine, dry, smaller pieces to start it. Fortunately, Peppino had two small barrels of water and offered us some, but we had to be economical with it as the wells were between the valleys on the top of the mountain and one could only go there in the dark and be back before full daylight. I heard Father say to Uncle that they would go and collect the rest of our stores the next morning. "We must be back before the dawn light," he said.

It was late in the afternoon when we all got up. I stayed by Father, who said to me, "As soon as it's dark I will make a very big fire and we will all warm up, boil potatoes and eat." There was hardly any light in the cave now.

Father went out many times to see if it was dark enough to prevent the Germans seeing the smoke. All I

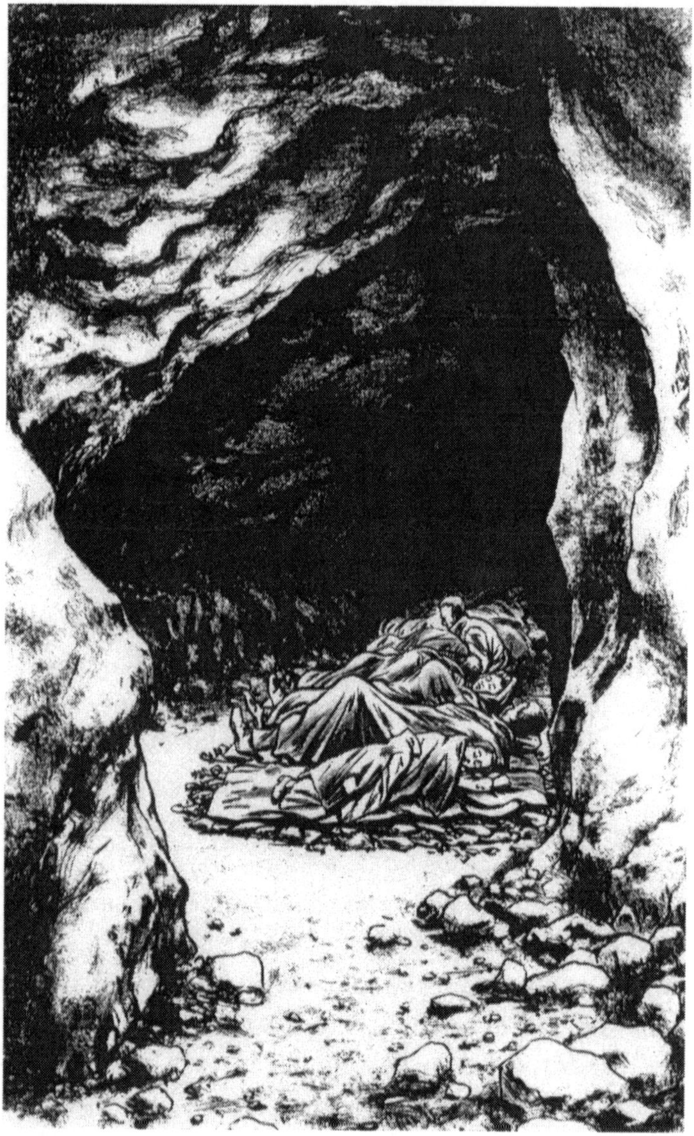

kept hearing was the others asking "E buio?" (Is it dark?) and Father answering "No ancora" (Not yet). Eventually Father looked out and turned to us with relief, saying, "E buio abbastanza" (It's dark enough) "I can light the fire now." Because he had carefully selected wood that was fine and dry, within minutes he had a blazing fire that lit up the whole cave and gave me my first clear view of it. The cave was shaped like a tunnel, slightly arched from floor to ceiling; the widest area was at the entrance, about two and a half metres and about the same height, then it tapered downward for about ten metres and there was a cavity that went on that looked mysterious and scary. A piece of canvas was placed over the entrance and held in position at the top with two poles placed diagonally against the rock and stones at the base so the wind wouldn't lift it off. It stopped only some of the wind blowing inside the cave.

Everyone was up now wanting to be by the fire, nine people from Peppino's family and we seven. There was no room for us all in the small space that remained where the fire was lit, near the entrance between our sleeping platform and the horse and goat. The only other space was along the end of the sleeping platform. We didn't know where to put ourselves, and just stood dazed by the cold. No one spoke, we just looked pathetically at each other, except Father, who was always active. He got a really good fire going, not just flames but solid chunks of wood burning and giving real heat. He had worked really hard that day, showing courage and hope, speaking words of reassurance, but when I saw his face lit up by the flames it revealed so much sadness, exhaustion and anxiety that it made me sad. Now with the fire blazing it was time to boil the potatoes, but to my disappointment Father asked Peppino if he wanted to do his cooking first, to which he answered, "Yes". We moved away from the fire and Peppino's family gathered around it. I asked Father why he had let Peppino do the cooking before us, since he and Uncle had gathered the wood and lit the fire. Father answered that Peppino was there before us and had offered us some of his water. Also, he had two very small girls who were not yet three years old and they were cold and hungry. We waited a long time for them to do their cooking while they took turns to be nearest to the fire. The flames enabled me to see all their faces, including the two little girls, who were twins, being held in the arms of their older sisters.

At long last, our turn came to warm ourselves and boil our potatoes. Saliva kept forming in my mouth thinking of eating the hot potatoes. Mother made my brother and me stand by the fire all the time while she, my grandparents and Uncle took turns to warm themselves. When the potatoes were cooked we peeled the skin and ate them still standing by the fire. I kept looking at the poor sad face of the horse that stared at us all the time with big shiny eyes. Father charged the fire with a pile of wood and we all went to sleep with our clothes and shoes on, on our spiky platform.

The next morning I woke up to hear the voices of Father and Uncle, who had just returned from collecting the rest of our stores. It was still dark in the cave but I could see a dull light on the side of the canvas hanging over the mouth of the cave. Father and Uncle quietly lay down in their sleeping places. It was soundless, except for the occasional movements of the horse's hoofs over the rocky ground and its heavy sighs. The raw mountain air of January was so cold that I buried my head under the blanket again. My back, ribs, stomach and thighs were very sore from the splinters from the branches of wood pressing against me and each turn I made only moved the pain from one area to other parts of my body, but I knew I had to lie there for many hours to come.

Waiting For Darkness

Time never seemed to pass and I wished that Father would get up so that I could get up too. Peppino passed the foot of our sleeping area and removed the piece of canvas from the entrance to let in some light. I looked at the long line of bumps under the blankets in the dim light, which nearly reached the bottom of the cave, everyone sleeping with their heads covered. What had made Peppino get up and remove the canvas, letting in a sea of cold air, I wondered? Then I watched him sweeping away the horse's and goat's droppings with a small bundle of twigs. Soon he replaced the canvas over the entrance and walked back to his sleeping place. I pulled the blanket over my head again, enduring the discomfort of splinters digging into my body.

At long, long last, Father and Uncle got up, but before I could say anything Father told us all to stay under the blankets. "It's very, very cold," he said, as he added his and Uncle's blankets to mine and my brother's. They sorted the stores they had collected earlier that morning. I kept lifting my head to look, but the cold was hurting me and it was painful to breathe the cold air, so again I was forced to put my head under the blankets. I heard Father and Uncle go out many times to collect firewood for when it got dark. On each return Father encouraged us to stay in bed a while longer, but the splinters were really hurting me.

It was probably near midday when Father said we would eat something, so we all got up and ate a piece of bread and a small piece of smoked sausage and drank water from a terracotta jug that was passed around. I didn't drink much because the water was icy cold.

My senses began to awaken as I stood in the desolate atmosphere of the cold, dark grey rock of the cave. I became more deeply aware of the situation we were in, the fact that we were hiding, that we had only a certain amount of food, that we had to speak quietly because if we were found it would be very, very frightening. I took my first few steps outside the cave and saw Uncle and Peppino's son Domenico watching the activities going on in the town while they lay on their stomachs on top of the thickly padded material put between the horse's back and the wooden saddle. I went and stood behind, them but as soon as they noticed me they both said, "Get down, get down". I thought they were trying to frighten me, so I didn't immediately squat down, but Uncle took my arm and pulled me down, explaining that with my head above the shrubs I could have been seen from a distance by the Germans patrolling the mountain area and those taking up positions with the anti-aircraft guns. I was told to speak quietly. We crawled back into the cave and Uncle told the others what was going on in the town, then to our surprise Grandfather said that he was carrying a pair of binoculars that they could borrow. The binoculars aroused Uncle and Domenico's interest and they soon went out again to their watching position. The thickly padded material was put down again and they lay on it and started looking through the binoculars. I stood away from them, watching as they spoke and passed the binoculars to one another. Uncle and Domenico were about the same age, twenty-one and nineteen years old, and got on well. I was afraid to go near them in case they told me off. After some time Uncle saw me standing alone in the cold and beckoned me to come over. They made room for me between them and I too lay on my stomach.

Uncle and Domenico kept speaking to one another about what they could see with the binoculars. I kept on asking "Where are you looking?" as I could only see where the groups of houses were, my school and the white main roads. Uncle handed me the binoculars and indicated where I should look, then I could clearly see soldiers going about and heavily loaded carts pulled by horses arriving. Motorbikes were speeding towards the piazza, where the church and town hall stood. It felt strange to see the place that was home, now forbidden to us. It felt as if it was an evil place now and that was why we had to hide and even speak quietly about it. I was pleased to be with Uncle and Domenico and felt I could always be with them now. It was cold but I felt good, though many times they told me to speak quietly. Then the wind became so bitterly cold that we went back into the cave to wait for the dark to come so the fire could be lit to warm ourselves by and have something to eat. We just stood around, as sitting on our sleeping space was almost like sitting on the ground and those splinters were so painful. I looked more carefully at

Peppino's family, who also stood looking cold with sad faces. The two little girls cried a lot, saying they were cold and hungry. They were further inside the cave and it was darker there but they didn't get the cold wind as we did. The horse and goat got the worst of the wind because they were at the immediate entrance to the cave, then us. It was so cold I wished it would get dark soon so that Father could light the fire. There were so many of us standing lifeless, entombed within the grey rock, waiting and waiting for the dark to come.

When darkness fell it seemed as if something really good had happened because Father could light the fire and we could have something to eat. The evenings were all the same. Father and Mother took turns with Peppino's family to cook, which was boiling potatoes or dried beans, and then back for more punishment on our spiky sleeping place. The thought of the long night ahead was upsetting and it took me a very long time to go to sleep. If I didn't put my head under the blanket I watched different spots on the rock being lit by the flickering flames of the fire and listened to the sounds of the horse's hoofs as it moved from time to time. There was no other sign of life.

Most mornings Father and Peppino would return in the dawn light, having gone for water to the well up the mountain. They had to be back before the Germans started carrying the ammunition with horses and donkeys. Peppino carried a small barrel on his shoulder, but Father only had a bucket.

Every day Uncle, Domenico and I went to our viewing position with the binoculars watching the

German troops moving about and loaded carts arriving. The aeroplanes carrying out reconnaissance of the German positions went back and forth above the town, tilting to one side and then the other, over and over again as the German guns relentlessly fired, filling the air with hundreds and hundreds of explosions and puffs of smoke. We knew that the aeroplanes were trying to find out where the big guns were positioned, but it took even us many days to discover where they were, among the clusters of oak trees inside our town and another big gun at the bottom of the town below the mountain among a huge cluster of canes. I really wished I could have told the pilot their position. Then the next day the fighter aeroplanes would come, firing at the targets. When the bomber aeroplanes dropped their bombs we rushed back into the cave as sometimes the shrapnel reached where we lay.

Life in the cold gloom of the cave was total misery. Most of the day we sat on the low sleeping platform enduring the discomfort, curled up, arms folded across our chests, our faces sorrowful. No one spoke very much, there were just the sounds of deep, deep sighs and quiet grumbling. Peppino's two little girls cried a lot, always saying that they were cold and hungry. My throat became sore and I felt numb around my neck. Inside my mouth it felt as if there was a stone that I couldn't swallow. The diet, the lack of movement and the cold weather made me constipated most of the time and I felt very uncomfortable, finding it impossible to relieve myself. I would go into the woods, but first I had to look for the largest leaves that weren't half rotted or wet with which to clean myself, then find a place that wasn't too steep, and squat for a long time, pushing and pushing, hoping and hoping to get movement in my bowels.

After a while Father would come and stand by me and wait. I felt so sad, wishing I could empty my bowels and that my throat wasn't so sore. After some time Father would say, "Let's go inside and come back before dark." We were always waiting for the dark to come so the fire could be lit. If the wood wasn't dry it smoked, and we coughed and coughed as we inhaled the thick, bitter smoke, which also made my eyes smart.

As each day passed we were becoming weaker and weaker. It was impossible to get warm. When it was our turn to be by the fire I used to stand as close to it as possible, slowly turning round and round trying to warm all sides of my body. I stayed near the fire until the heat was too painful to bear, but although my skin was sore with too much heat the bones inside my legs were always cold.

Mother tried to take my socks off to warm my feet but they were stuck to my skin, so I went to lie on my sleeping place and Mother kept warming her hands by the fire then quickly placing them tightly around my feet. She did this over and over again while Father warmed my shoes by the flames of the fire, then they did the same for my brother.

Our food reserves were running low and although Father had some bread left, now hard and dry, he still only gave us one slice a day each. Months before, Father had hidden some stores, including flour, in a vertical cave among the valleys on the top of the mountain. One

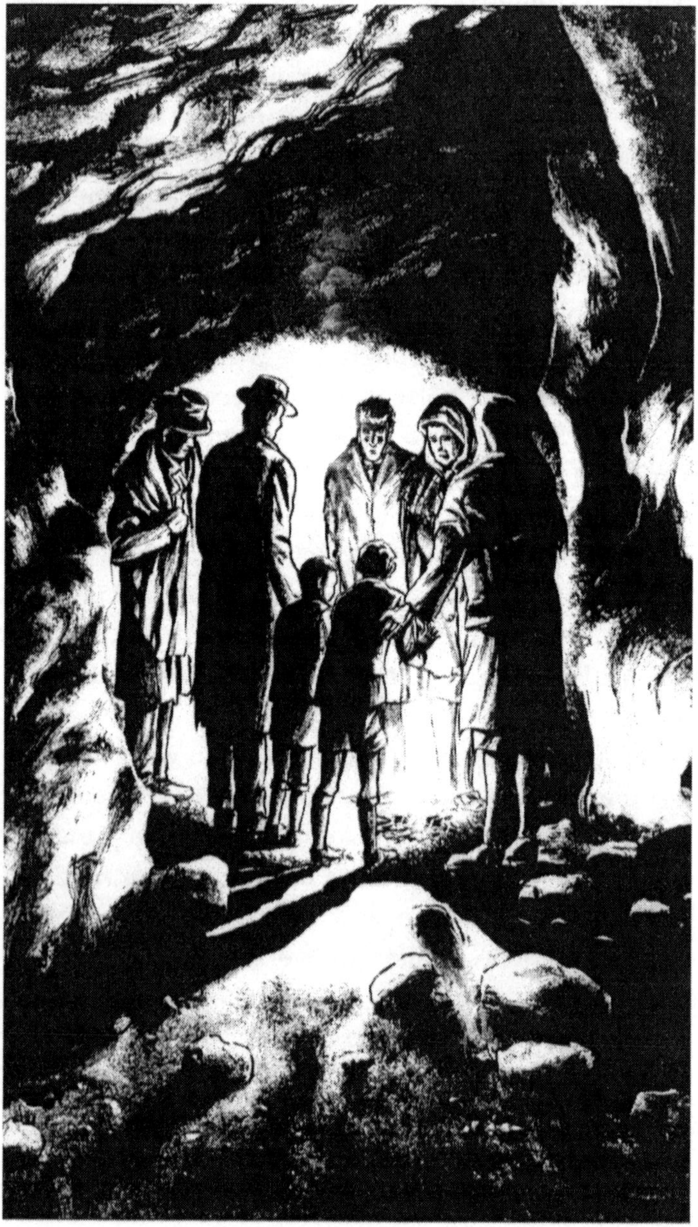

day he went to get some of the goods including flour and returned in the dawn light, but we had to wait until night-time before the attempt was made to bake the flour into edible food. That day Father and I went to find the more chunky dry pieces of wood for the baking. By now we had exhausted the already broken branches around the cave. To break or cut new wood was impossible because it would make a noise, so we had to go further and further to gather our firewood, which was difficult because the terrain around us was very, very steep, wet and mostly covered with decaying leaves. It was very slippery and we had to be careful not to disturb the loose stones as they would roll down the mountain and make a lot of noise. Father spoke very quietly, telling me to be careful and where to place my feet, and I would tell him if I had seen a broken branch or a chunky piece of wood that was too difficult for me to get. Father picked up a long dry branch too difficult to carry as it was, so he raised his leg, placed the middle of the branch below his knee and using all his strength broke it into two pieces. It made a loud cracking noise in the total silence of the mountain. Father looked fearful and I could see his regret at having done that. For a while we both remained still, looking into each other's eyes, listening to see if the noise had attracted any attention. They were very scary minutes, and fear made us take what we had collected carefully, and quietly return to the cave hoping that the noise hadn't attracted attention.

Later, Father and I went out again to collect more wood and about twenty of the biggest leaves we could find, the ones bigger than my hand Father said – not the ones on the top which were too dry nor the ones touching the ground that had began to decay, the ones in between that were still soft. That night, after Peppino's family had cooked their food and warmed themselves, our turn came. Father made a very big fire with the chunks of wood we had collected and we all warmed ourselves while Mother in the light of the flames mixed the flour with the water in a bucket into a stiff paste. Father moved the burning wood and ash from the centre of the fire, making a space which he lined with two layers of the leaves we had collected that day, then spread the flour paste on top of the leaves and covered it with several other layers. He covered the leaves with lots of ash and made a big fire on the top. Then, we waited and waited for it to cook while we all stood around the fire. After a long time Father removed the fire from the top of the paste and pressed the leaves with his hand. It was still soft. A big fire continued to burn on the paste for what seemed an endless time. Eventually, Father tested it again and it appeared to be cooked, so he removed it from the fire and shared it among the seven of us. It was very, very hot, the outside hard with the burned leaves stuck to it, and inside it was still just a hot paste, which was difficult to swallow. That was our main meal that day.

Grandfather made a great effort to join in when Father and Peppino discussed our situation. Mainly they spoke about how much food we had left, how many more days we could remain hiding in the cave and how long it would be before the Allied Forces broke through and liberated us. Grandfather wasn't at all well; his face always looked sad and he seemed deep in thought. Most of the time he sat on his sleeping space, bent forward, as if he were staring at the ground. I would see Mother and Father furtively looking at him with concern, then they would look at one another, frown, shrug their shoulders and move away. Grandmother often placed a blanket over his shoulders and carefully tucked it around him, asking sympathetically, "How do you feel today? What hurts you? As soon as we return home you must see a doctor." Grandfather would slowly raise his head, look at her, give a slight nod and return to his slumped state. Grandmother, looking disappointed, would slowly move away murmuring, "My beautiful Antonio".

Lucky Pee Pee

Grandmother took much comfort in looking after her pet chicken, which she carried with her. On the first or second day after we arrived at the cave I saw her collecting stones. With them she made a well-like nest at the end of the cave where it was dark and no wind reached. She half filled the nest with dried leaves and placed the chicken inside and there it stayed most of the time. When the chicken came out of its nest and slowly went over to Grandmother, it would get a gentle telling off and be put back inside. Grandmother treated the chicken as if it were a human being. It was incredibly obedient and when near Grandmother would only move one or two steps away from her, or just keep withdrawing one foot and then the other into its feathers. The chicken seemed to listen and understand what Grandmother said to it. I don't recall Mother or I or anyone else ever touching or referring to it, but its welfare was Grandmother's constant preoccupation. In the bundle Grandmother had carried was a small linen sack, like a very big pocket, which was full of corn. Twice a day Grandmother would put some in the palm of her hand and feed her pet while talking to it. The chicken was referred to as Pee Pee, so Grandmother would say, "Povera Pee Pee" (Poor Pee Pee, they are making you suffer too. Don't worry, this will pass and soon we will be back home). Pee Pee wasn't ill like Grandfather, nor did it have a sore throat like me. Pee Pee was fed with tender blades of grass and a handful of corn twice a day. Pee Pee looked warm in all her feathers. Lucky Pee Pee, I thought.

The Goat

We watched the squadrons of English and American fighter and bomber aeroplanes flying above us. Soon afterwards we would hear the deep, sinister resounding of the explosions carrying through the air, destroying people and places, causing the horrific scenes we had witnessed so many times ourselves and that brought fear and sorrow to our hearts. Then the muted sounds of the cannons indicated that the confrontation of the two armies was only a few kilometres away, and when we began to see the sky beyond the mountains filling with hundreds and hundreds of puffs of smoke from the exploding shells it really meant that the Allied soldiers were getting nearer and nearer. "In two or three days the Allies will arrive and we can go home," Father said. So, the more aeroplanes we saw and the more explosions we heard, the higher our hopes.

I heard Peppino say to his son Domenico that they had hardly any food left and he was thinking of killing the goat. Peppino also spoke to Father, saying that to leave the cave was too dangerous because we had refused to obey the German command to leave by the given date and they had said that anyone remaining after that would be shot. Peppino also feared that if he was recognised by the Germans and they had found out that he had deceived them while being paid to betray us, it would certainly mean death for him. Father too had been captured and escaped from them; he knew that it was crucial to be cautious. It was therefore decided to continue to remain in the cave until the Allies came to liberate us. So, the goat had to be killed to feed the nine people in Peppino's family. When Peppino's girls heard this, they began to cry. His wife, my mother and Grandmother also expressed their dislike at the thought and said, "We don't want to see the goat being killed. You'll have to do it outside." Then Grandmother said to Peppino, "Do you really have to kill the poor beast? Let's hope in a day or two the Allies will arrive and we can go home. You can see how upset your girls are." Peppino replied, "It's better if the goat dies and not us." I could see this answer worried Grandmother, and later that day I realised why she had protested about the goat being killed. She probably thought Father might suggest her pet chicken should also be killed – I noticed her speaking and stroking Pee Pee's feathers more than usual that afternoon. Peppino asked Father, Uncle and Grandfather for their help and planned how the goat was going to be killed. A narrow low stone platform was prepared immediately outside against the rock of the cave. Peppino sharpened his pen-knife and bread knife on a stone, passing the cutting edge back and forth many, many times. The goat was brought out and held in line with the stone platform. It stood still, just moving its head and eyelids, looking at the big stone slightly ahead where the two knives were placed. I wondered if it knew what was going to happen.

Peppino spoke very quietly, telling each of us what we had to do, and most importantly, he said, "there has to be no noise, no noise from the goat". I was handed a white shallow enamel bowl with handles on either side to catch the blood. I sensed the apprehension in everyone and I too was frightened that they were going to kill the goat, but I also felt good and brave that I was taking part with the men while all the others were staying inside. Peppino said, "Remember what each one of you has to do and speak quietly." He took up the pen-knife, looked at everyone and in a low, apprehensive voice said, "Allora, siamo pronti?" (Well, are we ready?). Anxiety showed in everyone's eyes as my heart thumped and thumped and thumped. The moment had now come. Peppino said, "Pronto, andiamo" (Ready, let's go).

Everything took place like a flash of lightning as the men simultaneously launched themselves at the poor goat. Father placed his hands around the mouth of the goat while Uncle took hold of the back legs and Domenico of the front legs and both tilted the goat on to the narrow stone base. Grandfather took hold of the ears to steady the head so that Father was able to keep the goat's mouth shut. The goat struggled and struggled, twisting its body and legs. Uncle and Domenico crossed the goat's legs and leaned on top of it, pressing it against the stone platform and the rock wall of the cave. The goat still struggled to get free but the men controlled it well. Peppino was having difficulty in making the first incision on the tough skin of the goat's throat with the pen-knife. When he went to use the bread knife it

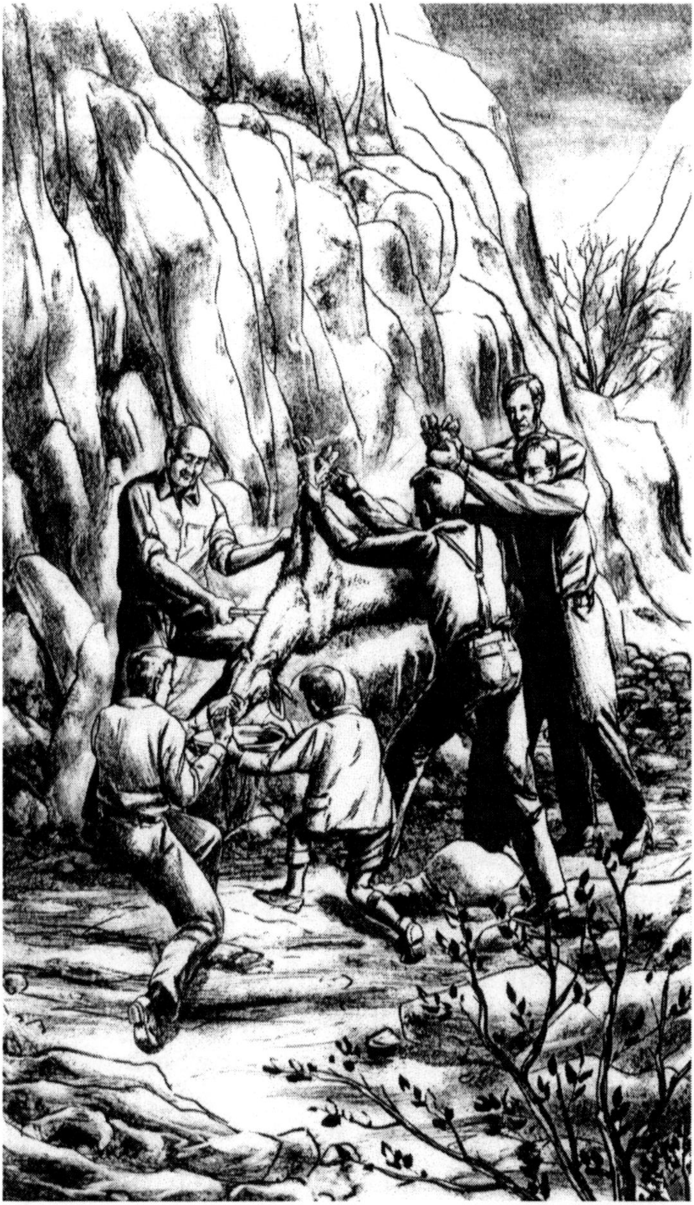

wouldn't enter the small incision so he had to take up the pen-knife again to enlarge the wound. When he was able to get the bread knife into the wound it wouldn't cut and he had to use it like a saw going back and forward, back and forward inside the goat's throat. Father was red in the face, gritting his teeth, using every bit of strength he had to keep the goat's mouth shut. Peppino had now enlarged the wound so the blood was rushing out and I was told to hold the bowl under the neck to collect it. I squatted with one knee on the ground, holding the bowl with both hands under the goat's throat. My face was near the goat's face. It still struggled and squirted some blood on my face and I was surprised how warm it was; it felt quite pleasant on my cold face. Huge gasps of air and thick froth came out of the goat's nostrils. I could see all of the men's feet planted firmly on the ground while they held it. The goat gave a jerk and stopped struggling and I saw that it was dead – its eyes were still. Then I heard Peppino say, "E morta" (She is dead). A big sigh of relief went up from the men that they had prevented the goat from making any noise.

I quickly went inside the cave and told the others that the goat was dead, feeling proud that I had contributed to the gruesome but necessary act. I wanted to stay out with the men, but my body felt so cold and my throat still hurt so I sat next to Mother on our sleeping space. Mother wrapped a blanket around me and held me tightly with both arms, close to her. After a while I felt eager to see what was happening to the goat, so I went out and watched Peppino, Father, Uncle and Domenico skinning and cutting it into pieces, mainly using the strength of their arms as the pen-knife and bread knife were useless.

That night a huge fire was made and a large pot was put to boil full to the brim with chunks of the goat's meat. The cave was filled with a nasty, steamy smell as the meat boiled and boiled, creating a pile of froth on top of the boiling water. Now and then it was stirred with a piece of wood, pushing the chunks on the top to the bottom so it would cook evenly. Eventually, when the meat was cooked, the receptacle was removed from the fire and all of Peppino's family gathered around the pot as Peppino and his wife tore pieces with their hands and handed them to each member of the family. When the flames of the fire lit up their faces I could see them all concentrating on eating, using both hands, holding the bone until there was no meat left. Then another piece was handed over and another until the whole lot was eaten up. Peppino gave us some meat, which we ate with cold boiled potatoes. That night we felt well, but Peppino's family had eaten so much meat that it made them ill with stomach pains and diarrhoea. It was a night of continuous lamentations from their side.

Ultimatum

The next morning, Father and Peppino went out as usual in the dark to get water from the well at the top of the mountain. It got lighter and lighter and still they weren't back. Everyone became concerned, especially Mother and Peppino's wife. The journey to the well had been made many times and they always returned in the dawn light. It was too dangerous for Uncle and Peppino's son Domenico to go and look for them now in full daylight and so we just waited, worrying and wondering what might have happened. Someone said, "Let's hope the Germans haven't captured them." This made one of Peppino's daughters start to cry and soon all of his daughters were crying. However, they returned about two hours later, Peppino empty-handed and father carrying the empty bucket and rope. They told us that on their way back they heard German voices coming towards them and the sudden shock made Peppino leave his barrel of water by the side of the track. Father emptied the water out of the bucket and took it with him then both quietly hurried some distance up the track until it was possible to go into the dense woodland and hide. The soldiers stopped where the barrel had been left and their voices, laughter and noise could be heard. Father and Peppino remained still for a long time, until they felt the soldiers were well into the mountain and out of earshot. They then went to collect the barrel of water, but sadly it had been rolled down the track and was smashed to pieces.

We had no water to drink or to boil the rest of the goat's meat or our potatoes. Father said it was now too dangerous to go to the same well again, even to go and return before dawn. They lost no time, Father with his bucket and Peppino with his other barrel, taking an uncharted route, climbing through dense woods and thorns to another well up the mountain to which there was no track but which was much safer. When they returned looking exhausted, Father's bucket was only half full. He told us that when he left the well the bucket was full, but during the difficult descent it was impossible to keep it balanced, so little by little he spilled some of the water. He filled the terracotta jug and it was passed round for us all to have a drink.

This was our seventh day in the cave. A dull and damp afternoon, the lack of proper food, the intense cold weather, and the squalor in which we lived all contributed to weaken us and make us feel sorry for ourselves. What took place that morning only served to continue to destroy our courage and hope. Father, Peppino and Grandfather sat at the end of our low sleeping space to discuss what they should do and decided to remain in the cave for a few more days in the hope that the Allies would soon come and liberate us. I could see their faces in the dim light looking totally lost as they shrugged their shoulders and shook their heads. Mother just stared ahead as if hypnotised, as if to say this will never end. Grandmother remained quiet too, spending most of the time looking after her pet chicken, stroking its feathers and saying, "Don't be frightened. This will pass. Later I will give you some food. It's too early now. Povera Pee Pee" (Poor Pee Pee).

It was difficult for me even to look at their faces, let alone speak. I felt that if I spoke I would do or say something wrong, as if I wanted pity, and I didn't want to add to their desperation. I was aware of our grave situation, so I went out to where Uncle and Domenico were lying on their stomachs looking with the binoculars to see where the shells were exploding over the town. Uncle always made room for me by his side, though I preferred it when I could lie between them where it was warmer. As the shells exploded they would say to one another, "Look, that one has hit the flour mill, that one just missed the blacksmith's workshop, see, that one just missed the last house in Via Roma", as each shell hit the houses or the ground, sending piles of smoky rubble and earth exploding into the air, leaving places destroyed and burning. It was all evil down there now and it felt safe where we were. Father said that even if the shells or bombs came near us, nothing would penetrate the tons and tons of massive rock which enclosed the cave. Then Domenico, who had the binoculars, exclaimed, "Look, look, there is a man leaving the town with a horse and cart piled with goods, he must be a thief, look at him whipping the horse to escape being hit by the shells." The binoculars were handed to Uncle, who said, "He must be working with the Germans, otherwise he would have been shot for being there." The conversation went on and we assumed that he was stealing from our houses in cooperation with the Germans. Uncle and Domenico cursed the man and I said, "I hope that one of the shells gets you." We just watched the scene as the shells were particularly concentrated along the main road, exploding away to the front and rear of the fast moving horse and cart. Uncle handed me the binoculars and I could see the man standing on the front of the cart whipping the poor horse again and again. We cursed and cursed him for his alliance with the Germans and for stealing from our homes. He was now reaching the bottom of the town, another four or five hundred metres and he would pass around the bend and disappear from our sight and perhaps escape the shelling.

I had just handed the binoculars back to Uncle when a shell hit the cart and everything was scattered over the road. Now I kept thinking of his family waiting and waiting for him that night, and went back inside the cave feeling bad about what I had said about the man and wishing I hadn't.

The next morning was our eighth day in the cave, around the 22nd of January 1944. I resisted staying in my sleeping place until about midday, got up and went outside, where I saw Father and Peppino in conversation. I went and stood by Father's side. They spoke very quietly to one another, as we always did now. We were standing on the right-hand side of the cave, where there was a little more daylight but it was still dull and very cold, when we were suddenly disturbed by a noise behind us and turned round to a horrifying sight. Only about three or four steps away stood two German officers, both pointing their pistols at us. Father and

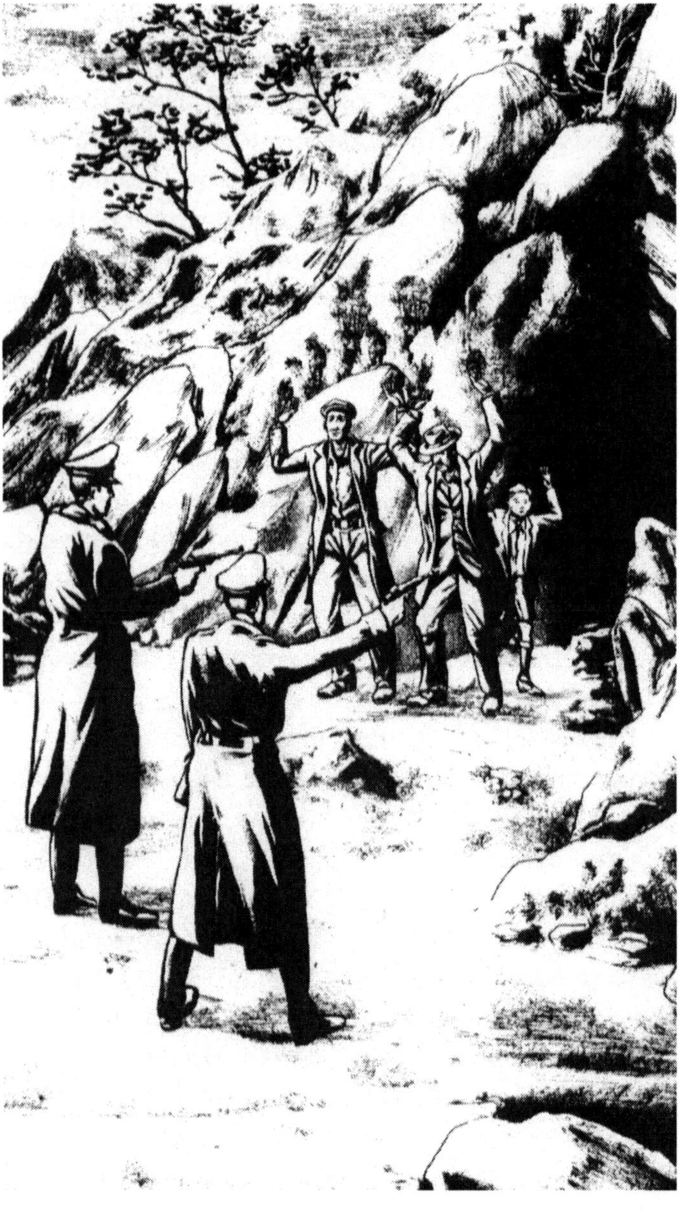

Peppino immediately put their hands up and I did the same. I knew they were officers because they wore peaked caps and had pistols; ordinary soldiers wore helmets and carried machine guns or rifles. One officer made a movement with the pistol and gave a slight nod to the right, indicating that we had to stand against the rock wall of the cave, where they began to question Father and Peppino. I hadn't seen such big pistols before with such a long barrel. The officers looked warm in their long coats and leather boots up to their knees. Their faces under the peaked caps looked serious, hard, their eyes fixed on Father and Peppino. I remember Father telling them that we were two families with young children and old people who were ill and couldn't walk; that was why we were unable to leave when the order was given.

After a while, the officers said that we had to leave by twelve o'clock the next day, when they would return. If we were still there, we would all be shot. One of them said all this using Italian words: "Andare via tutti" (Go away everyone) "Domani ritornare" (Tomorrow coming back). He pointed the index finger of his left hand to himself and then to the ground, signifying he would return there the next day, then repeated, "Domani ritornare" (Tomorrow coming back) and pointed to the number twelve on his wristwatch. I hadn't seen a watch like that before, with a dark face with distinct clear numbers. Then he said "Sole" (Sun), as he pointed to the sky where the sun would be at midday. Again he repeated the word 'ritornare' (coming back), waving the pistol from side to side, pointing it at us, and said,

"Uomini, donne, bambino tutti caput" (Men, women, child, all caput). His last words were, "Capito bene" (Understand well). They looked at one another, nodded and walked away, holding their pistols slightly away from their bodies, as if ready to turn and fire. We watched them depart then, when we couldn't see them any more, we went inside to meet the scared eyes and trembling faces of Mother, Grandmother, Grandfather and Peppino's wife, who had gathered together and were quietly listening. Their first words were, "Have they gone? How many were they?" Uncle and Domenico were lying on the ground at the end of the cave where it was dark. They stood up, but Father said, "Stay, stay down. Let's make sure they don't come back first", then casually walked out while we remained still. After a few minutes Father came back and said, "I think they've gone."

Everyone felt insecure. Uncle and Domenico went out with the binoculars, keeping watch on the part of the mountain where the Germans had to pass, making sure they were definitely going down in the direction of the town. Father was astonished how quietly they had approached us and the direction from which they came. The miracle was that they didn't enter the cave and find Uncle and Domenico, who would certainly have been taken away. The order was clear: we had to leave before twelve noon the next day, or else.

The rest of the afternoon was very miserable; everyone was tense, fearful and preoccupied as to how we could carry our stores, blankets and pots. We feared to walk loaded on the open road, for what might other German soldiers do? We worried about possible shelling or bombardments, and where we would go. We had no idea what had been happening in the past ten days. Father said that we would head for the town of Sora, where his parents had said they were going to stay. "We will walk there in two or three days, depending on whether we can manage the walk carrying our goods and if everyone is up to it." The situation was too serious for me to say anything, tempers were very frayed, and I knew it was better if I stayed quiet. I saw Mother and Grandmother with a small piece of white cloth making two small square pockets. They then made two ribbons from the same piece of cloth and sewed the ribbons to the pockets. Some time later, Mother and Father pushed the pockets inside my brother's and my vests and said, "Inside the pocket is your name and address and money. If you get lost or we become separated, tell people who you are and buy food with the money, but don't worry we will come and find you, avete capito?" (Have you understood?) "Non avete paura" (Have no fear) "we will come and find you." This was a terrible shock to me. I could not understand how we could get lost or become separated and I felt frightened and sad for the rest of that day.

Father, Uncle and Peppino's family were all preoccupied in preparing what had to be carried while there was still some daylight. Father kept packing and unpacking his big rucksack and his sack, trying to squeeze more and more goods into both of them. It was before dark when all was packed, including my and my brother's rucksacks. Some food for that evening, the blankets and the bucket with water were left out.

Peppino's family had done the same. We still waited until it was completely dark before the fire was lit, then had something to eat and warmed ourselves by a huge fire, using every bit of wood we had left, and went to sleep. All was ready for the next morning when we would descend the mountain and walk to Sora. I continued to worry about what I would do if my brother and I became separated from Mother and Father until I fell asleep.

The next morning I was awakened by Father, who said, "Get up. I'll fold the blankets and we'll go." He walked to the entrance and lifted the piece of canvas covering the mouth of the cave, then exclaimed in dismay, "Ma guarda, guarda, guarda" (Oh look, look, look). Mother asked, "Che è successo?" (What's happened?) and Father replied, "La montagna è coperta di neve" (The mountain is covered in snow) "we can't go, it's too dangerous, we can't see where to place our feet." Uncle said, "If the Germans come we will kill them before they kill us", but Father replied, "They won't come today, it's too dangerous to walk where you can't see a pathway. Stay under the blankets everyone, we can't leave today."

It was another day of suffering, staying under the blankets on top of those piercing wooden sticks which dug into all my body and made my back ache. Each time I uncovered my head I could smell the scent of snow in the cold air. Later, about midday, the snow began to melt. Uncle and Domenico kept watch with the binoculars to see if the Germans were coming while Father and Peppino tried to gather firewood for that night. No one said very much, everyone looked tense and frightened and every word spoken sounded sad and fearful. Time went so slowly. Late in the afternoon Father looked outside again and said, "The snow has nearly all melted, we'll leave tomorrow morning." When darkness fell the fire was lit but the wood was all wet and filled the cave with bitter smoke. Everyone coughed and coughed and our eyes streamed, even with our heads under the blankets. I hoped we could leave the next morning but I worried about being separated from Mother and Father. I wondered what Father and Mother knew that I didn't, and felt sad and scared.

The Descent

The next morning, I was again awakened by Father, who said, "Alzati" (Get up) "we are all ready to go, are you feeling well?" "Yes," I replied. "Get up, I want to put the rucksacks on you and Enio." Everyone was ready with their rucksacks, baskets and bundles. It was the first time that I had woken up in the cave and the horse wasn't there. Its place looked empty now as Peppino had already loaded it outside. It was hardly daylight and the air was cold and damp. Peppino came in with his rucksack on, speaking quietly as if he was frightened, and said, "Siamo tutti pronti?" (Are we all ready?) "Andiamo" (Let's go). He walked in front of the horse and one by one his family followed, then us, Father saying, "Be careful where you put your feet." Father and Uncle carried big rucksacks as well as a sack each on their shoulders, but Father's sack was very, very heavy. So there we were, in a long line, walking along the dark path on the steep side of the mountain.

Since the cave was in a deep recess, we had to walk along the narrow curving path before emerging from it to start descending the mountain. We had to walk slowly because the path was very narrow and full of rocky bumps and loose stones, now mostly covered with decaying leaves. All was engulfed in dense woodland with thin, very tall trees growing at an angle, which seemed as if they were about to fall on us because of the steep mountain. Peppino had to be very careful leading the horse, staying very close, walking in the front and holding it by a short rein. Now and then we had to stop momentarily as Peppino encouraged the horse to walk along the difficult passage before it came into its stride. The only sounds were the quiet words passed from the front to those behind, "Fai attenzione qui" (Be careful here) as we were about to pass really dangerous places where the path narrowed with deep, deep drops at the side. Peppino continually warned the horse of danger with muted sounds of "Eee, eee, eee" to make it stop and then "Ah, ah" to make it go. Once out of the recess we stopped for a rest in a sloping area cleared just enough for us to gather, but no one could sit on the ground as the rocks were still wet from the previous day's melted snow and there were areas where patches of snow still remained. We had intended to join the track to descend to the town here, but Father and Peppino decided not to go via the track as it was used by the German soldiers and to encounter them, particularly in isolated areas, would be too dangerous. Peppino thought we should descend via the section of the mountain that extended towards the end of the town, but there was no path on this part of the mountain to allow us to go down. Father suggested we might find one as we went along and Peppino said it would probably be more difficult for him because of the horse, so we should find our own way and meet at the foot of the mountain. It was very cold, every face looked numb, white and scared, and everyone just listened and did what Peppino and Father said. So Peppino with his horse followed by his family started on his way, Uncle helped Father to load the heavy sack onto his shoulder and one by one off we all went.

Peppino then went in a different direction because the horse couldn't go through a narrow sloping place, while we continued to follow Father forward and downwards. The terrain now was covered with small clusters of thin woods. The trees were not very high but well above our heads and there were many wild shrubs. The ground was mostly crumbling rock where it was easy to slip and fall, with no really solid rocks where we could get a good foothold. My brother and I slipped and fell many times, ending on our bottoms. Each time I tried to protect myself, the pressure of my cold hands and bottom on the sharp sandy rocks really hurt. Father decided on the best route to take every few metres and was followed by my brother, me and Grandfather. Mother and Grandmother were now following Uncle, who was working out his own route down. It was cold and soundless, except that now and then Father would quietly call Uncle, whispering, "Benedetto come andate?" (Benedetto how are you getting on?). When there was no response, Father would raise his voice slightly, "Benedetto come andate?" and Uncle would whisper, "Non hai paura andiamo bene" (Don't worry, we are doing well). Then all would go silent again and after a few minutes I would hear sounds from Peppino's family somewhere: "Not there, follow me, be careful" and Peppino's hushed voice speaking to the horse "Eee, eee, ah, ah", then silence again except for our exhausted breathing and the crunch, crunch under our shoes as we struggled against the dangers of the steep, crumbling, rocky surface.

Often we stopped momentarily as Father in front with his heavy load decided which way to go, then planted a foot firmly on the ground before taking a long stride over narrow slippery passages. My brother and I found it easier because we were lighter, but Grandfather, who was behind me, was having problems in walking over this difficult terrain. When I turned to see if he was coming, he looked unsteady and unsure of what to do, his feet seemingly unwilling to go forward. Father was very aware of this and more than once stopped and slowly turned with the heavy sack on his shoulder to guide Grandfather over the very difficult places, saying, "Dad, place your foot firmly on the side of the rock, hold on to the shrub on your near side and step over." Each time Father turned I could see his worried face bent to one side balancing the heavy sack, his eyes full of fear and despair. When we rested, Father had to place the sack on a piece of higher ground or rock, otherwise he couldn't reload it on his shoulder by himself. When we reached the foot of the mountain we continued on to our meeting point, where we sat on our packs in a long sandy ditch between the mountain and farmland. Uncle, Mother and Grandmother were still descending, but arrived soon after. We were all out of breath, with nothing more to say or give.

I hoped Peppino would take a long time to arrive so that we would get a good rest, but to my disappointment it wasn't too long before we heard them coming. Father went up on the verge, beckoned them towards us and they all slumped in the ditch too, the girls grumbling about their exhaustion, their scratches and that they were cold. The two little girls' eyes were watering and they looked cold and numbed by the whole ordeal, not being three years old yet; they were hugged and hugged by their mother, while she blew her warm breath on their hands then placed their little fingers in her mouth to warm them. So there we all were, slumped in a line in the long narrow ditch at the base of the mountain, including the horse, who couldn't turn and was desperately trying to eat the sparse blades of grass that he could reach. For a while there was total silence except for the sounds of the horse's movements over the sand and rocks. We sat on our packs, elbows resting on our knees, backs bent forward, heads bowed as if we were all praying. Peppino broke the silence as he quietly called to Father, "Crescenzo, è meglio se ce ne andiamo" (Crescenzo, it is better if we go). Father said to us all, "The land ahead is all flat, try to walk as quickly as you can and don't talk" – but we never talked. "Don't be frightened," he said, "the aeroplanes won't come today, it's too cloudy."

I sensed Father and Peppino's anxiety as they spoke, because now we were about to walk into the unknown, into the hands of those we feared so much, and possibly shelling or bombardments. There was no place to hide any more, just open fields and main roads ahead of us now. Everyone slowly stood up and gathered the goods they were carrying. Father put the rucksack on my brother and Uncle helped me with mine. Mother and

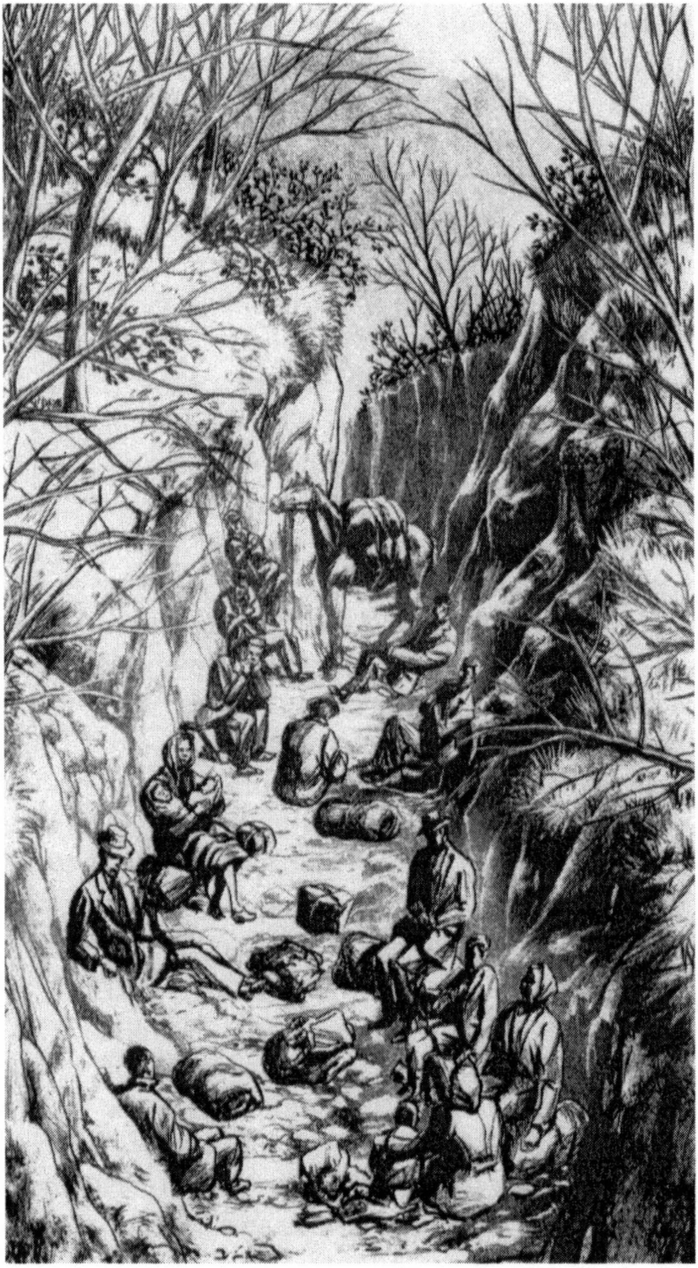

Grandfather tightly rolled the blankets they carried under their arms and Grandmother secured the bundle she carried in her arms with her pet chicken cosy in the middle. Peppino's family were all ready with their baskets, rucksacks and bundles while Uncle helped Father load the heavy sack onto his shoulder. Domenico squatted on the ground and lifted one of the little girls on to his shoulders and her tiny cold hands reached to clasp his forehead. He embraced the other little girl and stood up. Peppino said "Andiamo" (Let's go) as he pushed the loaded horse backwards a few paces so it could turn and come out of the ditch. One by one his family followed and then us. After many months in hiding places, we were now exposed to all that we feared. It was so scary.

In single file we followed Peppino and his horse across the first field. It was so much colder in the open and the wind numbed our cheeks, nose and knees. Then on to the next field, where we had to pass about two hundred metres from an isolated farmhouse that we had watched with our binoculars from the cave and where we had seen many German soldiers coming and going. I glanced over at the farmhouse – no soldiers to be seen but a small cannon on two wheels pointing towards us. After we passed I feared that we would be shot from the back. I didn't dare turn round. It was so silent, so empty, an emptiness full of fear – deep fear within me – until we had distanced ourselves from the farmhouse. We crossed ditches from one field to another and came to a field with long dried grass. Peppino, his horse and family walking across it before us made a channel-like path for us at the rear – we just had to lift our legs high over the partly flattened grass – but the frost still made my shoes and legs wet and my socks now refused to stay up. The wind from our left blew steamy puffs from our scared, exhausted breath to the right, creating a stream of cloudy air from each one of us and a very big puff from the horse at the front. It was as if we were all smoking a very big pipe. We reached a narrow stony footpath on a terraced area where the land on our right was as high as I was, our eyes always on the ground where the next footstep was going to be placed. I lifted my head once and jumped with fright, as my face was only a few centimetres from the face of a dead horse. We were about to reach the main road that would take us out of the town. Now we were going to fully expose ourselves to the Germans. "What would they do to us?" I thought. They would take Father, Peppino, Uncle and Domenico from us, that was for sure.

The Long Road

We reached the main road with open fields on either side. No trees, no woods, no place to go and quickly hide any more. The air was gloomy. The place was desolate, it felt evil and threatening and brought another fear to my mind, a fear bigger than confronting the armed German soldiers or being shelled or bombarded. It was a fear that overwhelmed me, making my heart thump, because I remembered Mother making the two pockets in the cave and Father pushing them inside my brother's and my vests, telling me they contained our names, address and money in case we became separated from them. He had told me twice not to be afraid because he would come and find us, and this had scared me. Now, in this God-forsaken place, my mind was in turmoil, thinking, "Is it now that it's going to happen? Why? How?" I was in the depths of fear, a fear I couldn't control or reason with. However, there was no time to brood, we just had to keep walking.

By a miracle, there were no German soldiers to be seen at this end of the town. Had they all gone to fight on the frontline that morning, somewhere beyond the mountains behind us from where we could hear the constant muted sounds of explosion upon explosion, causing us to walk faster? We were all walking in line, one after the other, on the left-hand side of the road, Peppino and his family leading, then Father, Uncle, Mother, Grandmother, my brother, me and then Grandfather, who was last. Then Father got out of line and walked across to the right side of the road, saying, "Move to the right, everyone walk on the right side" and we all followed. Peppino and his family did the same at the front and I soon realised why. About two hundred metres ahead on the left side was the cart, the dead horse and the dead man that I had seen from the cave at the very moment that the shell exploded on the cart. As we were about to approach the cart, Father said, "Look to your right, look at the trees by the river, don't look at the cart." We went along at a fast pace all looking to the right, but as I came parallel with the cart I quickly turned and looked and an immediate shock went through my whole body. Only about two or three metres from me lay the dead horse at the end of the shafts of the cart. The man's body lay scattered on the road with staring eyes, intestines spilled out, clothing red with blood. I wished I hadn't looked, I wished I had obeyed Father. I remembered when the man was going fast out of the town under the exploding shells; then, I wished that one of the shells would get him because we thought he was collaborating with the Germans and stealing goods from our houses. I was filled with so much remorse my whole stomach was churning and I wanted to vomit. I took very deep breaths and held them to prevent me being sick, but each time I released my breath I wanted to vomit. Again and again I filled my chest with air and held it as long as I could. I thought if I started to vomit it would have been so bad for Mother and Father as we couldn't stop. I felt so guilty. I imagined that the body might be trailing behind me, to curse me because I had wished him to die. I didn't dare look back. We were walking fast but I wanted to go faster to distance myself from the horrifying sight. The road came to a double bend, and after we had gone round it I felt that we had got away from the scene. I managed not to vomit and began to feel better.

We went on walking, walking, walking. The road now went along the foot of the chain of mountains on our left and then opened out to farmland on either side. Only one or two farmhouses were to be seen at a distance. It seemed that we were the only people on earth and I thought that we were being punished, but I didn't know why. We kept on walking on the right side of the road, one after the other, then Father moved to the left side where there was a ditch which he went down so he could put the heavy sack on the higher ground, reload it onto his shoulder, then come out and walk faster. Soon he would have to pause again because of the heavy weight he was carrying. Peppino, his horse and family were about twenty metres ahead of us. Father continued to struggle under his heavy load on the left side of the road while we on the right maintained a fast pace, walking in the same order. Grandfather was finding it difficult to keep up. Each time I turned he was transferring the bundle of blankets he carried under his arm from one side to the other. The road was grey-white, of crushed, hardened gravel. Now and again there were small areas where the gravel had been loosened. Mother

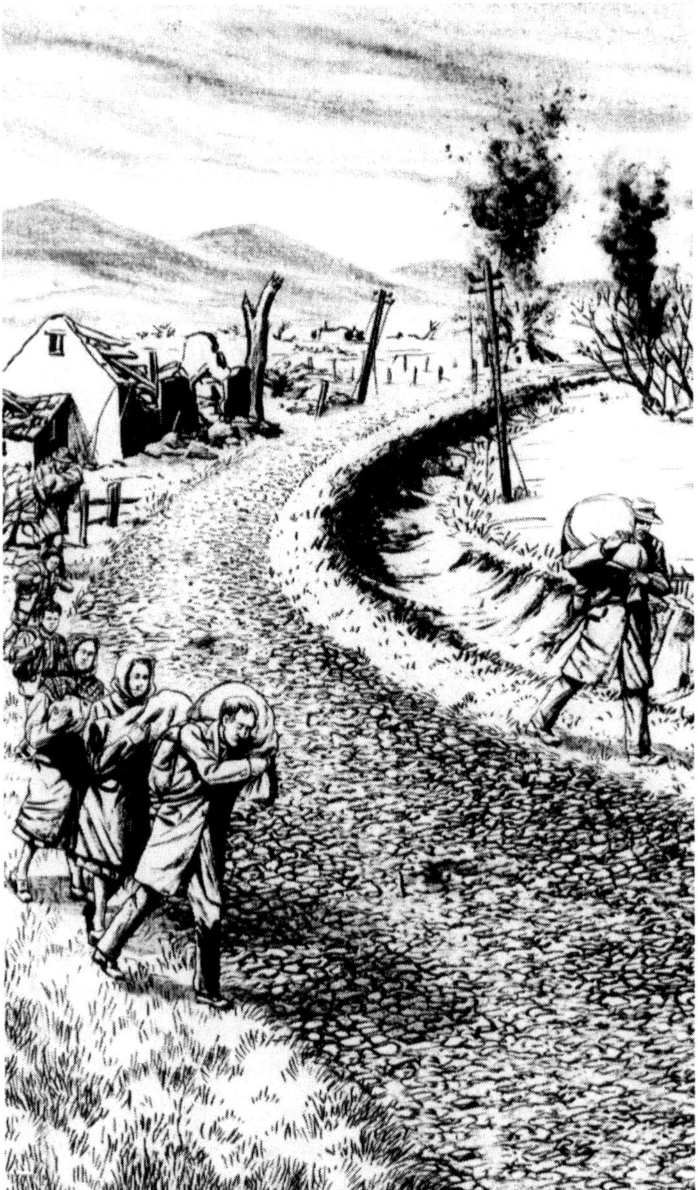

felt that these were where mines were buried, and each time she saw them on the road she made sure we walked on the grass verge, which was full of frost, making our shoes and legs wet again. Father kept on passing, walking very fast on the other side of the road and then pausing, the only way he could continue to carry his big rucksack and heavy sack. The sounds of the cannons and explosions behind us never ceased and made us keep walking without resting. My hips, my knees and my ankles were hurting as if they were on fire. I could hear Peppino's girls at the front moaning and crying and thought they were wrong to cry because it was making things worse for their mother and father.

Suddenly the shells began to fall nearer and nearer to us; we all started to walk faster and faster, but Grandfather behind me was having difficulty in keeping up. Father, on the other side of the road, was struggling, moving faster with his heavy load. Mother kept transferring the bundle of blankets she carried under her arms from one side of her body to the other, walking bent to one side to balance their weight. The merciless shells kept coming nearer and nearer, with their screaming, screeching sounds and then the deafening explosions. Mother continued to warn us of the suspected mines, saying loudly, "Walk on the grass, walk on the grass." One of my shoelaces came undone and I stopped to tie it, but Mother turned and said, "Lascia stare, cammina, cammina" (Leave it, walk, walk). It was awkward to walk with the shoelace undone, but I did my best to keep up. No place to shelter, just open spaces ahead. One shell after another exploded behind us where we had passed a short while before, each explosion stunning our heads, making us more and more dazed and confused. If the shrapnel was reaching us I couldn't hear it, but it didn't seem to matter any more.

Then the whole world collapsed on me – I heard Mother crying. She turned and looked at us with a face full of tears and between the sounds of the explosions I heard her sobbing. I felt so sad for her. I heard her say, "Cristo che male abbiamo fatto, se vi ho offeso, cosa hanno fatto questi due angeli?" (Christ, what harm have we done, if I have offended you, what have these two angels done to you?). This was the most devastating moment of my life. In my mind I asked Jesus to help my mother. I looked to my right, where some way away there was a cluster of very tall trees. They reminded me of a picture of the Madonna appearing above a cluster of trees so I expected Jesus to appear above the trees to help us, but nothing happened. A few seconds later I turned and looked at the trees again, but there was nothing to be seen except a sky full of dark clouds, no one to turn to. I felt so abandoned, insignificant, empty, just a worthless carcass moving along, walking, walking, walking, amidst a turmoil of fear and sorrow, tormented by sounds of death. My legs knew what to do to carry my body along but I was no longer in my body. My eyes saw me moving next to my mother, a streamline of bright light suspended in the air moving by the side of my mother as she walked. Was I there to comfort her? I don't remember. Was I there to be comforted? I don't remember. Was I there for ten, twenty, thirty seconds –

longer maybe? I don't remember. What I do remember is that I was not in my body, I saw myself next to my mother.

Father left the big sack on the bank of the road, came over, his rucksack still on his back, and walked beside Mother, trying to console her. "Non hai paura, le cannonate non ci arrivano qui" (Don't be afraid, the shells won't reach here), "Non ci sono Tedeschi qui" (There are no Germans here), he said. Grandmother answered, "Lasciala stare, falla sfogare" (Let her be, let her get it out of her system). Father stopped and waited for me to reach him, then walked by my side and with his right hand lifted my rucksack, relieving the weight on my shoulders for ten paces or so. We didn't speak. He did the same for my brother then left us to walk back and get the heavy sack.

We went on walking, the shells continuing to explode behind us and getting nearer and nearer as if they were chasing us. In that state of desperation, torment and sorrow, I descended into the depths of shame and selfishness, feeling as if I was committing a grave sin, because in that hell where my mother, father and everyone else were suffering, I began in my mind to sing a few lines of a sweet song that I knew and often used to sing. I sang the same lines over and over again, just like when the gramophone needle used to get stuck on our records.

O campagnola bella	Oh beautiful country maiden
tu sei la reginella	you are the little queen
Negli occhi tuoi	In your eyes

ce il sole	is the sun
ce il colore	is the colour
delle viole	of the violets
nelle valle	in the valleys
Tutte in fior	All in bloom

I knew that I was wrong, I knew that I should stop, but I just couldn't. I kept on telling myself that I would sing the lines just once more and then I would stop, and then just once more and I would stop, and once more and I would stop. I was torn between wanting to sing it once more and the guilt of how cruel I was to continue to do so.

When we reached the end of the long road, we turned right and saw a row of houses a few hundred metres away along the left-hand side of the road. Quickly we headed for them and made our way to the back, which gave us some protection in case the shelling reached us. I sat on a low stone wall, which was very cold, and curled up like a snail, just listening to my heavy breathing and heartbeats. My body felt heavy and my hip and knee joints felt as if they were on fire. I wasn't aware of what the others were doing or if they were speaking, though I sensed that they were there. I never turned or looked at anyone, the effort was too much.

Father came to me, took my rucksack off my back without speaking and gave me a piece of very hard bread and a small piece of smoked sausage. I took a bite of bread and a small bite of sausage and chewed, remaining detached and solitary. While chewing I made a discovery. I knew that the piece of bread and sausage was my ration for many hours to come, so each bite I took I chewed and chewed without swallowing it. The more I chewed the more it increased in my mouth, and when it had increased to a big mouthful of warm soft pulp, then I swallowed it. I felt that I had gained a lot more food by doing that and thought that I would always do the same when I ate in the future. When I finished my bread my mouth was watering, wanting more. I remained sitting, bent forward, hidden within myself, feeling alone, sad, confused, stunned by the sounds of death.

The Barrow

After a while my mental isolation was ended by Uncle calling Father's name as he walked back from a neighbouring garden. "Crescenzo, Crescenzo," he called on a note of surprise, as if something good had happened, "there is a barrow here." "Don't touch anything," Father commanded, thinking there could be a trap with explosives. They went off and within two or three minutes returned, pushing a barrow. Seeing it made me realise how lucky we were. Now we could put all our belongings on the barrow, Father didn't have to carry the heavy sack any more, Mother and Grandfather didn't have to carry the awkward bundles of blankets and perhaps, perhaps, my brother and I could ride on it. What a miracle! What a find! The barrow was ours now, because Uncle found it. These were my immediate thoughts and I couldn't take my eyes off it. It was ours to keep. The barrow completely brought me out of my withdrawn state and even took away some of the trauma of the last few hours. Father began to load everything we carried on to the barrow, placing the items carefully so they didn't fall. Then to my disappointment he said to Peppino's family, "Bring all your stuff over so I can load it and we'll go." This upset me because Peppino's horse hadn't carried any of our goods, but my main concern was that they might think the barrow was theirs too. As I saw it, the barrow was ours because Uncle found it, Father went to get it, and we were doing Peppino's family a favour.

With the sacks and rucksacks, baskets and blankets the barrow was loaded to capacity and I felt sad there was no room on it for my brother and me. Peppino and his family went out on the road first and we followed. Father took up position on the barrow like a horse with a cart and Uncle and I pushed it from the back into the road. The barrow was loaded so high that we had to make sure nothing fell off. I pushed as hard as I could to ease Father's pulling. Now and then I glanced at the side to see the chunky wooden wheel going round, hub, spokes and rim all painted red and a thick outer metal rim that would last for ever. I could also see Father's hand firmly gripping the staff. Then Father said, "Who's pushing? We're going downhill, try to pull back." All the time we were getting further away from the explosions. I wasn't too worried now we had a barrow.

We passed some bombed houses on either side of the road, windows and balconies hanging as if about to crash down any moment. Father wiggled the barrow through the rubble. No other human beings anywhere, it was all rather scary. A big dog crossed a little way in front, then stopped in the middle of the road looking at us. It was very thin, all its ribs showing, and it too looked confused and frightened as it slowly went on its way.

We were now travelling on a main road away from our town. Father said, "We have been fortunate not to encounter any Germans, let's not take any more chances, it's better if we find a way to go by the side of

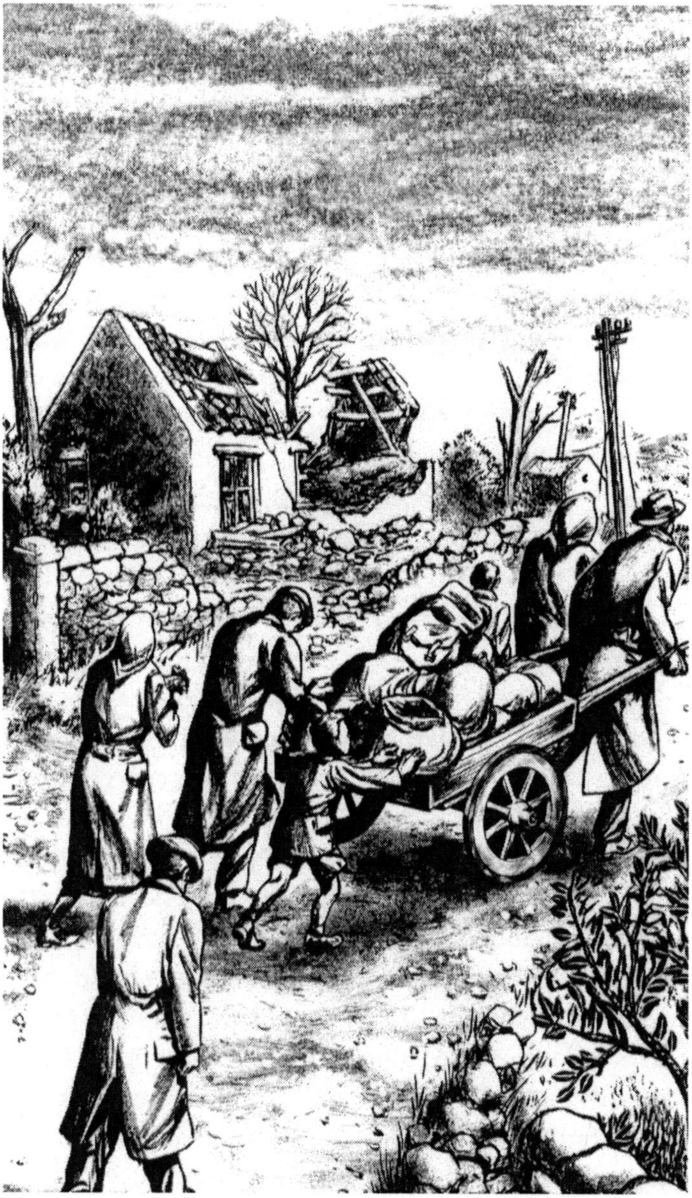

the mountains and forward from there." Soon we came to a side road on our left going towards the chain of mountains and turned down it. The road was full of stones, the barrow shook from side to side and the goods on the top began to fall off. At times it got stuck when the wheels sank into the soft earth and Uncle and I had to push really hard to get it through. Being at the back pushing and because the road was narrow and flanked by high hedges, I couldn't see ahead. It was a sudden shock, I didn't want to believe his words, when Father stopped and said, "Non si può andare più avanti con la carrozella" (We can't go any further with the barrow) "the road has come to an end." Uncle and I went to the front. Father was panting heavily, his face regretful, as he raised his shoulders and opened his arms as if to say, that's it, not much we can do. We had a rest, but I felt very sad that we were going to leave the barrow behind. It was very special to me as it had relieved Father from carrying such a heavy load, Mother and Grandfather from carrying the awkward blankets and me and my brother from carrying our rucksacks; what was more, it had taken my mind off some of the trauma of that morning. It had given me hope, been a wonderful companion, and now we were going to abandon it. Resting time was over. Father stood up, handed each of us the goods we were to carry and off we went again. I kept turning to look at the barrow as we crossed a field, and as we stepped onto a footpath flanked by high hedges I turned and gave it one last glance. It looked lonely and abandoned and I felt sad, as if I were leaving a friend behind.

We reached the foot of the chain of mountains where there was a narrow footpath. The earth had hardened in the centre where farmers had walked. The sides were full of long grass, now wet from the melted snow of the previous day. When I didn't pay attention to where I was taking my next step I accidentally placed my feet on the grass, which made my shoes and legs wet. On and on we walked, not knowing where we were going, just concentrating on keeping in the centre of the narrow path. Walking was completely automatic now, eyes down, looking where to place the next footstep. Numb from the cold, tired and tormented by the past hours, no words were spoken, there was just the sound of sorrowful breathing. We came to a small clearing where we were able to take a rest when I heard Father say to Mother, "There are two pieces of bread left, shall we give it to them now or later?" referring to me and my brother. Mother answered sadly, "Give it to them now." Father looked at me and said, "Are you hungry?". I said "No", so as not to worry them, then frowned at my brother, who also said "No" and bowed his head. I had never seen my brother's face looking so sad before, big eyes and sunken cheeks, and felt that I had made him say "No" as well, but I had been trying to make Mother and Father think that we were all right as I felt sorry for them too.

We were on our way again, all in line, walking into the unknown, placing one foot in front of the other, following the trail in the shadow of the mountains. All was quiet in a wilderness that made us fearful to speak, just brooding on what might lie ahead. Where was this unknown path going to take us? Would we find a safe place or were we delivering ourselves into the hands of German soldiers? Were they going to punish us just because we were there? What would they do to us? Father and Uncle would be taken for sure. What would we do without Father? It was a train of thoughts that made me fearful with each breath I took. Our home, with all its comforts, our relatives and friends were all forgotten now. No happy thoughts or wishes occupied our weakened and tormented minds, only fear for our survival. We continued to walk along the winding, narrow path and at some stage found ourselves joined by a small river on our right. It accompanied us with melodious sounds, rejoicing in the life and freedom we no longer had. The crystal clear water turned and flowed around all the obstacles it encountered, gushing between stones, through fallen trees, around rocks, speeding with ease to its eventual destination.

Often we were so closely flanked by trees on the mountain side and woods along the river bank that we felt enclosed in a dark tunnel. Then the gaps along the river impelled us to look for signs of life, a house maybe, a human being to ask where we should go, but only glimpses of abandoned fields appeared, revealing their own desolate state. Then, after hours of walking, we saw in the distance a road, offering hope that it might lead us to houses with people to help us but also involving exposure to the unknown.

After walking round bend after bend of the path – now dark, now light – we saw a bridge with walled sides. We all stopped and stayed very quiet, looking to see if civilians were crossing, only to be shocked by the sight of an armed German soldier pacing up and down the bridge. The walled sides meant we could only see the upper part of his body, his chest, helmet and the barrel of the machine gun he carried on his shoulder. We remained frozen, watching the scene and wondering if we were allowed to be there. If not, what would they do to us? Very quietly, Father said, "Listen, everyone, you all stay here, have a rest, but don't move from here, don't speak and don't make any noise. Peppino and I are going a little further to get a better view of the bridge and see if there are any civilians about. Have you all understood? Don't move and don't make any noise!" Moments after they left, Uncle also went and I followed. We soon caught up with Father and Peppino. When Father saw me he pointed his index finger at me and shook his head, indicating I should not have followed them. The four of us hid behind a cluster of dense woodland from where we had a good view of the bridge, the trees beyond it making it impossible to see further ahead. We fixed our eyes on the bridge hoping to see civilians crossing, which would give us the confidence to go into the open, but all we could see was the soldier going backwards and forwards, backwards and forwards, the length of the bridge. He would disappear for a minute or two then back he came on the bridge.

The minutes seemed like hours as we watched in silence except for the sound of our breath and pounding hearts. We remained as still as the stones, watching the merciless being pacing back and forth, back and forth. I saw Father looking at Peppino as he tightened his lips and shook his head, then a sudden gasp from Uncle, the first to see a civilian walking over the bridge, made us look at one another in hope as we saw a man wearing a jacket and hat going independently across. The soldier didn't stop him. We returned quickly to the others and Father and Peppino told them not to be afraid, it was safe for us to go ahead. So once again we continued to walk along the path with our loads to where it joined the road only a few metres from the left side of the bridge. I heard Father calling Peppino, who was in front, "Peppino, Peppino, go left. Don't cross the bridge. Go up, go up." Then he said quietly, "Don't be afraid, don't be afraid, just keep going and don't look towards the bridge. Don't look at the German." We continued on the main road full of fear and not turning round once, hoping and hoping that soon we would come to houses with people who would give us shelter for that night at least.

The Pigsty

We came to a small group of houses and entered a courtyard where Father began to beg for shelter for the night. "A room, a barn, anything," he said as he told them of our plight. People came out of their houses, looked out of windows, all expressing sympathy, but no one had any room for us. One woman said, "I have taken as many people as I can." Another said, "Mi dispiace, mi dispiace" (I am sorry, I am sorry) we are ten to a room." The place was overcrowded with people who had taken refuge there two weeks before; there were sixteen of us to be accommodated. A woman came forward and said reluctantly, "The only place I can offer you is where we used to keep our pigs. The pigs have been taken by the Germans, so it's empty."

So many people were looking at us and I wondered if my face looked as sad as my brother's, huge eyes and sunken cheeks. Being so exhausted, hungry and in a state of stupor, I felt no embarrassment or shame; nothing mattered very much.

We were still standing with our packs on our back when Father and Peppino began to follow the woman who had offered us the pigsty. We all followed and then entered the pigsty. It was a long, narrow room and only my brother and I could walk upright. We sat on our packs. The place really stank, a stench that entered the nose and stayed in the head. There was a small low, square opening with iron bars for air where a glimpse of light came in. Father said, "Let's go and find some straw before it gets dark" and he, Peppino, Uncle and Domenico left to find straw to sleep on. We remained slumped in that stinking place. Peppino's family were in first and settled at the far end; it was dark there, but it would be less cold during the night than being near the door and the opening with the metal bars where we were. Grandfather lay on the floor, resting his head on the blankets he carried. Grandmother sat next to him, clutching her chicken. My brother and I sat close to Mother, resting our backs against the wall; opposite us was the iron-barred opening that gave a little light and, more importantly, let in some air that diluted the stench, which in only a few minutes had given me a headache. Mother said, "We shall all get ill if we stay in this place too long" and Peppino's wife replied, "The smell is suffocating us down here." I felt so tired that I wanted to lie down and go to sleep. Peppino and his son returned bringing the straw for their family to sleep on, but Father and Uncle were taking such a long time to return that we became worried as it was now almost dark. After some time they came back but without any straw.

Entering the pigsty, crouched so as not to hit his head on the low roof, Father said, "Pick up what you're carrying and let's get out of here, I've found a room and we've already taken the straw there. Let's go, Peppino, we'll all fit in somehow, bring your straw." I was so exhausted that I felt disappointed we had to move again – and I was getting used to the stench. Without a murmur everyone took up their load and we were on our way again. It was dark now, just walking, not sensing anything, only aware of walking automatically, and I was feeling so tired that this short journey seemed longer than the whole day's travel. Now and again I closed my eyes for a moment or two as I walked. Twice I asked Father, "Do we have far to go now? When will we get there?" and he answered, "We'll soon be there and we'll have something to eat." I could hardly believe it when I heard him say, "Ecco, siamo arrivati" (Here we are, we've arrived) as he stopped by the side of a house. "This is the room," he said. There were two or three steps going down to a small door, as the room was halfway below ground. I followed Father, my brother in front of me, and entered the room in total darkness. My brother and I stood side by side, our bodies touching, waiting for Mother, Uncle and our grandparents to come in, and we gathered together in the dark room. Then Peppino's family began to arrive. A candle was lit revealing the room to be only three to four metres wide and about the same length, with a concrete floor, rustic walls and a small window which was very high up because the room was partly below ground level. Sixteen of us had somehow to settle ourselves in the confined space. Father had already spread the straw against the top wall for us to sleep in line next to each other. Peppino spread his straw around the rest of the room, just leaving a small space by the door where all our goods were piled up. The candle was placed on the high window-sill, its meagre light flickering on our worn-out, agonised faces as we bumped into one another, confused and sighing after the horror of our day.

When I woke up the next morning in the small dark room, we were so tightly packed that I felt warm but dazed as if only half conscious, and the dreadful experience of the day before seemed only a vague memory. I was lying between my brother and Uncle but managed to squeeze myself halfway up to glance around the room. A subdued light came from the high window, but there was nothing good to look at. I just stared at the bare, rough, dirty grey walls and the stub of the candle on the widow-sill. Except for the two piles of packs either side of the door, the floor was crammed with bodies under the blankets, only the tops of heads of hair visible amongst the straw. I was hypnotised by the sounds of deep breathing from all the sleeping bodies. I wriggled back under the blankets not wanting to get cold, wondering what we would eat when Mother and Father woke up.

It wasn't long before the room became full of confusing sounds as some began to mumble, others to complain of pain. The two little girls woke up crying, which mingled with the sounds of those who tried to give comfort. When we were all standing, bumping into one another, confused, lost, helpless, I heard Uncle say to Father that he wanted to go and find the rest of the family to see if they were well. He wanted to go to Sora, where Grandfather had said he would head for when we separated two weeks before. Father agreed with this, saying, "It will take you most of the day to get there and find them." Uncle replied that he would return by nightfall the following day, so we shouldn't worry about him. He left that morning as Father told him, "Be careful, always ask locals the best route to take – and don't get caught." Then I learnt that the man who let us stay in the room also allowed Peppino to keep the horse in his stable, and I think that's where Grandmother kept her chicken.

A little later that morning Father took me and my brother outside the room to relieve ourselves. As we went out I saw that we were quite near to a road and there were a few big oak trees here and there. When we had come to the place the previous evening we hadn't noticed anything because it was dark and we were so exhausted. Father took us towards some trees where there was also a high hedge, and here we had a big shock. The field beyond the hedge was full of Germans, some unloading lorries, some pushing a small cannon, one group attending to a big gun as they swung the long barrel from one side to the other, others carrying tree branches to camouflage the lorries. We quickly made our way back to the room, where Father told Peppino and his son Domenico not to go out unless it was really necessary. He added, "It's dangerous to remain here with all the armour around. It's bound to be bombed. We'll wait for Benedetto to return tomorrow evening and leave here early the next morning. Meanwhile, we men will stay out of sight. We must not attract attention to this room."

Mother, my brother and I went to collect bits of dry firewood from under trees and hedges, as well as dry leaves to start the fire, which we lit against a broken stone wall sheltered by some trees. The wood was damp and the day windy and that prevented a good fire. Smoke was blowing in all directions, but Mother did get a meal cooking in the only cooking pot we carried. Mother, her parents, my brother and I gathered around the fire, forming a shield to prevent the wind putting it out. It began to drizzle, but we remained by the fire watching and waiting for the meal to be cooked. I kept asking Mother, "Is it nearly cooked?" and she always answered the same, "It won't be long now". We ate in the same place standing, Father cautiously joining us as we shared the two spoons he had found among the goods he carried. We took turns as the spoons were passed round dipping into the pot. I felt very hungry but the food was tasteless, just wet and warm.

Inside the room Father kept telling everyone not to go outside unless it was necessary. "After tomorrow we will leave this place," he said. I felt extremely tired, my joints ached, I yawned a lot and Father kept telling me not to squeeze my eyelids shut. I tried and tried not to, but I couldn't help it and Father got more and more annoyed with me. There were sixteen of us crammed in that small room, lying or sitting on a thin layer of straw. I felt the cold hard concrete under me. Restlessness, tiredness and bad temper filled the air, together with prayers imploring the saints to help us. We dreaded the Germans coming to take Father, Peppino and Domenico away from us, because now the enemy were only a few metres away; we heard them speak, we heard them shout, we heard the crunch of their boots pass by the high window of our room.

Towards the evening of our second day we waited for Uncle's return. I missed him. Father began to repack his load to leave the next day and I felt as if we were going to be released from a cage. "Not long to go now," I thought, "just one more night on the cold hard floor, tomorrow we will find a better place. Perhaps there won't be any Germans where we're going to next. Perhaps Uncle will say that it's good where our other grandparents, aunts and uncle are." I rejoiced in the thought of seeing them again. We waited and waited and waited for Uncle to return. It became completely dark, but he still wasn't back and Father said, "He has probably stopped on his way and will be here early tomorrow morning." The room was now in total darkness and we were all sitting or lying in our space. Peppino said to his family, "Does anyone need to go out? It's better if we try to go to sleep and keep warm." The candle was lit for a few minutes for everyone to tuck themselves under their blankets then soon put out. It was all dark again, with murmuring sounds of prayers and a cough here and there as the bodies settled to sleep. I felt sad that Uncle wasn't back as I always slept next to him and he talked to me and never moaned, but I felt good too because when we woke up we would go somewhere much better.

Sometime during that night we were suddenly awakened by the deep whistling, screeching sound of a shell passing over us, rekindling our fear. This was followed by a deafening explosion and then another and another, horrifying sounds that had brought death to the people we knew, sounds that had nearly robbed us of our lives on more than one occasion in the past months. I remembered what Father had said the day before, that it was dangerous to remain in the area because we were in the midst of such heavy German artillery. Each explosion got closer and closer to us. I remembered the big cannon and other smaller guns we had seen in the field across the road from us; was that where the shells were aimed at?

Some of Peppino's girls were crying. Domenico lit a candle and placed it on the window-sill. Everyone sat up from their sleeping space, their eyes shocked and fearful, staring at each other, waiting for the sound of the next shell and hoping it would pass away from us. However, they began to explode so close that it made the window, the door and even the room tremble. Each explosion blew the candle out and Domenico kept relighting it. Peppino's girls were all crying now as their mother attempted to comfort them. Father tried to reassure everyone, saying we were safe as our room was partly underground. The shelling continued and we all began to pray aloud, imploring the saints to save us. Saint upon saint was called upon, "Sant'Antonio, Santo Giuseppe aiutaci" (Saint Anthony, Saint Joseph, help us). Domenico was the only one standing, relighting the candle after each explosion; even he looked petrified as if about to cry. I couldn't see the sense in him relighting the candle to be blown out soon afterwards by the next explosion. Then he tried to find spaces among us to place his feet in order to hand Mother and Grandmother small paper images of saints, saying in a frightened, trembling voice, "Pray, pray that the saints will save us". In her prayers Grandmother would say, "Santa Maria Madre di Dio aiutaci" (Holy Mary Mother of God help us), "Gesù mio abbia pieta di noi" (My Jesus have pity on us). The explosions increased, the shells sounding as if they were chasing each other. Faster and louder the prayers were recited and the room echoed with mournful sounds, which were frequently drowned by the explosions. Shrapnel could be heard continually hitting the stone wall outside our room, then a shell exploded on the roof, a terrifying noise as the roof collapsed on the floor above, making most of the old plaster ceiling in our room crumble on top of us and creating a cloud of dust. Father shouted, "Put your heads under the blankets, breathe under the blankets." We all coughed and coughed; the dust was just as bad under the blankets and we continued coughing as if we were choking to death. I felt the gritty stuff in my mouth and at the back of my throat and tried to spit it out but I couldn't. In the dark I was aware of Father next to me attending to my brother as he coughed and spat. Then I felt Father's hand behind my neck as he raised me to a sitting position and held a cup to my lips, keeping his hand at the back of my neck. He managed to say, "Drink only a little so the others can have some" then began to cough again. He lowered my head down, covered it with the blanket and moved on his knees away from me.

After what seemed an eternity the shells began to explode a little further away, but were still passing over us. Domenico relit the candle, revealing the dense cloud of dust in our room. We held shawls, blankets, bits of material over our faces with both hands, one above the nose and one below the chin, trying to filter the air as we breathed, but we still coughed and coughed, our eyes full of tears as we tried to clear the dust. Someone opened the door and a whoosh of cold, burnt, smelly air from the shells came in and created more dust from the pieces of plaster still hanging on the ceiling; it was quickly closed again. There were moments when the coughing lessened and then it would start again. When people began to speak, most of them complained of the grit in their eyes. The shelling stopped eventually but the coughing still went on. Water was again given to all of us, which helped. Our blankets were littered with large and small pieces of plaster and people's heads were covered with plaster that they hadn't noticed. The falling plaster didn't hurt anyone but the dust from it nearly killed us all. It took a very long time before we began to settle.

Peppino's girls needed to relieve themselves. It was too dangerous and frightening to go out of the room, so their mother went to the corner by the door where their goods were piled up, took a big cooking pot out, made room by the door and one by one all used the pot. Father asked me if I needed to relieve myself and I went to pass water. I was only three to four metres away from Mother and Father but I was frightened to be even that distance from them. I faced the door with my back to them, but I kept my head turned and my eyes fixed on Father, anxious to be back among them. Father removed the bigger pieces of plaster from our blankets and said, "Try to get some sleep. Tomorrow morning we will leave here." The rest of the night was spent lying there full of fear. Though the coughing subsided, the room was never quiet, as from time to time someone would cough, clearing their throat and spitting bits of grit onto the straw we slept on. I wondered what Mother and Father were thinking. I felt disappointed in Domenico; he was more frightened than anyone, and I had always thought that he was strong and courageous. I kept thinking of Uncle, what might have happened to him, and if we left the place in the morning how would he know where to find us? It was a long, harrowing night. I longed to fall asleep.

When I woke up the following morning, the door, immediately opposite me, was wide open. The cold air was biting on my cold face. My whole body was chilled, especially my lower back and legs, as my twisting and turning during the night had pushed the straw from under me to the sides of my body, so I found myself lying on the cold concrete floor. Father came in from outside and said, "Get up, we are going to leave in a while." He took my blanket and went outside and I could hear him and Mother trying to shake the bits of plaster and dust off the blankets.

Grandfather was standing in the space where he slept, leaning against the wall, Grandmother by his side. I stood too, looking at the ceiling rafters that were now exposed and at the pieces of plaster that were still hanging. It was very early in the morning; only a dull light entered the room from the open doorway and the small high window. Mother came in and knelt down by my brother, stood him up, gave him a long hug and took his blanket outside. I felt dazed; we didn't speak, just awaited Father's decision on what to do next. I saw him distributing the goods Uncle had carried but I did hear that most of it was going to be carried on Peppino's horse. I kept wishing that Uncle would return and wondered if he would ever find us. All of Peppino's family were standing too, waiting as we were, except for their mother, who remained sitting on the straw comforting her two little girls in her arms with blankets wrapped around them, just showing their tiny faces. Everyone looked weak, sad and lost. When our eyes met we said nothing, keeping all our thoughts to ourselves. We had nothing to say or to give and continued to stay by the wall motionless, speechless, almost lifeless, still tormented by that night's trauma.

Father gave us two cooked cold potatoes each, which had been boiled the day before, saying, "Eat this before we start walking". The potatoes were very cold, but I chewed and kept each bite in my mouth for a long time until it was soft and warm before I swallowed. I sensed so much anxiety in Father, everything he did was hurried, his face was sad, his eyes frightened as if at any moment we were going to be shelled again. Peppino and his son Domenico too hurried in and out of the room, taking all the goods outside to load the poor horse. They said it could carry much more now, as it was all flat land ahead of us.

When everything had been packed and taken up the few steps outside our room, Peppino came in saying, "Andiamo, andiamo" (Let's go, Let's go). One by one we slowly left the straw-covered floor and gathered outside in the icy cold grey morning air for each one to take up their load. The ground around us was littered with broken roof tiles, pieces of timber and stones caused by the night's explosions. The roof of the house where we had stayed had caved in and the houses around us were also devastated. The air itself seemed sad and smelly, the place filled with a menacing silence.

It was natural for my brother and I to stand side by side; the cold made our teeth chatter and he was pale with goose-pimples on his face and legs. I looked at my legs and they had goose-pimples too. Mother squatted by my brother and rubbed his legs, then took his hands and placed them next to her mouth and kept blowing her warm breath on them. She looked up at me as if to say, I'll do the same for you. I said that I wasn't cold, but I was really.

While we were waiting to start our journey, a man walked towards Peppino. It looked as if they knew one another and I think he was the man who had been kind to Peppino by feeding and keeping the horse in his stable for the last two days. What drew my attention to him in particular were his first words and the way he said them. "Che macello, che macello durante la notte" (What butchery, what butchery during the night). He went on to speak about the civilians who had been killed by the shelling and gave their ages. Then again he exclaimed, "Ma tu non lo sai che miracolo è che siete qui" (But you don't know what a miracle it is that you were staying here). Father, who had just come out of the room, joined in the conversation, saying, "Ma perchè, che è successo?" (But why, what has happened?). The man went on to say that had we stayed in the pigsty none of us would be alive now, because during the night a shell had actually hit it and exploded inside. Grandmother said, "Some saint helped us. God didn't want us to die. Sia fatta la sua volontà" (May his will be done). I really didn't care, it didn't affect me, I felt so stunned by the night's ordeal. I felt tired and cold, and just didn't want to be there.

A man handed Father a piece of cardboard and a pencil. Father wrote on the cardboard and nailed it to the door of the room we had stayed in using a stone as a hammer. It was a message for Uncle, saying: "Benedetto, we have left for the town of Casalvieri, find us there, Crescenzo".

As Father helped me put my rucksack on he said, "What you now have to do is to stop squeezing your eyelids shut." I didn't know I was doing that. Moments later he told me again, "Don't do that", then he said, "Andiamo primo che ricomiciano le cannonate" (Let's go before the shelling starts again, and when we encounter Germans just look ahead as if you haven't noticed them and don't be afraid).

One by one Peppino with his horse and family started to go and we followed all in line, carrying our loads. We soon encountered German soldiers going back and forward, all hurrying and looking worried. Other groups were moving guns and as we walked we heard their voices coming from behind clusters of trees. We passed immediately below the window of a house and heard several German voices speaking at the same time; it sounded as if a serious argument was going on. I thought the night's shelling must have given them a lot of trouble. We walked on, one after another, without turning then encountered two civilians. I did look at them, hoping that they would offer help, food or something, but their faces looked sad too as if they were in an equal state of despair. It was almost as if they didn't see us. We crossed the bridge with the German guard pacing back and forth with his machine gun on his shoulder; he said nothing. We walked along a narrow road with only farmland to be seen. Father kept turning to look how Grandfather, who walked behind me, was doing. More than once he caught me squeezing my eyelids closed and told me off, saying, "Leave your habit behind, leave it here in Sant'Andrea." Sant'Andrea was the name of the place we had stayed in for the last two days.

We reached the main road, which was heavily trafficked by German soldiers in lorries and loaded four-wheeled carts, each drawn by two huge horses, and motorbikes with sidecars, all speeding in the opposite direction to us, towards our town. We walked on the very verge of the road so as not to be in their way. Their presence decided us to leave the main road to the town of Casalvieri and take minor roads, lanes and footpaths.

We walked at a much slower pace now, but I felt so tired I could have curled up on the grass and gone to sleep for ever. Every time I turned to see if Grandfather was coming he was getting more and more behind. He kept transferring the bundle of blankets he carried from one side to the other, walking with his head bowed and taking short footsteps as if he was learning to walk. Father kept turning and looking at him too and most of the time told me off for squeezing my eyelids, but I had to do that. I wanted to stop doing it, but I couldn't. Then I would tell myself that I would squeeze my eyelids as much as I wanted until the end of that road or footpath and then stop. Sometimes I squeezed them so tightly for so long that I couldn't see where I was walking. At the end of the footpath I did try to stop but I just couldn't. Then, together with squeezing my eyelids, I found myself breathing out every bit of air in my body and resisting breathing in as long as I could. It was very uncomfortable, but it went on and on and on. I kept telling myself, "I'll do it once more then stop", but I just couldn't stop. The journey to Casalvieri was free from bombs, shells or interference from the Germans, but I caused myself so much misery squeezing my eyelids closed, resisting breathing in air, being told off by my Father and feeling sad for Grandfather as well.

Antonio's House

It was late in the afternoon when we reached somewhere in the vicinity of the town of Casalvieri. As we arrived at a group of houses Father and Peppino began to beg for shelter, only to hear the words "Mi dispiace, mi dispiace" (I am sorry, I am sorry) "my house is full, carry on, perhaps someone will have room for you". On we went, and to our surprise came face to face with Uncle Benedetto. We quickly gathered around him and Father anxiously asked how the rest of the family were. Uncle replied that he didn't know because when he left us, halfway into his journey to Sora, the Germans captured him and made him work for them unloading ammunition, carrying goods and chopping firewood; he'd been continuously under guard. He said that he worked really hard to be liked and on the second day he begged them to let him go so he could find his family, which they did. He decided to return to us but couldn't quite get there before dark, so he slept in a barn and reached the place where we'd been staying only an hour after we'd left and read the notice Father had nailed to the door. It felt good that Uncle was back with us and offered to carry Father's heavy sack.

We reached another group of houses with many refugees standing around. Father begged for shelter, even if it was just for the night, and a woman came forward and said that all she could offer was the room where they kept the farming tools and firewood. Father looked at Peppino, both shrugged their shoulders, then nodded, accepting the room. It was dark and cold with farming implements scattered around as well as a pile of firewood. Father said to Peppino, "Let's go and find some straw before it gets dark, we can organise the floor space later". Father and Uncle went in one direction to beg for straw to sleep on while Peppino and his son Domenico went in another. We remained outside the room because of the heavy farming implements that had to be moved to make space for sixteen of us. We were tired and cold and stayed huddled together. I was hungry, and my ankles, knees and hips were sore. Though there were people around we seemed to be so alone and dejected and must have looked as if we were at death's door. People stared at us and I felt they were talking about us, but I didn't care. We were all feeling half dead and beyond caring.

Because of our sorry condition and pitiful looks, somehow word of our presence and where we came from must have spread, and while we waited for Father and Uncle to return with the straw we were approached by a man. He was of medium height, had black curly hair, and looked strong, warm and confident. He wore a thick woollen jumper under his jacket, a style of trousers that buttoned just below his knees, long woollen socks and a second pair of socks rolled over the top of his boots. He looked like the men who climb mountains. Not addressing anyone in particular, he asked if there was anyone with us called Panetta, our surname. Fear made Mother come forward quickly and say, "No, we don't know the name, why are you looking for him?" The man answered, "He is a friend of mine, we were in the army together". Then Mother asked, "What's his Christian name?" and he replied " Crescenzo". Mother then told the man, "I said we didn't know him because one can't be too careful these days. He is my husband and has gone to find straw for us to sleep on." The man remained quiet for a moment or two, then said, "I will be back soon. When Crescenzo returns, tell him Antonio Morelli is looking for him" and went. About twenty minutes later the man came back, but Father and Uncle had not yet returned. He stood near us but neither he nor Mother spoke a word. We just stood there dazed, almost paralysed by the cold, the hunger and exhaustion, staring in the direction from which Father would return. A while later Father and Uncle appeared carrying a large bundle of straw each. Antonio moved towards Father, who quickly placed the straw on the ground. They shook hands vigorously then placed their left hands on each other's shoulder as if about to embrace. They didn't speak. Antonio moved towards Mother and said, "Come, we'll see how we can fit you in our house". Peppino and his son had now returned carrying straw and Antonio apologised that he couldn't accommodate them as he had already taken many people and we were going to sleep in his children's room. We all said goodbye to Peppino and his family, Father and Mother wished them well and we followed Antonio, who carried the rucksacks belonging to me and my brother.

Antonio's house was minutes away. We entered a large arched doorway in a high wall from the roadside into a courtyard with a well in the middle and there was a big house, like a small castle. We walked into the portico and entered a large kitchen where a big fire was glowing. There were many members of his family, who all stood and moved away from the fire and invited us to warm ourselves. "Venite, venite riscaldatevi" (Come, come and warm yourselves up), they said. It felt good, but it was also strange to be in a proper kitchen. The whole room was warm. We sat on proper chairs and the people were so very, very nice to us all. My brother and I were made to sit nearest to the fire, on either side of the fireplace. The warm glow on my face felt good, my legs and my knees were enjoying the heat and my clothes were hot too; it felt wonderful. Father was telling Antonio and his family of our plight during the last five months. Mother, Grandmother and Grandfather were very near the fire too and I saw their faces rejoicing in its warmth. It seemed too good to be true.

It wasn't long before a meal was produced for us all and we were invited to sit around the large kitchen table. I was told to sit on a small chair near a low side table positioned on the back wall and facing the fire and my brother sat opposite me. We were soon presented with deep plates full of food, rather like a soup. It had meat and vegetables and was so special that every mouthful was memorable. I felt the warm liquid making its way inside me and reviving me. I was enjoying it so much, but I was also in a dilemma, whether to eat it slowly and really savour, appreciate and enjoy each mouthful before

I swallowed it or eat it quickly in the hope I would be offered more. I felt torn between the two choices and I think I exercised a little of both, but sadly when my plate was empty there was no more left.

After the meal, Father and Mother thanked Antonio and his family warmly for their kindness. Antonio, his wife and the rest of the family apologised that they had no beds or bedding for us as they had given all they had to spare to other refugees accommodated elsewhere in the big house. The conversation continued as Father, Mother and my grandparents expressed their gratitude for what they were doing for us and they kept apologising that they couldn't provide any beds. The thanks and apologies went on for so long it almost sounded as if they were having a dispute. Soon afterwards we were shown to a room on the first floor with lots of straw on the floor and left to settle for the night.

When I woke up the next morning, for a moment or two I found it difficult to concentrate. I felt dazed, as if someone had hit me over the head, and couldn't think where we were or how we got there. It was late morning, nine or ten o'clock, because there was a strong beam of light coming through the slightly open wooden shutters on the glass window. I raised my head; everyone was still asleep, making different noises, deep breathing in and out, long powerful exhalations; the sounds resembled those of exhausted cows breathing heavily as they pulled the metal farming implements to plough the soil. Father made the loudest noises. Pounding hearts and exhausted lungs that for days had been forced to the extreme were now recovering. The air was cold and I lay back and pulled the blanket over my head to keep warm. I felt pleased that Uncle was back with us. Soon afterwards I heard Father say to Mother, "Come ti senti"? (How do you feel?) and Mother answered in a slow, sorrowful voice, "Mi sento male" (I feel bad), all my bones hurt. How long is this going to go on for? "E tu, come ti senti?" (And you, how do you feel?). With a deep sigh Father answered: "How do I feel. Since we left the cave my neck and my shoulders have been killing me. It's that sack, that sack has been killing me."

A voice called Father's name; it was Antonio. "Crescenzo come down, come and have something to eat, come and warm yourselves, come." Father answered, "Thank you, Antonio, we'll come soon." Since we always slept with our clothes and shoes on, it took only minutes for the seven of us to walk down the steps and enter the kitchen. I hardly remembered what the kitchen looked like from the evening before. It was a very large room with a wide fireplace and high mantelpiece, and there was a good fire burning that warmed the whole room. Antonio, his wife, mother and his two sisters all greeted us and asked if we had slept well. My brother and I were asked again to sit nearest to the fire, either side of the fireplace. Pots and pans hung above the table against the far wall, while the large centre table had a big round loaf of bread and a round piece of cheese on it. They all started talking about the war while the two sisters were by the stove preparing food. My brother and I rejoiced feeling the warmth of the fire. It comforted my body as I watched the red glow of the oak logs burning. The heat on my face was putting me almost into a trance, but what really occupied my mind was the wonderful smell of roasted barley. It reminded me of when, at home, in the morning Mother would give us a mixture of water from the boiled roasted barley with sugar, boiled milk and chunks of toasted bread in it. The thought brought a sea of saliva to my mouth. I felt very embarrassed and it would have been rude to turn and look at what was being prepared.

After what seemed a long time, my brother and I were asked by one of the sisters to sit opposite one another by the low table and were each presented with a china bowl with exactly the same food Mother used to prepare for us: boiled roasted barley water, sugar, boiled milk and chunks of toasted bread. With each spoonful I took my mouth watered and I breathed every bit of vapour into my head. I savoured every spoonful, I never wanted this joy to cease. Moments like that eased all our suffering. Mother sat facing us at the big table and with all the others kept looking at us with pleasure as we savoured such a gift. When we had finished, my brother and I went back to sit by the fire. I wished we could have stayed there, it was so comfortable and warm. We just stared at the fire; the tiredness and the heat of the fire on my face put me into a state of stupor and my brother's face looked sleepy too. The chatting of the adults was just a confusion of noises in my head. After they had had their food, Father stood up, saying, "Let's go back to our room". Everyone stood, Mother took my brother by the hand and I stood next to Father. It took quite a while before we left as they continued chatting and then Father, Mother, my grandparents and Uncle thanked them sincerely for their kindness. The restful night, the warmth of my body, the wonderful breakfast and the generosity and compassion shown by Antonio and his family began to awaken me to the reality of our situation. It was the first time since we left our home in September that we had entered a proper home and received so much kindness. It was at that moment that a feeling of humiliation overtook me. I felt embarrassed because of the situation in which we found ourselves, relying so much on other people's help for our survival. We were destitute. We were in despair. We were beggars. I felt so sad for us all.

We left the kitchen, again thanking Antonio and his family, and went to our room via the carved stone stairs. I began to be aware of our surroundings. Our room was small and narrow and on one side there was a small table and one chair. Father took some of the food out of his sack and placed some items on the table and the remainder underneath; the rest were piled up in the corner of the room. On the opposite side the floor was covered with straw, with our blankets on top. It was just enough space for us to sleep in line next to each other. The window had two panels with glass and inner wooden shutters to obscure the light. From it I could see the courtyard with the well and the high wall with the large arched entrance. As the minutes went by I realised more and more that we had hardly any space to move. There was only a very narrow strip between the table, our goods and the straw with our blankets. Grandfather sat on the only chair and we sat on the straw, our blankets over us, just staring as if lost. No one spoke. There was nothing we could do to improve our situation, nothing to say. We were lost. The room was cold. The cold even came through the straw from the concrete floor and made my bottom cold. I tried to rest my back against the wall, but the wall was cold as well. It was when we rested that our bodies told us how exhausted we were. This was the fifth day of our journey since leaving the cave.

Some time later that morning, Antonio came to the door of our room, from where he spoke to Father. He said: "Crescenzo, I want to warn you and your brother. The Germans often come to capture men. We have organised a good warning system so we can run and hide, but when they suddenly make an attack on the whole area using vehicles it makes it difficult to escape in time. So, if you hear me shouting your name from the bottom of the stairs, both of you run to the stables at the back of the building. From there just follow me, but you have to be quick." He looked at Mother and said, "La vita è triste signora, ma diamoci coraggio eh" (Life is sad signora, but let's take courage eh), nodded his head and left. Father turned towards Mother, saying, "Don't you worry, even if we don't return by nightfall, we do what Antonio says. He has contacts. He knows where to go." Grandfather, Grandmother and Uncle just looked, listened and said nothing. Antonio's warning had reawakened our minds to the full reality of our situation. We had distanced ourselves from the ferocious battle yet we still remained under the eyes of the enemy; the possibility that Father would be captured and taken away from us was our main worry. Each of us remained still, quiet and filled with our own private fear.

Somehow it felt strange to be in a room in a real house. For a while we remained motionless, keeping our thoughts to ourselves, our weakened bodies and tormented minds trying to recover from the endless traumas of the last five months. Father broke the silence, saying to Mother, "Che fortuna che ci troviamo nella casa di Antonio" (How lucky we are to find ourselves in Antonio's house). Mother replied, "Che brava famiglia, sono cosi gentili, cosi generosi" (What a good family they are, so kind, so generous). Father went on to say that we should not abuse their kindness and should go into the kitchen only when necessary. Antonio's wife had told Mother that she could go and cook in the kitchen any time, but Father said to Mother that she should be out of the kitchen before their normal cooking times. "Be out of the kitchen by eleven o'clock," he said.

It was dangerous for Father or Uncle to go out, so Mother went to local farms trying to buy food. We waited anxiously for her return. It seemed many hours before she came back, but we were pleased when she returned bringing potatoes, dried beans and bread.

As the days passed, I found it more and more amusing to hear the way people spoke with a different accent from ours and the way the women dressed in their traditional clothing, long flowing dresses to their ankles, frilly blouses and, what was really unusual, their stiffly ironed squareish head-dress with frilly sides. Also, because it was so cold, all the women wore a shawl of contrasting colours over their shoulders and arms. The most unusual thing about their customs, however, was on very cold days the women walked about holding a small earthenware pot with a long domed earthenware handle. It was just like a miniature bucket and they called it 'scaldino'. Before they left home the scaldino was charged with burning charcoal and then held with both hands close to the stomach under the shawl. Many times I saw two, three or more women chatting by the roadside holding the scaldino under their shawls, all looking as if they had a big belly.

I made friends with Antonio's son Italo, who was about my age. I used to go into the warm kitchen with him and became familiar with all the family, Antonio's wife, mother, two sisters and Italo's little sister Marisa. Italo took me outside and showed me the stables at the rear of the house. It was then that I became aware of how big the house was; it really seemed like a castle to me. I saw many other refugees who occupied the same house but used a different entrance. The area at the rear of the house was all farmland that sloped down into a shallow valley. I felt happy that I'd made friends with Italo, but sometimes he didn't want my company and that made me sad. I soon learned he only wanted it when he had nothing else to do. He was free to go about the house, especially into the warm kitchen. Also he went to see other boys in the next houses, but unless I was with him I was confined to the misery of our room. We spent most of each day in our room sitting on the straw with our blankets wrapped around us. It was tiring and very boring. Mother cooked our lunch in the kitchen some time during the morning so as not to be in the way of Antonio's family when they needed to cook and brought the food to our room. It was usually boiled potatoes, beans or polenta and we ate it about two or three hours later standing around the small table taking the food from the same pot or dish – it was always cold. We ate as late as possible so we wouldn't be very hungry towards the end of the day.

Each evening for a short while we went to warm ourselves by the fire in the kitchen and then quickly went back to our room and lay under the blankets in order to keep warm. It was always so very early in the evening that I found it difficult to go to sleep. In the small oblong room, Grandmother slept nearest to the far wall from the door, then Grandfather, Uncle, me, my brother, Mother and Father. When they slept I could recognise the sounds they made as they breathed in and out. Grandmother had a particular way of breathing. She inhaled a long breath of air, then there was a short pause and then she exhaled through her mouth, which remained closed until the air exploded through a small opening between her lips, making soft popping, blowing sounds. One evening after everyone fell asleep except Uncle, me and my brother, Uncle began to imitate the way Grandmother exhaled, exaggerating a little as he exploded the air through his lips, ending in a quiet whistling sound. This made me and my brother laugh. Then he would stop for a few moments and do it again. We laughed and laughed, keeping our heads under the blankets so as not to wake the others. These were moments when all misery vanished from my mind, the experience of laughing being such a great joy. It felt as if to laugh and be happy was a beautiful discovery and told me that to live was good. Unforgettable moments!

It was in our last place, Sant'Andrea, that my head began to feel itchy. Now Mother discovered that we had lice. She searched our heads and killed them, but there were always more, even among our clothes. I searched for them too, slowly and gently passing the tips of my fingers though my hair, feeling them trapped under my fingernails and crushing them between the nails of my thumbs. Some of them were massive!

Since the Germans forbade us to listen to or own a radio, people were always asking one another sorrowfully if they had heard any news about the war. The muted sounds of the exploding bombs and shells coming from the direction of our town never seemed to stop. That was where the big battle continued, but it was a long way from us now. Our big worry was that we kept hearing that more and more German troops were moving into the area where we were staying. A deep fear began to cloud our lives again; we knew how cruel they could be. Were we going to return to the dangers, the horrifying experiences we had already gone through? Our hopes always were that in a few days we could go back to our home. The news that so many Germans were coming to our area disheartened us completely. Antonio kept coming to our room to speak to Father; everyone was nervous now. Father almost closed the wooden panels on the glass window, making the room dark, and at every slight sound he and Uncle jumped to the window, looking through the gap between the shutter and the glass. In our state of anxiety we all knew that it was better not to talk, but our silence signified fear.

A few days passed. It was a dark drizzling afternoon and we were all in our room when suddenly we heard Antonio rushing up the stairs shouting Father's name and "Tedeschi, Tedeschi, presto, presto, andiamo via" (Germans, Germans, quickly, quickly, let's go). Antonio had hardly finished his sentence before Father and Uncle disappeared from the room after him, then we heard the commotion of all the refugee men staying in the other part of the house calling to each other, trying to keep their voices down, and running down the valley at the rear of the house. Mother opened the wooden panels of the window, letting the light in so as not to cause suspicion. Grandfather, who was so ill, lay on the straw with most of our blankets over him and we remained motionless with the door left open. Minutes later we heard the sounds of boots as German soldiers rushed towards the house and then their angry voices echoing within its walls. Within moments the sound of boots on the stone stairs made our hearts tremble. One German soldier rushed into our room waving his machine gun at us and stood with his back against the wall. Grandmother, Mother, my brother and I stood grouped together, watching his vicious eyes under that horrible helmet. Mother held my brother and me in front of her with her arms over our shoulders and hands on our chest, pressing us close to her body. Soon the shadows of two tall officers fell across the light in the doorway as they walked in with their shiny leather boots up to their knees and those horrid peak caps telling of their power to commit evil actions as they pointed their big pistols towards our faces. They came close, looking behind us,

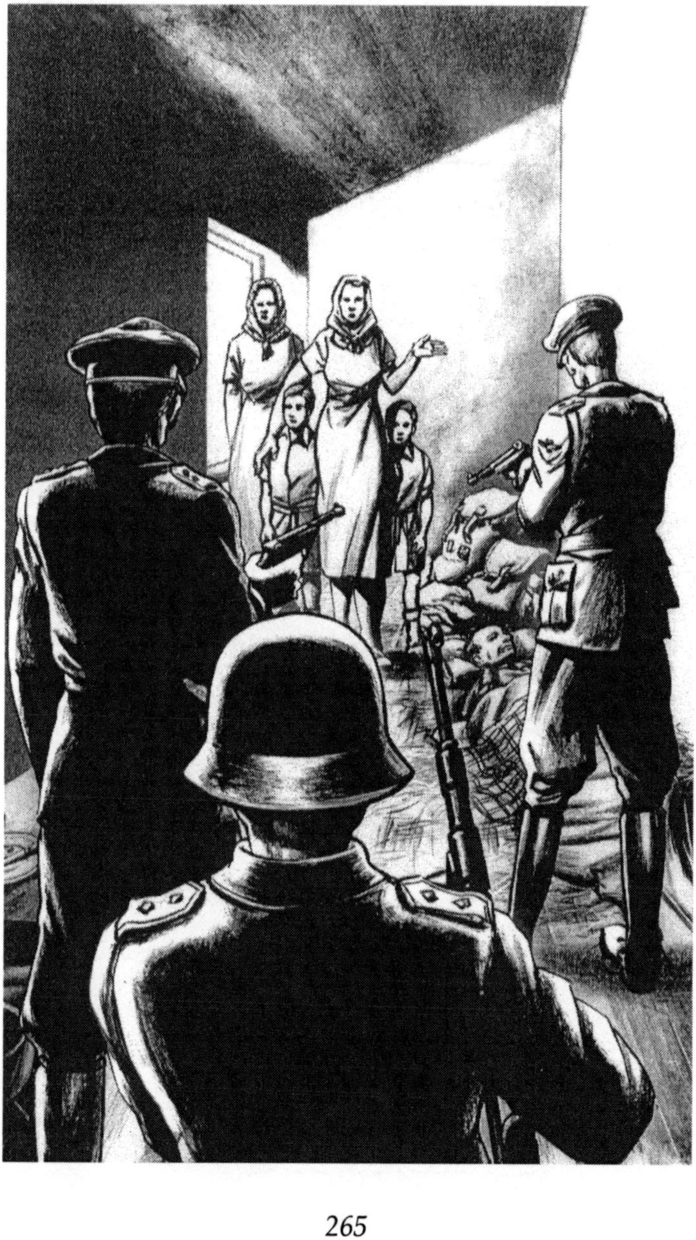

and took a long look at poor Grandfather, whose eyes remained still and sad as if to say, I don't care what you do to me. They then walked backwards out of the room and the one still pointing the machine gun also walked backwards, never talking his cruel eyes off us.

This happened many times while we were in Antonio's house, when they were looking for food, farm animals and, above all, when they wanted men. On one occasion they took two of Peppino's daughters to work in their kitchens; the oldest was fourteen years of age. Peppino, who was at an advantage as he spoke German, went with his daughters to protect them. On another occasion they discovered Antonio's food store and took everything away. We heard the women crying.

The men didn't come back for hours and hours, until it was dark. I was glad it wasn't me who had to go and tell Father, Uncle and Antonio when it was safe to come back, because I didn't know where to find them.

The Courage of Elisabetta

On another day, in the afternoon, I saw Antonio and his sister Elisabetta coming from the rear of the house where their farmland lay, walking calmly, accompanied by two German soldiers carrying rifles on their shoulders. They went into the kitchen and I heard them speaking to one another, trying hard to make themselves understood in Italian and German. It sounded friendly. I walked into the kitchen to see what they were doing, pretending I needed a drink of water. There was a big fire burning and they were all sitting around the table with a loaf of bread, a piece of ham, a flask of wine and glasses. I came out of the kitchen feeling rather disappointed with Antonio because he was being so friendly with the soldiers and, more so, that he was giving them food. I was hoping that the soldiers would soon come out. Perhaps I would be offered some of the food they were eating? I waited and waited, feeling hurt, trying to listen to their conversation and laughter and Antonio saying again and again "Unaltro bicchiere di vino"? (Another glass of wine?).

When the soldiers eventually came out they looked happy; the jackets of their uniforms were unbuttoned, rifles were on their shoulders, helmets in their hands. They looked young with blonde hair and rosy cheeks. They shook hands with Antonio and Elisabetta, who smiled and smiled while they were all saying, "Arrivederci, arrivederci, arrivederci" (Goodbye, goodbye, goodbye) as the soldiers walked away. Before they left, one of the soldiers turned and waved, saying, "Niente guerra, noi amici" (No war, we friends). It was obvious they were drunk. The soldiers looked very friendly, but I still felt annoyed with Antonio for giving them food.

Antonio and Elisabetta went back into the kitchen. Father appeared wanting to know what was happening and went into the kitchen too. I followed Father and stood by his side, anxiously waiting to hear why such kindness was offered to the people who were terrorising us. Antonio's mother, wife and other sister were there too. For a moment there was silence as if nothing was going to be said. It seemed that Antonio and Elisabetta were deep in thought. Then Elisabetta looked at Antonio, moving her head sideways as a sign of disapproval, and said, "Madonna, che miracolo, che miracolo" (Madonna, what a miracle, what a miracle). Antonio's mother said, "Ma che è successo?" (But what has happened?). Elisabetta looked frightened and as if she was about to cry, but she remained quiet as though she didn't want to reveal what had happened. Antonio, who had not spoken a word, looked at Elisabetta as if wanting to reassure her and said, "Non hai paura, e tutto passato, non hai più paura" (Have no fear, it's all past, don't be frightened any more). Elisabetta gazed at Antonio then said, "You could have been killed – and me." She then talked on and on as if she had to unburden her fear and I learnt what had happened that afternoon.

Antonio had buried an amount of produce in the farmland. This was something familiar to me because Father had done the same at home. That afternoon, Antonio and his sister had dug out of the ground a demijohn, which is normally used to keep wine and holds about ten litres. For protection, the demijohns are always enclosed in a wicker basket made of thin strips of cane interwoven around the demijohn with two handles. It had been filled with broad beans. They had pulled it out of the ground, refilled the hole with earth and were almost ready to lift it and go back to the house when the two soldiers suddenly appeared and said, "Questo è nostro" (This is ours) as they pointed to the demijohn. Antonio answered, "Questo è per la mia famiglia" (This is for my family). The soldiers answered, "Tutto nostro" (All ours). Antonio pleaded with them, saying: "You have taken my cows, my pigs and all my produce. I have nothing left to feed my family." The soldiers ignored what Antonio was trying to tell them, speaking among themselves, and one of them made a sign with his hand to Antonio to move away, saying, "Via, via" (Away, away) as they both bent forward to pick up the demijohn by the handles.

Antonio lost his temper and launched himself on the two soldiers, bringing them to the ground, holding one between his legs in a scissor hold and placing the rest of his body weight on the other, his hands around his neck, trying to strangle him, so that his tongue protruded from his mouth and his eyes stared at the sky. He shouted to his sister, "Give me the hoe, give me the hoe, I want to kill them both." Elisabetta, seeing what was happening, was horrified and didn't move, refusing to hand the hoe to Antonio. Within moments the struggle was over as Antonio was overpowered, ending with his hands up facing the two soldiers, who were pointing their rifles at him. Elisabetta threw herself in front of Antonio crying and pleading for mercy and Antonio also begged for mercy, keeping his hands up and saying that he had nothing against them, it was the war that had made him act like that as he had no food left to feed his family. It took an enormous amount of pleading, especially by Elisabetta, to appease the two soldiers. Antonio asked them to have a glass of wine with him, and that was why they were treated with so much kindness.

The next day, in the afternoon, I was with Antonio's son Italo walking along a path at the rear of the house through the farmland. Suddenly we saw Antonio running towards us. He stopped and hurriedly told us to go back to the house and if the Germans asked after him we didn't know who he was, telling Italo if they asked where his father was to say he had been killed in the war. Then he disappeared, running down the valley like a frightened fox.

We returned to the house, now surrounded by soldiers all armed with rifles and machine guns held ready to fire. They looked restless, their angry eyes visible under their helmets, talking in loud voices like an enraged pack of dogs. Italo and I walked slowly, pretending not to be frightened of them. What scared me most was the picture of the skull on their uniforms, because the only other place I had seen such a thing was on the large black mantle that was always placed over

It was this sinister sign (the SS insignia) on all their uniforms that made me even more frightened, especially after Father said, "They are the really bad ones."

the coffins in church while the requiem mass was being said. For me that was a mark of death. Italo went into the kitchen and I went into our room on the first floor. I could see that Father, Mother and Uncle were scared, wondering what was going to happen. I asked Father why they had 'La Morte', the picture of death, on their uniforms. He replied, "They are the really bad ones" (SS soldiers). Their angry voices were now in the house and soon we heard the sound of boots running up the stairs and two soldiers appeared in our room, waving the machine guns from side to side, pointing at us all. Father and Uncle put their hands up and kept them up. There was another door in the corridor outside our room that was closed. They kept shouting outside the door, "Raus, raus". Mother, pretending to be helpful, said, "Non cè nessuno" (There is no one there). Then one of them kicked the door open and the other leapt into the room shouting. There was no one there so it was "Raus, raus" to us as they waved their machine guns and indicated with their heads for us to go outside. Once in the courtyard, we had to stand in line with some people from the other part of the house who were already against the wall.

We heard men screaming from the other part of the house and the women saying, "No, no, no". One man came out holding both hands in front of his face, which was covered with blood, another could hardly walk and was crying. I learnt later that they had been beaten with the butt of a rifle. There were so many who were staying in the other part that I had not seen before. Now we all stood in line looking at each other, not saying anything. I recognised the two soldiers from the previous day, now

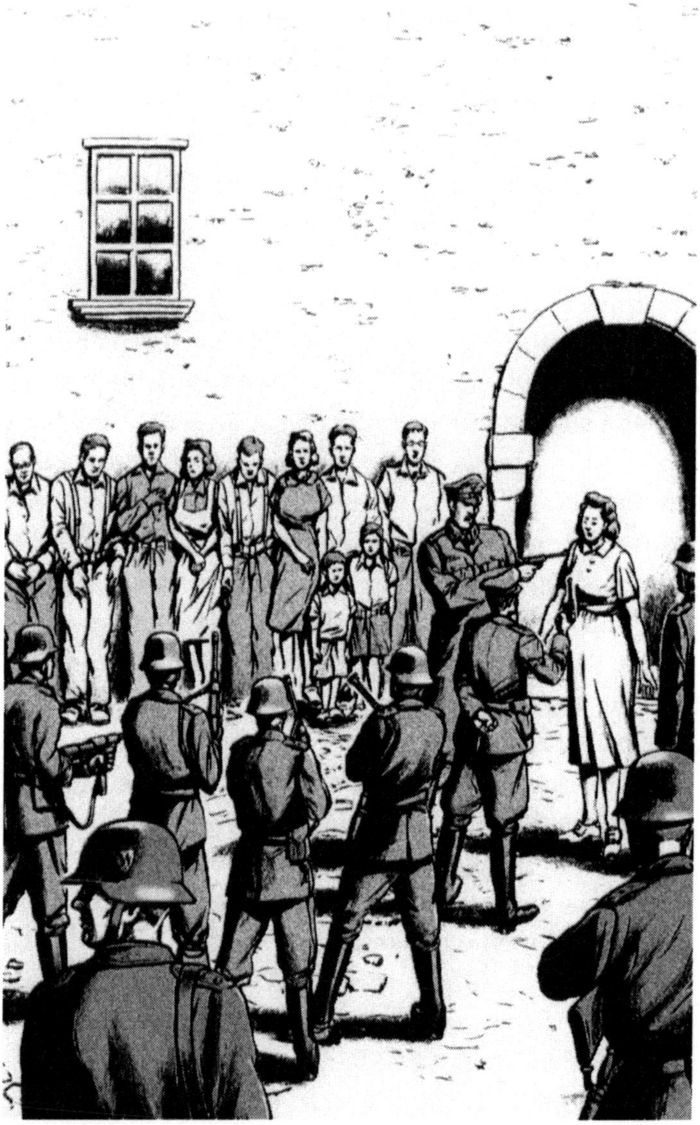

disarmed, standing separately between two officers with pistols in their hands. Officers always wore caps and carried pistols. When the house was emptied of all the people, some of the soldiers were ordered to search it again. The two soldiers from the previous day were made to look at all of us to see if the man they were searching for was there, but they only picked out Elisabetta, who had to stand away from us all like the two soldiers. Other soldiers paced back and forward looking at us, holding the rifles and machine guns in a firing position. I stared at them: they all had the picture of 'La Morte' on their uniforms. I looked at their faces, never a smile. Only merciless faces under the helmets, eyes full of hatred. Father was right, they really were the bad ones. The soldiers who went to search the house the second time came back with no one. Then they said that the women and children could go, but they kept poor Elisabetta behind standing alone.

Back in our room with Mother, Grandmother and my brother, our fear now was whether they were going to take Father and Uncle away. Poor Grandfather, who was so ill, remained standing in the cold too. We stayed very quiet listening to the men being interrogated. There were so many loud, angry voices that we couldn't understand what was being said. Then there were screams from some of the men who were being beaten. We remained motionless, terrified, staring at one another as if paralysed, listening for the next scream, hoping that it wouldn't be Father, Grandfather or Uncle's voice.

A miracle – Father came in bringing Grandfather, who had to be helped to his sleeping place, where he lay with most of our blankets on top of him. Uncle came in with a bleeding face. Mother took a piece of cloth and held it tightly against his face. Father said we should not stare out of the window as it would look suspicious. He closed the wooden panel leaving a small gap through which he watched poor Elisabetta, who was all alone among the fearsome soldiers. Everything went quiet for a moment and then they started to interrogate Elisabetta, their angry voices carrying on the air. Our room was soundless and almost dark as we remained standing, waiting and listening to Elisabetta's answers.

The soldier's voices became louder and louder, saying, "Dove è l'uomo? Dove è adesso?" (Where is the man? Where is he now?). "Non lo so, non lo so" (I don't know, I don't know) replied Elisabetta. "You were with him yesterday? He came into the house. You know who he is, tell me now." "I don't know, I don't know, he was a refugee in our house for only a few days, there are thirty or forty people in this house now, I don't know who they are or where they come from. He moved on after a few days here, because he found more room for his family. He has a big family." "Tu sai il nome?" (You know his name?). "Si, si chiama Giuseppe" (Yes, he is called Giuseppe).

"Il cognome, il cognome, dimmi il cognome?" (The family name, the family name, tell me the family name). "Non lo so, non lo so" (I don't know, I don't know), why should I know, we don't take any names. We don't ask for payment, we are just trying to help people. "Dove, dove è andato adesso?" (Where, where has he gone now?). "I don't know, I could tell you that he has gone to one of the many towns near us, then I would be lying to you." "You know him, you were in the field with him?" "Yes, yes, he had buried the broad beans in our field and came to collect them. He borrowed our shovel and our hoe. I was trying to help; he told the soldiers that he had no more food to feed his family. You ask them, you ask them." "Why did he come into the house?" "He wanted to thank my mother for accommodating him and his family. I know now that he is a bad man but I refused to cooperate with him when he wanted to harm the soldiers. He shouted at me, I refused to cooperate, I was on the soldiers' side, I was sorry for them, that's why I invited them into our house. I know the war is bad for all of us."

Now Elisabetta's voice was angry. Father saw Elisabetta's mother and sister going towards the interrogating soldiers, shouting, "Lasciala, lasciala stare" (Leave her, leave her alone), we don't know who the man is. Mother said to Father, "I think I should go and support them." "It's better if I come too," said Grandmother. Father remained looking through the gap between the wooden shutter and the glass window. I followed Mother and Grandmother downstairs because I used always to be with Mother when Father was away, but I remained in the portico because I knew if Mother saw me she would tell me to go back to our room. It was cold and I was frightened and trembling. I felt my heart thumping and heard my heavy breathing as if my body and I were two different entities. Mother and Grandmother went to stand by the side of Elisabetta's mother and sister, a few metres from the officers and

Elisabetta. From the portico I watched all the soldiers scattered around standing still as statues. Only their vicious eyes moved from side to side under the helmets as they continued to hold the machine guns with both hands in a firing position.

Elisabetta was still being interrogated by loud angry voices. She kept answering, speaking fast in her now strained voice. She waved both her arms to emphasise what she was saying and her annoyance. All of a sudden there was a burst of voices from Elisabetta's mother and sister, my mother and grandmother that made the two interrogating officers turn as the women cried, "Basta adesso" (Enough now), don't you see that we don't know who the man is? Then Elisabetta pointed one arm, shouting angrily, "He went that way, that way, I know now he is a bad man. You find him. I stopped him harming the two soldiers. He frightened me too. He went that way, you find him."

All went very quiet for a moment while the two officers spoke to each other. Then one shouted to all the soldiers and within seconds they regrouped in a perfect formation of threes and stood to attention as the officer spoke to them for a short while in a loud aggressive voice as if they had done something wrong. I could not understand why he spoke to his own soldiers in such a way. He then gave the order to march away. The two soldiers from the day before marched behind separately, followed by the two interrogating officers, still holding their pistols by their sides.

The moment all the soldiers were out of the courtyard, Elisabetta's mother and sister and my mother and grandmother rushed to Elisabetta, who sat on the ground she had been standing on for such a long time. She bowed her head and cried and cried and cried, her eyes overflowing with tears. The women tried to soothe her and praised and praised her for her courageous act, but Elisabetta just cried, unable to speak.

The following days we lived in a state of fear, thinking the soldiers with the death mark on their uniforms were going to come back and discover that the man who tried to kill the two soldiers was Antonio, Elisabetta's brother and the owner of the house. Then they would know that all the men knew him and, together with Elisabetta, they would suffer the consequences. We stayed in our room all the time, again with the wooden shutters almost closed, making the room dark. We had to speak quietly so we could hear any unusual noise. Father and Uncle were nervous and irritable. Mother and Grandmother looked frightened too.

It was scary, tiring and cold just to sit on the straw with the blankets over us, and resting against the wall made our backs so cold. Uncle's face became more bruised and swollen and he kept holding a piece of cloth to his face to keep it warm. Grandfather, tormented by pain and discomfort, hardly ever spoke, his eyes dulled, just blinking occasionally. If he wasn't lying on the straw, Grandfather sat on the chair, his upper body slumped on the table; when he raised his head he looked distantly at everyone, as if he was no longer there, and soon slumped on the table again, his head resting on his folded arms. We remained in misery in our dark, cold room with little food, which was now difficult to find at any price.

A few days later, Elisabetta came to our room to let us know that a man had told her that the soldiers with 'La Morte', the death mark, on their uniforms had now moved away. The new battalion that replaced them didn't carry that mark. That was good news. The next day Antonio returned to the house, but everyone had to be on the lookout in case we saw soldiers marching towards us. At night Antonio went to sleep elsewhere in case there was a sudden attack on the house to catch him.

Family News

Early one afternoon Father and I were in the kitchen when a thin, tall man came to the front of the house selling packets of paper to make cigarettes. We immediately recognised him; he was a close friend of Father and lived near our home. On Sundays he played the organ in our church. Father and he became very emotional, shaking hands, looking into each other's faces; all they could say was the other's name, "Crescenzo", "Ermenegildo". He was invited to come to our room, where he shook hands with everyone, saying, "Miei cari, miei cari, come state" (My dear ones, my dear ones, how are you?). Mother exclaimed, "What a surprise, where are you staying? Who would ever have believed we were all going to be reduced to this?" Grandfather, who was sitting on the only chair in the room, offered him his seat as he went to sit on the straw. The rest of us formed a half circle crowding around him, exchanging details of what had happened to us in the last few months. The man looked very weak, with sunken cheeks and a thin neck. Each time he inhaled he lifted his head and chest as if he had to reach for air. Mother gave him a small amount of cold polenta, about three spoonfuls, apologising that that was all she had. He thanked Mother very much as the polenta disappeared into his mouth. Father also apologised that he couldn't offer him any space to sleep. He told us that when he was forced to leave his house he ended up in a town where by chance he came across a supplier of paper for making cigarettes and now he had become used to walking from one town to another selling the paper and slept wherever he found himself at the end of each day. He told us that because of his obvious ill health the Germans didn't bother him. On his travels he had met many of our neighbours and relatives, including Father's and Uncle's parents and family. Father and Uncle both immediately interrupted, exclaiming, "Dove, dove, come stanno"? (Where, where, how are they?). Ermenegildo told us exactly where they were in the town of Sora and that they were well. That was good news. After about two hours spent in forgetting for a while our tormented lives, he stood up, put on his rucksack, said his goodbyes, picked up his suitcase and left. Father accompanied him down the stairs and we waved from our window.

Now that Uncle knew exactly where the rest of the family were, he said to Father that it was better if he went to them. He wouldn't be using the small amount of food we had left and perhaps it would be safer there. Father agreed. The next morning Mother gave him a piece of bread and a small piece of cheese to eat on his journey and he left with his rucksack containing all his belongings to walk to Sora and join the rest of the family. I felt sad to see him go and wished we could all have gone there too. I was always pleased to be with them.

Grandfather

Grandfather became seriously ill. Elisabetta gave up her bed for him; it was placed in the hallway immediately outside the door of our room, which was now left open all the time. From my sleeping place I could see diagonally across our small room into the hallway where Grandfather now slept in a bed with white sheets, his head resting on a pillow, which seemed almost strange now. Elisabetta managed to find a doctor to come to see him. He carried a bag like a small squashed suitcase. My brother and I were told to go downstairs and stay there while the doctor was seeing to Grandfather and when we saw him leaving we returned to our room. Mother, Father and Grandmother's eyes and faces looked sad and they moved around with their heads slightly bowed as if they couldn't face one another. Each stayed in turn near Grandfather's bed. To go in or out of our room we had to squeeze between the bed with Grandfather and the wall. It was sad to see Grandfather so distressed. He had always been kind to me and at home he often took me and my brother by the hand and we went to the piazza to buy chocolate.

That night I was awakened by the noise of Mother and Grandmother crying, coming from where Grandfather lay. I thought that Grandfather had probably died, but I wasn't sure. Then I heard Antonio saying, "Mi dispiace signora, adesso non soffre più" (I am sorry signora, but now he isn't suffering anymore) and felt sure that he was dead. I kept the blankets over my head and just listened to Father, Mother, Grandmother and Antonio speaking nervously and abruptly to one another. "Let me do it." "You move out of the way." "Aspetta, aspetta, porta la candela qui" (Wait, wait, bring the candle here). "Fammi passare" (Let me go through). "Antonio, you come this way." "This is the best shirt." "I'll lift, you put the arms through." "No, no, not that way." "Lift the candle up so I can see." "Lift the candle higher." "Wait, wait, let me help from the back." "Now put the other arm through the sleeve." "Do the button up." "No, no, let's put the jacket on first, this has to be done now." Then Grandmother would burst out crying. Mother said, "Gesù mio aiutaci" (My Jesus help us) and she would start to cry again. It took a long time before I heard "E tutto fatto, va bene cosi" (It's all done, it's good this way). Only once did I uncover my head and lift myself up to look. It was dark and all I could see were the shadows made by the candlelight moving against the wall.

Later that morning, when it was light, I heard Mother say, "The boys are still sleeping, I'll wake them up." She came close to us and called, "Berto, Enio, it's getting late, it's time to get up." My brother started to get up but I didn't want to face all that sorrow so I pretended I was still sleeping. I wished I could have slept for ever. Mother knelt by my side and shook my shoulder, quietly repeating, "Berto, it's getting late, get up", and I pretended then that I was just waking up. Mother's face looked sad, her eyes full of tears as she told me, "E morto nonno" (Grandfather has died), "He has gone to heaven." I got up and we walked the few steps towards the bed and stood near Grandfather's white face on the pillow. Mother said to say a prayer for him. I felt sad that he had died, but I thought his face looked more peaceful than when he was alive. Grandmother sat on the chair placed at the foot of the bed facing Grandfather's body. She caught me looking at her, gave a deep sigh, bowed her head, shook it and quietly cried. After some time standing by the bed, Mother said we could go downstairs to warm ourselves by the fire and Elisabetta would give us something to eat, but before my brother and I left she told me to kiss Grandfather on the forehead. I stretched to reach and kissed his forehead and my brother did the same. I was surprised how icy cold he was.

That day, Father had to pluck up courage and go out to make arrangements for the funeral the next day, finding a priest, the undertaker, the gravedigger and other things relating to Grandfather's death. He kept coming back to see how we were, told us what he had achieved and rushed out again. He did say how fortunate he was that there were hardly any Germans about that day. "Most of them must have gone to the battlefront," he said. We remained by the bedside and at times members of Antonio's family or Peppino or his wife came to keep us company as we crammed into the corridor outside our room. We stayed quiet, sometimes saying prayers while we watched Grandfather's body.

Time went by very slowly in the cold, mournful atmosphere in the dismal light of the corridor. Sometime in the afternoon Father came back and said the undertaker would come at about eleven o'clock the next morning but was so heavily booked that he didn't have time to go and get a coffin. He told Father where to go and buy one and that he would have to carry it back himself. The carpenter's works where the coffins were made was a long way away and Father was concerned about how he was going to carry it back. "It's the awkwardness of it, not the weight," he said. Peppino suggested that his daughter Olgetta could help carry it and when they returned the coffin was placed upright in a corner of our room. Father and Olgetta both looked tired and upset. Olgetta anxiously told us how lucky they were not to be injured, as on their way back carrying the coffin they had passed a German encampment with cannons, carts and lorries when suddenly a group of fighter aeroplanes dived down, machine gunning all around them. They had quickly placed the coffin upside down on the ridge by the roadside with the coffin lid next to it and Father sheltered under the lid and Olgetta under the coffin. Olgetta, who was about fourteen years old, spoke very quickly, moving her hands and body as she told of the ordeal. Her father gave a slight cough to attract her attention and placed his index finger to his nose indicating she should be quiet near Grandfather's body. Olgetta slightly bowed her head, remaining still and quiet as if ashamed of voicing her fear. Grandfather's body was never left unattended. I dreaded each time I had to go out or return to our room and squeeze between the wall and the bed with his body. When my body touched the bed it made me feel bad; it was a very long, sad day and night.

The next morning I was awakened by the voices of Father and Antonio saying, "Let me take hold of the shoulders. You take hold of the legs." "Gira la cassa prima" (Turn the coffin round first), that's where the head goes. "After we move the bed we can pass by." "Sei pronto?" (Are you ready?). "Be careful, it's heavier on your side." "Pronto adesso" (Ready now). "Si" (Yes). "Ready then." "Lift." Then there was the noise of a hammer fixing the lid to the coffin as Mother and Grandmother sobbed.

When my brother and I got up the bed had been taken away and the coffin was on the floor. Grandmother sat on the chair slumped forward at the foot of the coffin, as if wanting to be as close as possible to it. When she raised her head she looked tired and worried and kept wiping away the tears on her face. We stood in silence just looking at the coffin. Some time later I heard a noise outside so I went to look out of the window and saw a highly ornate hearse drawn by a horse. The hearse was painted black with glass on its sides and back. Soon we were on our way to the cemetery, walking behind the hearse. It had rained a lot that night and the unmade road to the cemetery was full of puddles, which we tried to avoid so as not to get our feet wet. The sky was full of black clouds that looked as if they were going to burst at any moment – and they did! In the cemetery the ground was very muddy and the pile of earth around the grave had spread out with all the rain; it was like glue under our feet as we moved nearer to the grave. The rain continued. The priest tried to say the prayers quickly as we became more and more soaked. I heard the sound as the coffin was lowered into the water at the bottom of the grave. Two men with shovels began to push the muddy earth on to the coffin as we all reluctantly started to move away, looking back until we were out of the gates of the cemetery. We walked quickly back as it was still raining and went into Antonio's kitchen. My brother and I were asked to stand nearest to the fire as we tried to dry our clothes, which were sticking to our bodies. My brother copied me as I turned my body round and round and smelly steam came off our clothes. Antonio's family had prepared food for us all and after some time, my clothes still wet and sticking to my body, we returned to the deathly silence of our room. There we were with two of us missing. Grandfather was no more and Uncle had left us. Just Father, Mother, Grandmother, my brother and me now. Mother pushed the straw from where Grandfather and Uncle had slept and put it where my brother and I slept. Grandmother sat on the only chair, in the same position Grandfather used to sit, facing the door and resting her elbows on the table, her face between her hands, staring at the table top. Mother placed a blanket around her shoulders. Father, Mother, my brother and I sat on the straw as usual, with blankets around our shoulders and one covering our legs. Only a dim light came through the window of our small, gloomy room.

Our weakened bodies, the heartbreak of Grandfather's death, the nights without sleep, were all showing on Father's, Mother's and Grandmother's faces. Father, who had all the responsibility for our safety, food and needs, looked so exhausted and now, with his pronounced cheekbones and eyes full of anxiety, often remained staring deep in thought. Mother's face too had changed, revealing so much sorrow, and her eyes had sunk in. She kept her hands on my brother's head. My brother had fallen asleep, his head resting on her lap. Grandmother remained bent forward in her grief beside the table; now and again she raised her head and glanced at Father, who was now her protector and on whom she depended for all her needs. Sitting on the cold concrete floor was so uncomfortable. The crumpled straw didn't help much, the air was damp and cold and our clothes were still damp and made us shiver. It was so lonely, nothing to look at or speak about. We just stared at the wall, avoiding eye contact because the eyes gave away the truth, and the truth of our situation was bad and sad, the future unknown. To face one another would have brought more tears to our eyes, and more tears and more crying would have been bad for us all. The rest of that day was spent within ourselves in silence, because on top of all our desperation death had come to our room and taken Grandfather away.

Following Grandfather's death we spent day after day in the gloom of our room. It rained a lot and the room was always cold, the damp air penetrating our clothes. Grandmother kept sighing deeply and crying, while Mother, tears in her eyes, tried to console her. We didn't speak much as it was difficult to find something to say. When our eyes met they told only of the depth of our misery and sorrow. Father was always concerned that we shouldn't become a hindrance to Antonio's family, so I tried not to go into their nice warm kitchen. Mother continued to cook our food in the morning and brought it to our room. Later in the day when it was time to eat it was very cold, but I always chewed for a long time to make it last longer.

The German Doctor

For many days I had an abscess on my hand. Mother kept bathing it with warm water and squeezed the pus out, but it became bigger and bigger as the days passed. It was very painful and throbbed a lot; I couldn't rest or sleep. No one knew where I could see a doctor any more. Mother went out to buy food and when she returned she brought back some bread, cornflour to make polenta and two eggs. Father immediately took the two eggs, carefully placed them in the pockets either side of his jacket, took my hand and said, "Vieni con me" (Come with me). Walking along the road I asked Father, "Dove andiamo?" (Where are we going?). He answered, "We are going to see that your hand gets better." I said, "But there isn't a doctor here any more" and he answered in subdued tones, "Non hai paura, andiamo all'ospedale Tedesco" (Don't be frightened, we are going to the German hospital).

After a long walk we came to the front of a big house, pushed open a large double door and entered. We found ourselves in a long corridor with doors on either side and a long staircase at the end. We remained still; there didn't seem to be anyone there. Father carefully took the two eggs out of his pockets, held them in his right hand then took hold of my hand again. He looked worried and I wondered if we should have come to this place. Then an officer came out of a room towards us. Father told me to show him my hand and asked if it was possible to see a doctor, slightly moving his hand forward to show the two eggs. The officer indicated that we should wait outside a particular door on the left-hand side of the corridor and went away. Now and again a soldier came out of one room and went into another or up the long staircase. We remained in the silent corridor alone, Father holding my hand tightly. I could see his eyes were full of anxiety and sensed the intense fear he was feeling. I felt he had become as small as I was and wondered if he was thinking he had made a big mistake in bringing me there, exposing himself to the people we feared so much, the people who had turned us out of our homes and reduced us to our present disastrous state. They were the ones he was always hiding from, the ones who had captured him at gunpoint, but from whom he had managed to escape. Were they going to take him away this time? Was that why we were kept waiting so long?

Then, alone in the soundless corridor, we suddenly heard two loud, arrogant voices coming down the staircase.

This made Father's hand jerk and frightened me too. They were two tall officers wearing peaked caps and leather boots up to their knees. As they passed they gave us a scornful look while still aggressively speaking to one another. The longer we waited, the more fearful we became. It was such a relief when we saw the officer who had told us to wait by the door, because he had a kind-looking face. He acknowledged us and went into the room, closing the door; within a minute or two he came out and indicated to us to go inside as he walked away. Father and I walked into the room towards an officer who was sitting behind a desk where his frightening peaked cap rested. I extended my hand across the desk showing the abscess as Father carefully placed the two eggs near to the peaked cap. The officer looked at my hand, got up, went to a cupboard and brought out a box with cotton wool and bandages. He squeezed a lot of pus until a thick stream shot out, then blood. It hurt, but not as much as when Mother squeezed it. He put some stuff in the cavity and carefully bandaged it. Most of the time I looked at the two eggs, wishing we could take them back and eat them. I looked at the officer's face several times, searching for some sympathy because my hand hurt. I also wanted to smile at him because he was helping me, but our eyes hardly met. After he finished bandaging my hand, he indicated to Father that I should keep my arm folded, resting my hand on my chest. He looked serious all the time and never smiled, which made me sad. Father thanked the officer several times as we walked backwards out of the room but the officer never replied; I don't recall him saying one word. With my hand well bandaged, throbbing with pain, we came out of the hospital door. Father took hold of my hand again and held it tightly. He asked, "How does your hand feel. Does it hurt?" and I replied, "It does hurt. It's throbbing like my heart does." He then said, "We'll be back in our room soon, don't be frightened, don't look back. Walk slowly." With my hand held against my chest we walked at a normal pace. When we were about to turn a corner Father asked me to look back and see if anyone was following us. I looked and said, "No, there is no one on the road." As we turned the corner out of view of the hospital Father said, "Let's see if we can walk a bit faster now", and holding my hand began to take such long, quick strides that he was pulling me along and I had to run to keep up with him.

Back in our room, Father looked proud of his achievement as he told Mother what had been done to my hand; he seemed relieved we were now both safely back in our room. Mother was pleased to see my hand well bandaged and told me that now it would soon get better, and if I lay down and tried to go to sleep it would help to take the pain away. I did lie down and Mother placed lots of blankets over me. In about two days my hand began to feel better.

Grandmother and the Chicken

There were some afternoons and sometimes days when it was felt the Germans weren't going to come searching for men, farm animals or produce because we had learned that a blitz raid for men had been made that morning in a nearby area or because most of the soldiers had suddenly moved away. At these times everyone cautiously relaxed by gathering outside the houses, particularly if it was sunny, but someone would always be on watch. Men grouped in a sunny spot and women did the same. I always stayed by Father's side but my brother usually remained with Mother.

The gathering of people in the open seemed to give us moments of hope, as if our tragic situation would soon be over. Everyone chatted, discussing what each one thought about the outcome of the war and how soon it was going to end. People asked one another if they had found a place where food could be bought. All anxiously waited for the man who secretly listened to the radio to hear what the latest news was, hoping he was going to bring good news. As he approached, the men quickly moved towards him, excited, apprehensive, all asking questions at the same time, hoping for encouraging information, but there were never any good tidings. Only the sun gave comfort. When we were back in our room, Mother and Father exchanged what each had learned and then we returned to our downhearted state.

Since Grandfather's death, Grandmother seemed less interested in what was being said. She just looked and listened as if she didn't care any more, often sighing deeply and saying, "Who knows what's going to happen to us? Gesù mio aiutaci" (My Jesus help us). Since Grandfather's death her care and preoccupation with her pet chicken had become greater. She went to the stables more frequently and when she returned to our room she would say something about the chicken. On one occasion she told us, "The chicken knows things are bad, I can tell the way it looks at me." One sunny afternoon I went to the stables with Grandmother and as we approached the chicken Grandmother began to speak to it. "Pee Pee, let's go out in the sun, you will warm yourself up. That's the only thing that hasn't been taken away from us." She picked the chicken up and we went to a nearby field where the chicken ate tender blades of grass or scratched the earth with its feet looking for worms. There was no fear it would run away. It felt good to have the sun on my face; it warmed my clothes too. Grandmother moved back and forth following the chicken and speaking to it. "Pee Pee, where are you going now, can't you see I can't come there? Pee Pee come back, don't go there." Then she would give a big sigh. "Oh, we are alone now."

Back in our room, the reality of our situation returned. Father kept the wooden shutters on the glass window almost closed all the time; the room was nearly dark. At the slightest sound he would jump up and go to the window, telling us to be quiet even if no one was talking, and remained looking between the gap of the shutters and the window in case he had to run into hiding. When Antonio came to our room to speak to Father about what he had heard it always felt reassuring, even if he only stayed for a moment or two.

A Night with Grandmother

It was now about two weeks since Grandfather had died and Mother's and Grandmother's sorrow remained as great. It rained and rained, which kept me confined to our room, so all I met with were sorrowful faces and deep sighs. I felt as if at any moment something bad was going to happen because nothing good ever took place. Father and Antonio spoke to one another quietly and secretly – I knew why, because someone had listened to the radio, which was forbidden; if the Germans found a radio in the house the punishment was very severe. There was never any good news. We wanted to hear that the Allied soldiers were getting near, that our town had been liberated, that the war was soon going to finish, but it was never so. Often we heard the faint sounds of explosions, of bombardments or shelling coming from the direction of our town, horrible, frightening sounds. That was where the ferocious battle went on and on. There seemed no hope for us.

The scarcity of food was everyone's main concern. Father, like many others, had hidden a good amount of storable food well before we had to leave our homes, things like potatoes, dried beans, olive oil, flour and jars of preserves. The big problem was that the Germans had absolutely forbidden people to go into many of the towns in our area. I remember it well – facing the huge pistols and being emphatically told that they would come back in twenty-four hours and if we were still there we would be shot. We heard of people who had taken such a chance and managed to bring food back, but it was not until after the war that I learned of a distant relative who had tried to go back to his house and was shot and his body left by the roadside. His name was Pietro. He was always kind to me.

It was such a dilemma for Father as he spoke about wanting to go back. He felt sure the food he had hidden hadn't been discovered. Then he said, "The danger is if it's one of the days when the Germans are looking for men to carry ammunition up the mountains, then the other danger is of bombardments and the ceaseless shelling." He talked about taking minor roads, country lanes and crossing fields in the hope of avoiding the Germans for most of the way, but from the way he spoke, his head down, his voice subdued, I think he also felt that if luck wasn't with him it could be a journey of no return.

Our desperate need for food made Father decide to take a chance. Once the decision was made, Mother immediately exclaimed, "I'm coming with you!" Grandmother, who had sat motionless during the discussion, immediately reacted, turning to Mother sorrowfully and saying, "No, no, è pericoloso per te, è troppo pericoloso" (No, no, it's dangerous for you, it's too dangerous). Father said the same, adding, "I can hide, I can run. If they get me I may be able to escape like I did the last time." Grandmother anxiously supported

Father, saying, "Listen, listen to what Crescenzo is saying, he stands a better chance without you." Nevertheless Mother insisted, saying, "If you go I am coming with you" and went on, "When the Germans stop us, I can plead with them. I can tell them that we have children who are starving. You know they don't take any notice of men. I can carry things too, you know." The argument was over. Complete silence made it clear what was going to happen. Grandmother looked very upset and the atmosphere between them was tense. I kept quiet, because to be without Mother and Father for the whole day felt scary. Somehow Mother contacted her friend Assunta, who had stayed with her almost to the end trying to protect our home and hers. Mother said that Assunta was courageous. She was asked if she wanted to join them in this dangerous task and she agreed. The day it stopped raining, the three of them decided to leave at daybreak the following morning and return the same day. "We'll definitely return before the curfew," Father said.

Early the next morning I was awakened by hearing Mother and Father getting up and preparing to go. It was still dark. Father lit the candle and mother was speaking to Grandmother telling her not to worry, not to be afraid. Mother saw that I was awake, knelt by my side and said, "We are going now, look after Enio and be good to Grandmother. We will return this evening and bring lots of food back. Grandmother will give you something to eat later." In the dim light of the candle I saw Father cutting a piece of bread. He put some in his rucksack for their journey then turned to Grandmother, who was sitting on the floor of her sleeping place, and said, "I have left the bread for you and the boys, give it to them when they get up and there is a plate of polenta. Share it between the three of you later." "E poi mangiamo quando ritorniamo questa sera" (And then we will eat when we return this evening). Mother put her and Father's blankets on top of me and my brother, repeating to me, "Be good to Grandmother and say a prayer to the Madonna and Jesus to help us." Then I heard Father say, "It's getting light, let's go and meet Assunta." He picked up the rucksack, blew the candle out, and said, "Non avete paura, ritorniamo questa sera prima del coprifuoco" (Don't be afraid, we'll be back this evening before the curfew). "Be careful," Grandmother said, "La Madonna vi accompagna" (May the Madonna accompany you) "and look after yourselves." Raising her voice she added, "Don't take any chances, do you understand? Be careful." As they went out of the room Father muttered, "We understand, we understand." I curled up under the blankets feeling the benefit of the extra one Mother had added and listened to Grandmother quietly praying to individual saints for their help.

We tried to stay under the blankets as long as possible to keep warm. It was usually about ten or eleven o'clock when it became too uncomfortable to remain lying on the straw. I sat up and my brother followed, always doing as I did. Grandmother, who was sitting on the chair looking at us, said, "Do you want your portion of bread now or a little later?" I answered "Now". She handed each of us a piece of bread and left her portion on the table. My brother and I remained sitting on the straw with the blankets covering our legs and began to eat our bread. It was stale and hard and crumbled easily. As always, each time I took a bite I placed the palm of my hand under my chin to catch the crumbs and then sucked them into my mouth. I ate slowly. My brother waited until I took the next bite, then he did the same. It was so delicious savouring my bread and I made it last a long time.

Our room was small and narrow, the table placed against the wall near the window. We slept in a line facing the table and the window. Grandmother always sat at the right-hand end of the table facing the door, with her left side towards us. My brother and I slept about one metre from the table, so it felt as if Grandmother was almost on top of us. She kept her piece of bread in the cloth in which it was wrapped, broke off small pieces with her fingers and gently placed them in her mouth, concentrating on picking up any small crumb. If it was a very small crumb she pressed her index finger on it and conveyed it to her mouth. Her head remained bent forward staring at her piece of bread with a deep hungry look, and when she had finished she carefully folded the cloth, placed it to one side, rested her elbows on the table and placed her face between her hands. Sometimes her headscarf moved forward and her face became completely hidden from us; now and again a deep sigh came from her covered face. A few minutes later, from her bowed position, keeping her face between her hands, she slowly turned towards my brother and me, looked for a few seconds, then with a big sigh said,

"Madonna, let them come back" and turned her head, again staring at the table. A while later she raised her head, looked at us and said, "Have you prayed? Have you prayed that your Mother and Father will come back? Say the Hail Mary to the Madonna so she will help us." She took the rosary out of her pocket and began to pray. After a few minutes she looked at us again and said, "Don't worry, later on there is the polenta to eat. Get under the blankets and keep warm."

We lay down. I kept looking at her sad face as she prayed with her eyes closed, moving her lips as her fingers jumped over the beads. It was tiring and very uncomfortable lying on the straw. Grandmother said her prayers quietly as if whispering and now and again gave those deep sighs that made me feel sad and lonely. Time seemed to have stood still. No Mother or Father present, no Uncle, Grandfather gone for ever, the room seemed quite desolate. I was hoping to go downstairs where I might see someone and perhaps I would be asked to go into the kitchen and warm myself by the fire. I would then ask my brother to come too. But I was frightened. I sensed Grandmother's anguish and feared she would tell me off. It was now early afternoon. After long thought, I plucked up courage and slowly stood up and took two or three steps towards the door when I heard Grandmother say sternly, "Where are you going now?" "Downstairs," I answered. "Stay in here," she said. "If you go your brother will want to go too. If you hurt yourselves, what am I going to do then? Get under the blankets if you are cold and be good." So under the blankets I went. I felt very sad because Grandmother

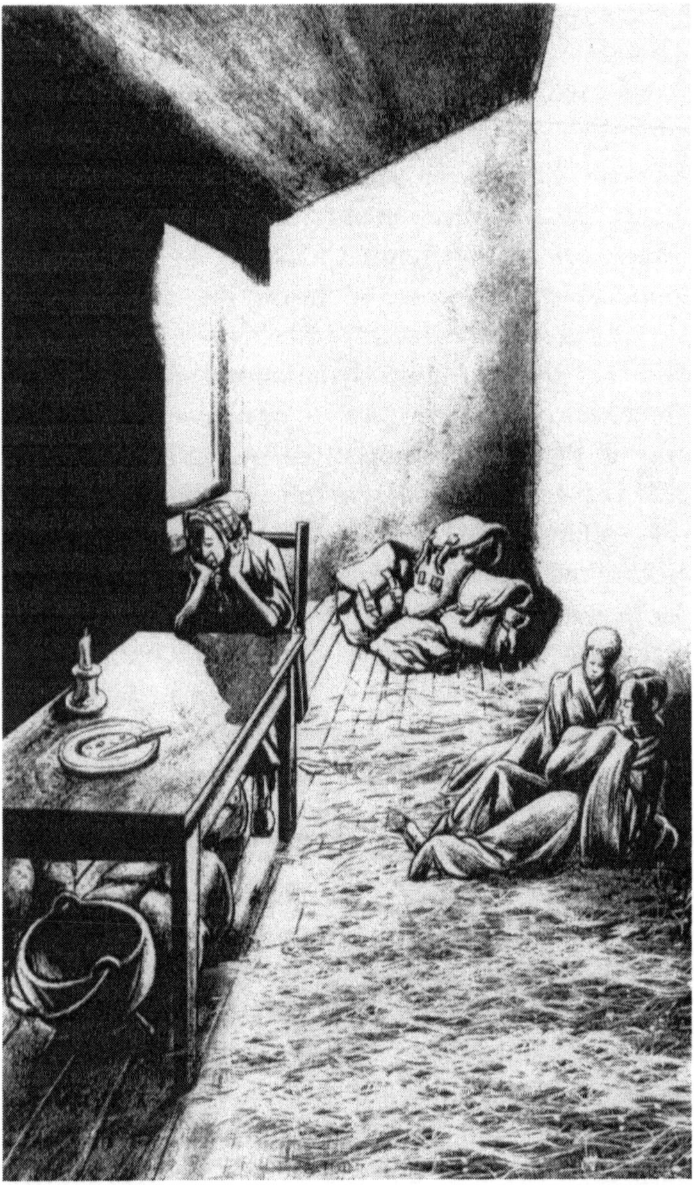

was being so severe. To remain in the room just hearing her deep sighs and laments even when she prayed made me even sadder. I fell asleep with my brother next to me. When I woke up, Grandmother was quiet. I looked at her sad face waiting for her to look at me, and when our eyes met I asked if we could go downstairs just for a little while. She answered, "Just for a little while, and stay where I can see you from the window." I felt so relieved to be liberated from her and the confines of the room.

We did stay in the courtyard where she could see us. The wall that surrounded the house was very high. There was no one to be seen, no one passed on the road outside the entrance, the place was desolate. It was bitterly cold and the sky was full of black clouds. There was nothing to do but make sure that we stood within view of the window. After a while my dilemma was to decide which was the better of the two places, but I knew that once we returned to the room Grandmother wouldn't let us out again. We stayed for a while longer but my whole body felt very cold; the cold air was biting my face. Then I saw my brother's goose-pimpled face, and that made me go back before we were called. As we entered the room Grandmother said, "You look frozen. Get under the blankets. I shouldn't have let you out of the room." So under the blankets we both went.

It must have been sometime late in the afternoon. It wouldn't be too long before Mother and Father would be back. That was good. The day seemed to go on and on, but it was getting a little darker in our room. When Grandmother said, "Let's eat the polenta before it gets dark", it was really good news. We ate very slowly, making the small portion of polenta last a long time. Grandmother gave us an extra spoonful each from her share when we had finished ours. I felt much better after we had eaten and by now the room was almost dark. It wouldn't be long before Mother and Father came back and all our problems would be over.

We waited and waited for total darkness to come, so that we could see Mother and Father back before the curfew. Grandmother spent all her time sitting in her usual place. She pulled the candle-holder near her, took a match out of the match-box and placed it on the box ready to light the candle when Mother and Father returned. Now and again she stood to look out of the window, but it was too early for them to return because it wasn't really dark outside yet. Each time Grandmother vacated the chair I really wanted to jump up and sit on it just for a little while, but she was in such a bad mood that I felt sure I would be told off. I went to look out of the window too, but with the window closed I could only see if someone entered the doorway in the courtyard wall. Sometime later, when it was really dark, Grandmother opened the window and stretched out to look further down the road, when she said, "Oh Madonna, it's raining, let them come back soon, they'll be soaked." As she moved away I quickly went to the window, stretched my arms to reach the end of the windowsill and pulled myself up to see further down the road. It was very dark, there were no street lights, nothing to be seen. Soon Grandmother said, "Close the window, it's letting the cold air in." I did so and went back to my sleeping space.

A while later Grandmother opened the window again. I went there too and pulled myself up to see, but more to listen for the sounds of footsteps. It was very dark, soundless and raining hard. Again Grandmother, sounding rather annoyed, said, "Shut the window, it's letting the cold air in. Can't you hear it's raining hard?" My brother and I stood by the window in the darkness of the room with our eyes fixed on the courtyard doorway. Grandmother told us to move as she placed her chair there and sat looking out; we stood by her side. The three of us remained looking out in complete silence, but it was useless because it was too dark to see anything. We had nothing to do but keep a lookout. The rain began to hit the window panes and Grandmother exclaimed, "Madonna, che mal tempo, che mal tempo" (Madonna, what bad weather, what bad weather, they are going to be soaked). It seemed we were in her way; she told us, "Go to sleep otherwise you will freeze standing here." Under the blankets we both went again. I felt very sad for Mother and Father out there in the dark, cold and now so much rain. Why were they not back, I thought, had they been captured like Father had been before? I heard Grandmother praying again to the Madonna, to Jesus, to St Anthony, to make Mother and Father return quickly. Quietly I prayed too.

At some stage I woke up as the cold air was hitting my face. It was very dark but I could just see Grandmother's body stretched over the window-sill. It was raining violently and I could hear the rain hitting the flooded area in front of the house as if buckets of nails were being dropped from high above, but what was worse now was the sound of exploding shells coming from the direction where Mother and Father had gone. Even when Grandmother closed the window, the noise of the torrential rain and sounds of exploding shells were so violent. It sounded a real hell out there.

I don't know why, I got up and took one or two steps towards the window. Grandmother said, "Why have you got up? Your mother and father haven't returned. Who knows what's happened to them? Don't you hear the shells exploding? I don't know what we're going to do. St Anthony, Madonna, perform this miracle for me, let them come back." I just stood in the dark as she spoke, not knowing what to say. It was very cold so I went back under the blankets yet again, where the continuous noise made me curl up, holding myself very tightly.

Buried under the blankets, still hearing those wild sounds, brought back memories of the horrors of when we had been under heavy gunfire. I thought of Mother and Father among all those explosions now, and it made me feel so very sorry and scared. I tried to imagine that all that was happening wasn't true, perhaps I was dreaming, but when my imagination failed it was back to reality, back to all our sadness. Each time Grandmother opened the window to look into the dark, into nothing, a gust of cold air filled the room and increased the sounds of the never-ending hell. I wished it wasn't true, but it was. I couldn't sleep. I just stayed quiet. Grandmother lit the candle and I raised my head slightly and watched her face in the glow of the candlelight as she peered at Grandfather's pocket watch as if unable to believe the time. The candlelight showed me a different face, a face

I didn't know. It was drawn, small, eyes sunken in the skull, having a look of total despair. It wasn't like Grandmother's face any more. She blew out the candle and started to moan at the saints again, but this time it was all to do with my brother and me, saying, "St Anthony, St Joseph, what have I done to deserve this punishment?", "Madre di Dio, come faccio con questi due?" (Mother of God, what am I going to do with these two? Who is going to feed them? Who is going to bring them up? Why, why has all this happened to me?), "Gesù mio, abbia pieta di me" (My Jesus, have pity on me).

I began to accept that Mother and Father would never come back. Curled up like a snail under the blankets, I thought that to remain with Grandmother would be terrible. She was so severe and now she was saying that we were such a problem. Feeling so very sad for myself and my brother, I thought of what to do and decided I would take my brother by the hand and walk to Sora where our other grandparents, uncles and aunts had gone, but I didn't know where the town was. I would have to ask lots of people the way, and then I would hopefully find them. I kept visualising we two walking to Sora and hoped my brother would be able to keep up. I went over and over these thoughts in my mind before I fell asleep.

A sudden thrust of cold air woke me up again. It was light now. Grandmother was looking out, craning over the window-sill as she talked to the saints, now really convinced that Mother and Father would never return. I sat up and my brother sat up too. He asked me, "Why aren't Mum and Dad back?" and I answered, "I don't know." "Are they coming back when it's dark?" he said, and again I answered, "I don't know." He remained still, his head slightly on one side, staring ahead, looking abandoned and sad. I knew he was hungry, but I didn't say anything. We were both dazed and weak. The rain and the explosions had all stopped and there was complete silence. I felt lost and very frightened about what Grandmother was going to say next. There was no one for me to turn to. My brother was my responsibility. Grandmother came away from the window and as she turned she saw us sitting up. For a few moments she just stared at us; she looked consumed by fear. Her first words were, "You're awake. You slept during the night and I've been awake. Your mother and father haven't come back, who knows what's happened to them?" She spoke in a trembling, disjointed voice and kept undoing the knot of her headscarf under her chin and doing it up again, then pushing her headscarf forward onto her forehead, then back and then forward again. She kept her eyes on me, saying, "What are we going to do?" I didn't know what to say so I remained silent. It seemed as if it was all my fault. Grandmother continued looking at us, not saying a word as she blew warm breath on her cold hands, then turned to look out of the window again. This gave my brother and I the chance to quickly bury ourselves under the blankets and escape those looks that suggested we were the problem in this situation. The window had been opened so often that the air was cold and uncomfortable to breathe and the hunger and cold air made my head feel numb and dizzy. I knew there was no food in our room. Curled up in a ball under the blankets, the more I thought, the sadder I felt for myself and my brother. I felt lost and very frightened because everything Grandmother was saying was becoming fixed in my mind. There was going to be no Mother or Father any more. It was all real now.

Each time I heard the slightest noise from outside I imagined it was Mother and Father returning, expecting them to come through the door at any moment, but alas, it was never true. Every few minutes I heard Grandmother say the time. I wanted to remain under the blankets forever. Again I heard Grandmother say the time, "Gesù mio, sono passate le undici, aiutaci" (My Jesus, it is past eleven o'clock, help us) "What am I going to do with these two?" I heard the window being opened again. For a few moments all was silent, then Grandmother suddenly exclaimed, "Santa Maria, Gesù mio" (Holy Mary, my Jesus). She shouted to us, "Your father is coming!"

I threw the blankets to one side, jumped up and launched myself on to the window-sill, pulling myself up to look further down the road, and saw Father with his rucksack on his back. I only got a quick look because Grandmother pulled me back to look again herself. She said, "It's only your father, what's happened to your mother, she's not with him." My brother and I scrambled for the door, raced down the stairs as fast as two bullets and met Father as he turned into the doorway of the courtyard. He touched our heads and said in exhausted tones, "How are you, are you all right? Mother will come back later." He took us by the hand and we walked the few steps to the house in silence. As we entered our room, Grandmother looked directly into Father's face and said sharply, "Where is Lisetta?" (Mother was always referred to as Lisetta). Father put his hand forward as if to say be calm and said, "Don't worry, don't worry, Lisetta is all right, she couldn't walk any more. I have left her in a farmhouse resting, about five kilometres from here. I'll collect her later and the other goods we carried." Grandmother moved her chair towards Father saying, "Sit down, you look exhausted, sit down." As Father sat, he gave a loud sigh of relief. His clothes were drenched, the brim of his hat had flopped down. His unshaven face was drawn and his cheekbones seemed to be sticking out more than when he left. He kept looking at me and my brother as he tried to regain his breath, lowering and shaking his head as if to say, "Why all this, this can't be true." My brother and I stood each side of him as he took hold of our hands, turning to us and saying, "Don't be scared any more. Mother will be here later today and we'll all be together then." He added, "I managed to buy some bread and cheese on the way, let me change into dry clothes and we'll eat." Grandmother left the room so that Father could change and my brother and I stayed with him. When Grandmother returned, Father took the bread and cheese out of the rucksack. The first piece he cut he put aside, saying, "I'll take this with me for Mother to eat", then gave each of us a good portion of bread and a small portion of cheese. I relished each bite of bread and a small bite from the piece of cheese while looking at the rest still in my hand, waiting to take the next bite. It was so delicious. It was so good.

I could see that Grandmother wasn't so tense now, but I also sensed she was holding something back by the way she kept looking at Father and not saying anything. Father said to us, "In a while I'll go and we'll be back well before dark with the rest of the food." Then Grandmother unloaded her feelings. "Come back quickly. Don't make me pass another night like last night. You don't know what I've been through, I thought you were both dead. I didn't know what to do with these two. I haven't slept since you left yesterday morning." The tone of Grandmother's voice made it seem it was all Father's fault now, and he stood up and cried, "Mother, listen to me, you don't know what we've been through, so I'll tell you. Yesterday when we left here and met Assunta everything went well for the first hour or so, then we were stopped three times within a few kilometres, when Assunta and Lisetta had to plead, to beg to be allowed to continue going home. Many times they went ahead to see if it was safe for me to go while I hid until they beckoned me on. We mostly walked in wet and mud, field after field. When we were only fifty metres from the house two soldiers wouldn't let us go any further. As Lisetta pleaded and pleaded with them, one saw the rings on her finger and said we could only go through if he could choose a ring for his girlfriend in Germany, which he did. Soon after we started coming back, loaded like donkeys, shells began to explode all around us. We spent the night at the bottom of the town in Alemerinda's house, in the dark and cold and without anything to eat. Since daybreak this morning we have been walking in torrential rain. Do you understand what

I'm saying? I'm going to go now, because Lisetta is alone. Assunta came part of the way with me then made her way to where the rest of her family are staying." Grandmother turned and went to the window, murmuring "Gesù mio, aiutaci" (My Jesus, help us).

Father placed his hand on my shoulder and said, "I'm going to see if I can borrow a wheelbarrow." I felt pleased about the way he had spoken to Grandmother because I didn't think what was happening was my or Father's fault and it quietened Grandmother down. He soon came back to collect his empty rucksack and said, "Don't be afraid, we'll be back well before dark." Grandmother said quietly, "Look after yourselves." My brother and I watched him go from the window, pushing the wheelbarrow and taking long quick strides. As he disappeared from view a sudden feeling of loneliness came over me and I felt scared that Grandmother was going to scold me. My brother and I went to sit in our sleeping space. I avoided meeting Grandmother's eyes because she had looked angry ever since Father had spoken so sharply to her.

The rest of the afternoon we remained in our room waiting for Mother and Father to return. Grandmother sat in her usual position while my brother and I sat on our sleeping space with lots of blankets over our shoulders and legs. Time went very slowly. We kept getting up to look out of the window until Grandmother told us off for moving around so much. The three of us waited in silence. Whenever I heard a slight noise I still went to the window to see if it was Mother and Father returning. It was always a disappointment, but I felt sure they would be back before dark as Father had promised and I kept visualising us all together a little later. Patiently we waited. Grandmother kept looking at Grandfather's pocket watch. It was beginning to get dark in our room. Grandmother again pulled the candleholder towards her and prepared a match to light the candle for when Mother and Father returned. It was nearly dark now. I listened attentively for the sound of the wheelbarrow in front of the house when suddenly the door of our room was pushed open and Father appeared with a heavy sack on his shoulder and a rucksack on his back followed by Mother, who immediately put everything she was carrying on the floor and spread her arms out with a joyful smile, embracing me and my brother. She held us very tightly as she said, "Berto, Enio, non vi lascio mai, mai, mai più" (Berto, Enio, I shall never, never, never leave you again). Being embraced by Mother and having Father there, I felt as if the heaviest and most horrible thing had gone away. What we had endured and our present situation no longer seemed so bad as long as we were together. Grandmother said, "Grazia a Dio che siete ritornati" (Thank God, you have come back) as she came close to Mother, who was still holding us both in her arms. She said, "How are you? How are you feeling? If you only knew what I have been through, I thought you were both dead." Mother answered, "Don't tell me, Mother, because I can't tell you what we have been through." Father, a look of satisfaction on his face as he unpacked the goods they had brought, said, "Be quiet now, it's all over, let's see what we have to eat." I felt good that even

Mother had told Grandmother to be quiet. Now I knew she was wrong in what she had suggested the night before, that my brother and I were such a problem, I didn't feel guilty any more.

Grandmother lit the candle, Father gave us bread and a piece of smoked sausage each and we ate in total silence. The candlelight on Mother's face revealed the agony she had endured in the last two days – the exhaustion of walking, the stress of carrying a heavy load, the fear of explosions and, even more, the terror of her courageous battles with the unpredictable human beings who were the cause of our despair, who were notorious for carrying out arbitrary acts of terror regardless of their consequences.

That night, Grandmother's lack of sleep and the stress she had suffered took her into a deep slumber. Mother and Father too soon fell asleep as for the last two days they had had to call upon every bit of strength and courage they possessed. I could hear their heavy breathing. My mind closed down on my two days of fear and sadness as I listened to the sounds of bodies recovering from their ordeal.

The Road to Sora

Each day we continued to live under the shadow of misery and fear, our bodies weakened by the lack of food, the cold weather and the conditions in which we lived. We were in a permanent state of anxiety, hopelessness and sorrow. When we woke up each morning, finding ourselves in that bleak room, lying on the crumpled straw with the cold concrete floor beneath our bodies, we felt immediately depressed, worrying about what catastrophe, what horror, the new day would bring. That was what we had become conditioned to.

There was a sudden increase in the number of German soldiers in our area. They were everywhere. Some patrolled in twos, but most of the time they marched about in group formation. Each time we were told or suspected they were coming towards our place, Father and Antonio disappeared to their hiding places down the valley at the rear of the house. My brother and I ran back to our room with Mother and Grandmother, where we remained still, in total silence, our hearts pounding. We listened to them marching towards our place, the powerful sound of their boots hitting the road, and only when the sounds began to get fainter and fainter as they marched away from us did we begin to relax. But it was the times when the marching suddenly stopped near our place that made us tremble as we waited for them to blast into our room. We always had to stand in line against the wall as they mercilessly waved their machine guns at us only an arm's length away, feeling helpless, terrified, unable to understand their horrific actions. Why, why, why? There was no respite. A new order was issued by the German command in the area telling people who were not permanent residents to leave by a specified date. If they were still there after that date, they would be moved away.

This meant that we now had to leave the hospitality of Father's friend Antonio Morelli and move even further from our home. Since we now knew where Father's parents and family had gone, Father decided we would go to find and join them. This would be our seventh move from the time we left home and began to hide on the mountain, about the end of September or early in October 1943; it was now March 1944. When my brother heard that we had to move to another place, he exclaimed "No un'altra volta!" (Not again!).

So, our next move was to go to the town of Sora. Father managed to find a man who owned a horse and cart and hired him to carry our goods there. We went the second day after the order was issued. We got up early, carried our possessions downstairs, piled them up in the porch of the house and waited for the man with the horse and cart. We had always carried our possessions ourselves and I felt confident my brother and I would be able to ride on the cart to our new destination. Father had said it would take us most of the day to reach Sora and find the rest of the family.

While waiting, we all went into the kitchen to say goodbye to Antonio and his family. A rattling noise made Father go out of the kitchen and I followed. There was the man with the horse and cart, but for me it was an immediate disappointment. The more I looked, the more I could see that there was no chance of my brother and I riding on the cart. It was small, the same type that Mother's parents used to hire every Monday morning to go shopping to the market in the next town, and it had two big wheels and a short platform with two seats at the front and two at the back with space under the seats to carry the shopping. It was very old, which was why it rattled so much as it approached the house. Then I espied the poor horse. It was very old too, with patches on its body where it had lost its hair, and it looked spiritless, moving its head slowly. It seemed an effort for it to open and close its big eyelids. The poor thing: it had lived its life out and had no more energy to serve. I realised it was going to be a very long and tiring day ahead, but at least this time we didn't have to carry our possessions. Father and the man carefully piled our goods up in the limited space of the cart and we stood waiting as Grandmother clutched and caressed the feathers of her pet chicken.

When our goods were loaded on the cart, the man took hold of the reins, stayed close to the horse's head and started to move. We said our last goodbye to all of Antonio's family, who came out to see us off, saying, "Arrivederci, arrivederci, buona fotuna, ci rivediamo dopo la Guerra" (Goodbye, goodbye, good luck, we'll meet again after the war). Then we followed the cart as

Mother and Grandmother shed tears on parting from Antonio's family, who had been so kind to us. Here we were, Father, Mother, Grandmother, my brother and I, following the rattling cart pulled by the half-dead horse. It seemed strange being en route again with no Uncle, no Grandfather any more and none of Peppino's family, who had already left for another place. The man always walked close by the horse's head, as if he were propping it up. We walked immediately behind the cart without speaking, our heads bowed so as not to trip over the stones and bumpy road, longing to reach our destination for a place to rest, a place to sleep. On and on we went, bend after bend, uphill and downhill, then along stretches of deserted roads. At times we saw other families moving away from the area taking different routes. Sometimes we passed close by one another, but no one turned or spoke. Only empty glances were exchanged as each family confronted their despair, most of them loaded as we used to be, some with a donkey carrying a heavy load. All had sorrowful faces, all heading to unknown destinations, to places where it might be safe, where the aggressors might leave them and us alone. Now and again a lorry full of German soldiers would go by, or motorbikes, some with sidecars, all speeding in the opposite direction to us, towards our town, where the battle went on and on. We passed huge guns camouflaged under the branches of trees and smaller guns in fields pointing towards the road with soldiers by them. Father kept on telling us and the man leading the horse, "Don't let them see you're looking. Look straight ahead. Pretend you haven't seen them."

Grandmother always walked upright with a straight back, proudly clutching her pet. Now and again she would look at it and say "Pee Pee, Pee Pee" as we continued to walk and walk and walk. Then I noticed Grandmother getting closer and closer to the rear of the cart until all at once she pushed a bundle on the cart forward and placed the chicken in the space she had made. The chicken stayed there seeming a little frightened at first, but Grandmother kept reassuring it by staying close and saying "Pee Pee, Pee Pee". Exhausted and lethargic, I wished my brother and I could have a ride on the cart too, but there was no room even if I'd asked. There was no choice for us but to keep on walking. Lucky Pee Pee, I thought.

Family Reunion

It was late in the afternoon when we reached the town of Sora. Father began to ask people if they could direct us to the road where we'd been told his parents and family were living and we found we still had a good way to go as it was out of town in the countryside. Eventually, we reached the road with isolated farmhouses, where Father asked if anyone knew a family from our town who had taken refuge in one of the farmhouses. We were pointed to a small group of houses with several smoking chimneys, accessed by a long narrow path. The cart remained by the roadside and so did Mother, Grandmother and my brother. The man with the horse and cart asked Father if he would be quick because he wanted to travel part of the way back before the curfew.

Father and I went up the path to the houses to make sure his parents and family were there. Though very tired, the thought of seeing my grandparents, uncles and aunts again made my heart thump with excitement. It was almost like being frightened, but a good frightened feeling. We stopped by a door, Father knocked, a man answered and we were pointed to a door on the ground floor only a few metres away. Father knocked, the door opened – it was Grandfather! He threw his arms around Father then embraced me. We took two or three steps into the smoke-filled room and there they were, all sitting around the fire, Grandmother, my two uncles and two aunts. For a moment they remained still, as if unable to believe we were there, then an eruption of sound – Oh! …Ah! … Eh! … Grandmother stood up, opened her arms and launched herself to embrace Father, just saying "Figlio mio" (My son). I was hugged by my aunts, then by my uncles. Everyone was almost speechless, there were just sounds of joy, spontaneous embraces, smiles and tears as we looked into each other's faces. Father went to pay the man with the horse and cart and Grandfather and my two uncles went to fetch our goods. Soon Mother, Grandmother and my brother joined us and there were more embraces, more kisses and more tears. Then came more surprises – Grandfather's brother, his wife, son and daughter. Moments later came Grandfather's sister, her husband, two sons and two daughters, all greeting us with kisses and embraces – moments of great joy, moments when we forgot the war and why we were there as we rejoiced in our reunion.

Father asked if there was any room for us to sleep that night. Sadly there was none. Each of the three families shared one room and a communal kitchen in which we were all crowded at that moment. Father and Grandfather went to nearby houses to find a place for us to stay and Mother went out to see if she could find straw for us to sleep on. Grandmother, my brother and I remained by the fire and were given something to eat. When the excitement of our reunion was over, I saw in the glow of the firelight how thin and sad everyone's face was, reflecting the reality of the situation in which we found ourselves. It made me sad.

It was almost dark. Father and Grandfather returned having found a room for us and Mother came back with a small bundle of straw in her arms. She told us she had had to beg a woman farmer if she would give at least a small amount of straw for my brother and I to sleep on. She looked pleased to have managed to get the straw for us two. Grandmother had some food for Father and Mother as well, and soon after we made our way to the room Father had rented, my two uncles helping to carry our goods. Fortunately, it was only two or three minutes' walk from the rest of the family. We settled on the floor of our room, where only my brother and I had straw beneath us. Numb and worn out, we slept and slept and slept.

A New Beginning

Life in Sora wasn't so lonely or bleak for me because we were near other members of our family. No one had anything to do so we saw a lot of each other. Since it was now March, the weather wasn't so cold and for the first time we didn't seem to be in the midst of the German soldiers; they were in the centre of the town and only patrolled where we were a few times a day, sometimes on foot and sometimes in a slow-moving lorry.

The house in which we lived was very small, more like a cottage, set back from the road and quite secluded, with vines and other fruit trees at the front. We lived in the attic, accessed by an outside wooden staircase fixed against the wall on the left of the house. It had a small platform on the top and a low narrow door to enter the attic, which was empty. There were no windows, rough walls, no ceiling, just rafters with tiles on the top. The wind came in from all directions, as even the small ancient door had gaps where the wooden panels had shrunk and pulled apart from one another. Putting our heads under the blankets was the best way to rest or go to sleep.

The owner of the house was a man with a wife and grown-up son and daughter. My brother and I called him Uncle Agostino; he repaired and tuned church organs and accordions, but alas, because of the war he had no work. His son Mario was a professional musician who played the accordion in bands, at weddings and parties. Now there was no demand for his art, so they were pleased to receive our rent for the attic space in which we lived. They were always friendly towards us and it was never any trouble for us to be in their kitchen to warm ourselves or if Mother had something to cook.

As always, each morning Father encouraged us to stay under the blankets as late as possible so as to keep warm. When we were all up, we would go down into the kitchen. Mother would boil water with roasted barley to make a hot drink for us, in which we dipped our slice of bread.

Father was always busy. He cautiously went to the hills somewhere to get firewood, and some days he worked for a local farmer, who fed him and at the end of each day gave him some broccoli, a cabbage or a cauliflower. Father always carried a small sack to bring home what the farmer gave him. One day Father produced from the sack not one, not two, but three big cauliflowers, handling them like precious gold as he showed them to Mother, whose eyes lit up with delight. At times there were days and days when there was no food to be bought, then Father learned that there was a place far, far away that hadn't been occupied by the German army. He and Uncle walked the long distance through the countryside, over hills and across mountains, taking almost a day to reach the place in order to avoid areas occupied by the German army. There they bought potatoes, salt and cornflour to make polenta and carried the goods in their rucksacks as well as heavy sacks on their shoulders, making their way back on foot. They would start making the return journey the same day and slept in some barn when it was dark. When they were very late getting back on the second day, everyone worried in case they had been captured, but on their return, although exhausted from the two-day journey and heavily loaded, Father had a pleased look on his face as we now had another week to ten days' worth of food. Each time we thought that before the week's food ran out the war would be over and we could return to our home.

Apart from our drink and slice of bread in the morning and at lunchtime some boiled cabbage, cauliflower or a small amount of polenta, our main meal was always before nightfall, boiled potatoes and a slice of bread. Mother boiled the potatoes and Father did the sharing, the same amount of bread each and one large and one small potato, or two medium-sized, or three smaller ones. It always looked as if each one of us had exactly the same quantity. Mother used to eat very slowly, and when my brother and I had finished our portions she gave us some of hers, convincing us that she wasn't hungry. "I'm full," she used to say. "I'm full, I can't eat any more."

Father often told us not to make any noise, so as not to attract the attention of the Germans when they patrolled our area. He also told Mario that it was not a good idea to play his accordion, as sometimes he rehearsed pieces of music. "They can take your accordion if they want," Father told him. But whenever

I heard Mario play I always went and stayed by him; I think he liked me to watch him play too. The people there hadn't gone through the experiences we had suffered.

Aeroplanes went by and dropped their bombs, but it was usually some distance from us. They bombed where the mass of German soldiers were and where ammunition or petrol was stored; we just watched the smoke rise into the sky. Later we would hear about the damage the bombs had caused to the German positions. Sadly, there were always civilian casualties too. The adults continually spoke about the war, saying where the Allied soldiers had arrived and how many days it would be before they reached where we were and liberated us. I just listened; I had heard the same thing so many times for so long that I didn't believe anything any more.

Then the activity of the German army in our area became more and more intense. Groups of soldiers hurried past our road, then I saw guns and ammunition arriving, but what frightened us most was when we heard they had begun to search for men. Again we had to be on the lookout for groups of soldiers coming towards our area so the men could run to their hiding places, and again I felt responsible for looking out and listening for the sound of lorries coming our way. Father's hiding place was at the bottom of a field at the rear of the house in which we were staying. There was a brook, now dry and at one point quite deep, with wild shrubs growing along the sides where he ran to hide, lying down in the brook. Father's father, brothers, uncles and cousins prepared a hiding place within their house.

At the rear of the house, attached to the kitchen wall, was a small room used to store firewood. The door was taken away and then closed with blocks, leaving a few airholes. The whole wall was then smoothed with sand and cement, wooden poles were placed upright against it and a huge pile of firewood scattered on the ground around, all to distract attention from the new work. I used to watch Grandfather, my uncles and others hurriedly doing all this and was instructed many times not to tell anyone about the hiding place. From inside the kitchen, immediately next to the fireplace, an opening was made by knocking down the wall at ground level, about half a metre high and the same width, so that the men could crawl under it and get into the small closed room. A large tin bath was placed against the opening filled high with logs, and bits of chopped wood were scattered around it. The opening to the hiding place was now well concealed.

In Hiding

A few days after the hiding place had been prepared I was with my grandparents, uncles and aunts. It was mid-afternoon and I was standing outside the kitchen watching Uncle chopping firewood. In the peacefulness of the country air we heard the sound of a lorry, which appeared to be coming towards our place. Uncle stopped chopping and we both stood looking across the field towards the road waiting for the lorry to appear. When it did, it was a German lorry. It suddenly stopped about three hundred metres from where we were and soldiers jumped out from the back and rushed towards a house. Uncle threw the hatchet on the ground and hurried inside, shouting in a subdued voice, "Tedeski, Tedeski" (Germans, Germans). Within seconds the kitchen was crowded with men, who one by one lay on the floor and crawled on their stomachs after each other into the opening in the wall leading into the small closed room at the rear of the house. They drew themselves forward on their forearms, wriggling their bodies and pushing with their feet. Uncle Benedetto gave a loud cry as he hit his knee against the wall, but otherwise, without a word, they disappeared as swiftly as foxes. Grandmother and Grandfather's sister pushed the tin bath full of logs against the opening, piled a few more logs on top, spread more bits of wood on the floor around the bath and placed some chairs around the fireplace. The opening was now well concealed.

Grandfather's sister Annunziata went out, picked up the hatchet and continued chopping firewood, while Grandmother, Aunt Benedetta and I remained in the kitchen. Moments later, Annunziata called quietly, "Some are coming through the fields at the back of the house, some are coming along the path at the front." Soon the house was surrounded and every room was searched at gunpoint. Two soldiers burst into the kitchen, searched the adjacent rooms, came back to the kitchen and immediately began to interrogate Grandmother as to where the men were hiding. Annunziata stopped chopping the wood and came into the kitchen too. Each question the soldiers asked was answered promptly and loudly by the women so as to blot out any sound the men might inadvertently make like coughing or sneezing as they were only on the other side of the wall.

The women spoke continuously and all at the same time, making a loud, confusing noise, saying, "Cosa volete, non ci sono uomini qui?" (What do you want, there are no men here), "You took our men a month ago. We pray every day that they will come back soon. Where have you taken them? When are you sending them back? The war is a horrible thing." Grandmother moved towards the door, beckoning the soldiers, "Venite, venite, voi venite a vedere" (Come, come, you come and see). We all moved outside, where Grandmother pointed to the fields around the house pretending it was her land, saying, "Look, look at the state of our land. Who is going to do the work if our men don't come back?" and this took the soldiers further away from the men's hiding place.

The women continued to talk, but the soldiers were taking no notice of what they were telling them. They just stood tall in front of us, looking in all directions with piercing eyes under those sinister helmets, pointing and shouting to other soldiers, indicating various windows as if they should go back into the house and search the rooms again. Then they stared into our eyes for a moment, turned, gathered together the other soldiers and walked down the path towards the road and their lorry. Immediately the women took up a hoe and two forks, told me to follow them and we went to the nearest field pretending to be working the land by pushing the forks into the ground and turning the earth. Grandmother told me to bend down and pretend I was taking weeds out of the freshly turned earth. When I looked up, the soldiers were getting onto their lorry and leaving. We remained in the field for another ten or fifteen minutes in case the soldiers came back unexpectedly then returned to the kitchen, moved the tin bath full of logs from the opening next to the fireplace and told the men they could come out. One by one they crawled out of the hole on their stomachs. Uncle, who had hurt his knee, was in pain and Grandfather's brother, who was quite a big man, said he nearly suffocated as there wasn't sufficient air in the small room, which was meant to hold seven men standing – they were eleven!

I ran back to see if Father was all right. Mother didn't know the soldiers had gone so I went to call Father, who was lying at the bottom of the dry brook in the field behind the house. Back in the attic we sat on the floor, staying quiet because Father looked very worried. We had now returned to the fears of the past with the bombardments getting closer but, most of all, because of the dreaded thought that the soldiers might come at any moment and capture Father and my uncles.

It was back to a severe scarcity of food, because it had become too dangerous for Father to venture out for it. The world had collapsed on us once more; only the weather was gradually improving. During the day we followed the sun, sitting around the house. We even ate our potatoes and slice of bread sitting on the treads of the staircase if it was sunny. When the sun went in we stayed in the darkness of the attic until it was time to go and warm ourselves in the kitchen. One evening, while we were sitting by the fire in the dark so as not to attract attention to the house, the owner's daughter took a large copper pot of boiling water off the fire. I didn't notice she had put it on the floor immediately behind me and when Father said, "Let's go to sleep", I turned on the stool where I was sitting to put on my shoes and plunged my right foot into the boiling water. The pain was excruciating and I screamed. Mother and Father jumped to my aid, took my sock off and blew on my foot, but I was crying because of the terrible pain. The owner of the house and his wife angrily told their daughter off for having left the boiling water in such a dangerous place, but Father, not wanting to create a bad atmosphere between us, said, "It's an accident, it's an accident, it's no one's fault." Mother poured cold water over my foot and told me, "The pain will soon go, don't be frightened, don't be frightened, the pain will soon stop," then Father lifted me in his arms and carried me up to the attic. My foot swelled like a balloon and Mother kept blowing on it, but the pain was so unbearable that I went on crying. Grandmother said to slice a potato thinly and cover the huge blister with it, which Mother immediately did. The coolness of the potato slices soothed the pain, but only momentarily. That night Mother and Father took turns in staying by me, most of the time blowing on my foot. It was a horrible, horrible night. It took many days for the pain to go completely and before I could walk again.

Soon after I was able to walk again, my brother and I fell ill, our bodies covered with red itchy spots. No one knew a doctor who could see us. Early the next morning Mother went in search of a doctor or a chemist. Many hours passed and she still hadn't returned and Father and Grandmother became worried. Father made two attempts to go out to look for her, but was afraid to go too far in case he was seen and captured. Eventually Mother came back and told us that no one knew where she could find a doctor or a chemist's shop that was open. She spent many hours trying to trace the house of a chemist and managed to get a bottle of lotion. She gently washed us from head to foot then smoothed the lotion all over our bodies and wrapped us in two white sheets she had managed to buy. It took a long time before the itchy spots began to go and we could sleep at night. Some people said the disease was due to lack of food, others that the heat and movement of our bodies had turned some of the straw we slept on into dust and caused the skin infection. So now my brother and I had to sleep on the bare floor too.

It had become almost impossible to buy any kind of food, but Father always managed to provide some bread and potatoes. Sometimes he managed to buy cornflour to make polenta, but this was always reserved for our measured ration at the end of each day. During the daytime we ate very little food that had any substance, a boiled cabbage or cauliflower, but even this wasn't always available. Mother and I used to go to the nearby lane and look in the grass for dandelion leaves to pick; on our return Mother washed and boiled them and that was our lunch for several days. We were always hungry.

One afternoon I was going alone to see my grandparents two or three minutes away, but instead ventured down one of the lanes and saw a donkey grazing. I watched and listened to the sound it made as it snatched each mouthful of tender grass and wished I could have eaten the grass too as there was so much of it wherever I looked, soft, tender and rich green. I picked a few blades and tried to eat them, but they were so rough on the tongue that I spat them out. Then I saw a short distance away a patch of onions whose stalks had been cut down. My hunger was so great that I was possessed with the desire to eat a raw onion – I thought of taking two, one to eat and one to take back to Mother. It meant I would have to steal them, though, and the very thought filled me with fear. I hadn't taken anything that wasn't mine before; stealing was a grave sin. Then I thought that if the owner caught me stealing the onions he might beat me up. My mind was in turmoil, but the desire to eat a raw onion was overwhelming.

Near the onion patch was a narrow path that led to a group of houses. For a while I slowly ran up and down the path using my hands to pretend I was driving a tractor. I had little energy to do this, but it was necessary while I looked around to see if anyone was about and might see me. I looked particularly at each and every window in the group of houses nearby. Satisfied that I wasn't being observed, trembling with fear, I crawled to the onion patch and lay on my stomach. The onion stalks had been cut so short I couldn't pull one up, so I tried to dig the earth around it with my fingers, but the ground was hard so I had to give it up and crawl back to the path. I just wanted to get away from the place now because the guilt had made me so frightened, but having walked a few steps along the path I saw a small chip of wood just sharp enough for me to dig with. I picked it up and decided to have another go at stealing two onions. The thought of stealing brought the fear back, but the desire to eat the onion won. Once more I pretended to be driving a tractor up and down the path, making sure no one was looking, then I crawled to the onion patch, lay on my stomach and with my sharp chip of wood and trembling hand I dug all round a big onion and pulled it out of the ground. Fear would not allow me to dig up a second one to take to Mother as I had first planned. I crawled back to the path, stood up and walked slowly away pretending nothing had happened, but my heart was thumping and thumping with fear still. I went over to a group of trees to hide, peeled the onion and took a huge bite out of the beautiful white crunchy pulp. It felt good, but it was so bitter that my eyes were full of tears and I couldn't see anything, but I didn't care and went on biting into the onion until I finished it. As soon as I had finished eating it I felt a pain in my chest like a fire burning inside me. I had to wait a long time for my eyes to clear and to see properly before I could go back. I felt bad for the rest of the day, but I didn't tell anyone what I had done and stayed away from everyone so they couldn't smell my breath.

The Accordion

After many months of danger, oppression and fear and with little food, the endless misery had drained every bit of energy, courage and willpower from our bodies. One night, while a bombardment was taking place a little distance from us, each horrid explosion made the whole house tremble. Dust and debris from the old roof rafters made us cough and cough. Putting our heads under the blankets was the only way to subdue the coughing and not choke, and we always kept our eyes shut to prevent grit going into them. It was the in-between moments after each explosion that were the most frightening, because I always thought that the next bomb would get us. When the bombing stopped, Father lit the candle, gave us all water to drink and said, "Don't be frightened any more, see if you can go to sleep." Soon after, I found myself crying. I didn't know why I was crying but I couldn't stop for a long time, curled up in my sleeping space with my hands over my face, hoping that Mother and Father wouldn't hear me. Waking up each morning was always depressing because I didn't know what catastrophe, what sadness we might have to suffer that day. Nothing good ever happened.

Awake, I waited for the time to get up, listening to Father and Mother mumbling words of fear mingled with yawns and sighs of desperation. When I opened my eyes there was only gloom. We were encased in the crude attic with the low-pitched roof, rough stony walls and crumbling concrete holding cobwebs and dust from years and years ago. Those ancient warped rafters with splits and cracks holding the terracotta concave tiles were far too close. I knew I had to remain on that hard, cold floor for a long time yet, so I closed my eyes, curled up my aching, hungry body and felt drowned in sorrows for us all.

During the day, if it was sunny, I would spend much of my time in front of the house sitting on a log with my back against the warm wall and letting the sun comfort me. I closed my eyes and held my face up to the sun until the heat dulled my senses into a numb, sleepy state. I was there, I wasn't there. That's what I did on sunny days. When the sun went away from the house I would start to shiver and goose-pimples appeared on my arms and legs. Then I would go back to the gloom of our dark attic, where Mother would greet me with a glance and half-smile, saying, "Hey, you are back, has the sun gone now? In a while we'll have something to eat," but soon her face would become melancholy again. Then we all remained quiet, sitting on the floor of our sleeping space until there was another glance, a slight movement, or a quietly murmured meaningless remark, "It's getting dark now", "We'll soon have something to eat", "It's Wednesday tomorrow". We waited for the hours of the day to pass in the hope that tomorrow something good would happen to inspire us, that soon we would be liberated from this tyranny and be able to return to our home, to our happy way of life.

We waited for the time when Mother had boiled the potatoes and Father would carefully hand out our slice of bread and portion of potatoes, making sure that each of us had the same amount, and when Mother insisted on giving me and my brother some from her share. Then, still hungry, we would survive another night to face another day and to continue to suffer the misery and the fear – or worse.

It was a beautiful peaceful, sunny afternoon and I was sitting in my usual place in front of the house when Mario came out carrying his accordion and a chair. He sat on the chair near me, facing the sun too, and started to play. I stood by his side admiring and rejoicing in the beautiful sound of the music and watched his fingers moving so fast over the keys, just the two of us. Sometimes we looked at one another and smiled; he could see how much I was enjoying his music. Sometimes he moved his head from side to side with his eyes closed, expressing the emotions of the music. We were both absorbed in a world of excitement, a world of beauty that made us forget bad things in our lives; all I wanted was to be Mario. While he and I were rejoicing in our dream world, a sudden shadow made us look up. The music stopped. We were facing two tall German officers standing intimidatingly before us, leather boots up to their knees, revolvers on their belts. Two stern faces under those evil peaked caps that usually only conveyed terror tried to smile at us. The joy of the last twenty minutes or so was immediately destroyed, as if a bomb had exploded beside us. It was an immediate return to the reality, the horror, in which we lived.

340

The officers said, "Bravo, bravo, suona ancora" (Bravo, bravo, play more). Mario played another piece of music for them, but he never looked up while he was playing or made gestures with his head any more. He kept his head still, looking down all the time. I looked up at the officers' faces; they smiled at me and I smiled insincerely back as my eyes went to their uniforms. Suddenly I was overcome with a deeper fear which I tried not to show, a fear that made my skin twitch, because they were the really bad ones, the ones who had 'La Morte', the death mark, on their uniforms – SS officers. Mario finished playing the piece of music and looked up. The officers again said "Bravo, bravo" and went on to ask Mario about the accordion. "What does this do?" "What does that do?", pointing to the different keys on the accordion that changed the sound to imitate various instruments, which Mario demonstrated. In no time one of the officers said, "I want to buy the accordion." Mario responded by shaking his head, saying emphatically, "No, no, I am a musician. This accordion is part of my life and my living. I wouldn't sell it for any amount of money." One of the officers took his wallet out of his pocket, produced some money, extended his hand to Mario and said, "Take this for it." Mario said again, "No, no, I wouldn't sell it to anyone, anyway the money you're offering wouldn't buy a bottle of olive oil." The officers looked at one another, exchanged a few words and then moved towards Mario, placed their hands on his shoulders, took hold of the leather straps and pulled the accordion off him as one said arrogantly, "Take this money or we'll take it without giving you anything." Then they walked away with the accordion happily chatting to one another, while Mario left me and walked back into the house with a red face and tears in his eyes. I remained standing by the chair alone until the officers were out of sight, then I ran back to our attic to tell Father what had happened. He told me he had heard everything and exclaimed, "I told Mario he should not play the accordion, remember!" For days it seemed as if a funeral had taken place in Mario's house.

The Deepest Fear

The more days that passed, the more everyone feared that the war would go on and on and we might be killed or starve to death. We had been living on our hopes for such a long time and now they were almost destroyed. The discussions I used to listen to were always about "la guerra, la guerra" (the war, the war). With no newspapers and because the Germans had made it clear that if anyone was found to have a radio they would be severely punished, no one knew what was really happening, except for the information passed from one to another about what had taken place in a nearby area or town that morning or the previous day.

It took only two people to meet and start talking for others to gather anxiously around them. The desire to know what was happening was so great that people immediately broke in, asking: "What's the news?" "What's happening?" "Where have the Allies reached?". But any information was always about the destruction the shelling and bombardments had caused, family members who had been injured or killed by the bombs, the ransacking of houses by the German soldiers, and the men they had captured. It was hearing about the captured men that upset me most because I thought they might capture Father again. When the gathering dispersed to return to their homes, they walked slowly, heads bowed, lost in thought. Back in the misery of our draughty attic, sitting in line on the floor quiet and withdrawn, I felt afraid because what I had heard brought home the reality of our situation. I couldn't stop thinking of our plight since we had left home, the fear and cold we had suffered in the mountain hideouts, the demanding journeys, the horrific shelling and bombardments, the terror of facing those machine guns held by merciless soldiers. To have to endure all that again would be terrible, I thought, as we waited for the time to pass, waited for when Father would give us our slice of bread and portion of potatoes, waited and waited and waited in the gloom of our attic, not knowing if the day would ever come when we would be liberated. We had thought that by coming to Sora we had distanced ourselves from the deepest horrors of war, but the situation changed rapidly as the town became increasingly dominated by the German army and it too was subjected to heavy shelling and bombardments. Those loud, deafening explosions, particularly at night, often took place in total darkness as each blast would blow the light of the candle out. When the whole house trembled and the attic became full of dust and debris from the old rafters and roof tiles that made us cough and cough, I thought of saints, especially St Anthony. Quietly and earnestly I would say, "My St Anthony help us, don't let us die, help us St Anthony, help us." Then I would quickly say a Hail Mary prayer to the Madonna: "My Madonna, save us, don't let the bombs explode near us." At the same time I could hear Grandmother also begging the saints to save us. Father and Mother would speak to one another then Father would say quite loudly, "Non avete paura, non avete paura" (Don't be frightened, don't be frightened). "The bombs are aimed where the Germans keep the ammunition, don't be frightened." But I hoped and hoped the next one wasn't going to get us.

They were horrible, devastating explosions that it was pointless to reason with – "Don't hurt me. Don't kill me, I've done nothing wrong, nothing against you." Each explosion seemed as if it was never going to stop. When it did, we were left stunned, disorientated and trembling. As I slowly recovered, I felt thankful that I and the people around me were not hurt but sad for those I didn't know who were hurt or killed, because I knew this was what I would learn at daylight the next morning. Yet our deepest fear was always of the human beings who terrorised us. The very word 'Tedeski' (Germans) was frightening in itself. It was now fixed in our minds that the word meant 'terror'. It was the fear we woke up with each morning and went to bed with each night; it was those uniforms, those evil caps the officers wore, even those shiny leather boots up to their knees were frightening. All those merciless looking faces struck fear into the heart; they told us the wearers were cruel, unreasonable, as merciless as the exploding bombs.

Fear never left us now. It was in our minds and bodies, obvious in everyone you looked at and every voice you heard. Father became irritable and impatient with me when I said I wanted to get out of the confined space of the attic. He wouldn't even allow me to stay for a while with his parents, brothers and sisters, who were living only two or three minutes' walk from us. I would say, "I'll only stay out for a bit then I'll come back." "No, no," he would reply, "It's dangerous even to stay in here; if the Germans go by you'll attract attention to this house." However, sometimes he did tell me and my brother to go and sit in the sun in front of the house, but always with the words, "Don't move from there, do you understand?" It was only after the war that I learned Father had known then of the atrocities being committed, so no wonder he was so strict with me.

Many times the soldiers came to capture the men and Father would run to his hiding place while Mother, Grandmother, my brother and I remained still and silent. First we would hear the sound of boots over the stony path, then the rush up the wooden staircase, accompanied by loud, aggressive voices. We stood together, the door purposely left open, trembling, our hearts pounding, waiting to be shouted at and confronted by the perforated barrels of the machine guns and the eyes full of hatred under those sinister helmets. I always hoped that Mother wouldn't be subjected to a lengthy interrogation about Father and other men's whereabouts. The raids didn't last long but always left an atmosphere of fear. However frequent they became, we never got used to them; each time the feeling of devastation and disbelief they caused lasted until our minds and bodies had had time to calm and we were ready to return to our normal state of sadness. Hours would pass before Father returned, hoping it was now safe to stay with us at least for the rest of that day, but the insecurity and fear never really left us.

Father kept stressing that we had to remain inside and be silent so he could hear any noise coming from outside: the sound of a lorry from a distance or voices warning of their coming. There we were, Father, Mother, Grandmother, my brother and me, sitting on the floor in the dismal atmosphere of our attic with no windows and full of draughts even with the door closed. The only light was what seeped through the uneven roof tiles and shrunken panels of the ancient door. When a face was caught in a dim streak of light, it was revealed how it had become shaped by the unending sorrow in an atmosphere of restlessness, irritability and above all fear, fear that allowed the mind no respite from the continuous nightmare. I knew I was not to cause annoyance, not to speak, and to avoid eye contact.

'Liberation'

It was now the month of June, the tenth month of our struggle to survive. One afternoon Father had allowed me to go and sit in the sun in front of the house when I heard the sound of an aeroplane. The sound of aeroplanes always brought fear because they dropped bombs or dived and fired, but this was only one aeroplane and it seemed to be flying much higher than usual. Other people came out to look at it too, when it suddenly began to pour out streams and streams of leaflets that looked like millions of large snowflakes tumbling in the sky. We wondered what they said as we watched them floating to one side then the other. It seemed they were going to drop a long way away from us, but eventually some came our way too and we chased them as the wind slowly blew them about. They were printed in large letters, telling us to have courage, that in the next few days we would be liberated from the Germans. This was such good news! – it felt as if people knew that we were suffering and that they cared and it gave us the confidence to go outside. We felt almost as if we were free. Father said, "Adesso vedi i Tedeski cominciano a fuggire" (Now you will see the Germans start to run away), "Soon the Allies Forces will arrive and we can go home." It seemed unbelievable that Father, his brothers and others were discussing and planning our return home within the next few days. It wasn't just the sun that was shining that afternoon, people's hearts and eyes were shining too. Hour after hour we waited anxiously for the moment when we would set eyes on the Allied soldiers.

Early in the afternoon of the next day everything was quiet. No German soldiers were to be seen. Father decided to visit a family who were our friends at home to plan the return together; they were staying about fifteen minutes' walk from us. I went with Father and we walked through country lanes and footpaths to the rear of the house and went inside. Father was soon deep in conversation with the family about when to leave and the route we should take. I was bored just listening, so I went into the kitchen garden and slowly made my way to the front of the house, which was by a main road. To my surprise the road was full of German soldiers, all preoccupied and serious-looking, speaking quickly to one another as they went backwards and forwards bringing goods out of the houses in which they were staying. They loaded their big four-wheeled carts very high and huge horses were harnessed to pull them.

Everything was being done with intense urgency. It seemed such noisy confusion as they hurried in all directions preparing for their departure to the battlefront that afternoon. A young soldier came out of the adjacent house, a huge rucksack on his back with a blanket rolled on the top and a rifle on his shoulder. An old man and woman came out from the same house and walked the few metres to the main road, where they shook hands with the soldier as the woman said, "Buona fortuna, quando la guerra è finita ritorna a trovarci" (Good luck, when the war has ended, come back to see us). The soldier looked at the woman and said, "Domani io morto" (Tomorrow I dead). The woman quickly said, "No, no, you will be all right, come back to see us." The soldier bowed his head slightly, shook it a few times and said with conviction, "Si, domani prima mezzo giorno io morto" (Yes, tomorrow before midday I dead), turned and started to walk alone towards the battlefront. It made me sad to see how convinced he was that he was walking towards the place where he would be killed before twelve o'clock the following day. More soldiers kept appearing from the neighbouring houses, all heavily loaded with rifles or machine guns and wearing helmets, walking one by one towards the battlefront. They looked lonely and sad, as if they had been abandoned.

It was only about ten minutes after we arrived that Father came anxiously looking for me. He took hold of my hand, glanced at the armed soldiers who were in such turmoil and said quickly, "Come on, let's go from here. I didn't know there were still so many about. It's been a mistake coming here." We hurriedly started to walk back to our place, but this time instead of going along the lanes and footpaths Father looked for the shortest route across the fields. He took long strides and he looked worried. I sensed his anxiety as he kept glancing back to see if we were being followed. He didn't speak to me, except to repeat, "It was a mistake coming out so soon." I couldn't understand why he was so worried, because the Germans weren't looking for men that day. They seemed focused on going to the battlefront and the leaflets the aeroplane had dropped the day before had said that in a few days we would be liberated. Father continued to walk quickly, pulling me along by the hand as we squeezed through hedges and jumped over brooks. I had to anticipate when he was going to jump because he didn't tell me, concentrating only on looking ahead to see where best to go next. He really didn't seem to know how much he was pulling me along and I kept wondering why he was so worried.

When we arrived back in our attic, I soon learned why Father was so worried. His first words to Mother and Grandmother were, "Non vi spaventate, ma la nostra sofferenza non è ancora finita" (Don't be frightened, but our suffering isn't over yet). "Ma che è successo?" (But what's happened?) Mother instantly asked. Father replied, "I have come back quickly because a man came to tell the people in the house I went to that the Germans are taking people away." I didn't know where, but I could see by the expressions on Mother and Grandmother's faces that it must be a frightening place. Father said quickly, "I'll be back soon, I'm going to see what other people are saying." Mother and Grandmother said together, "Fai attenzine e ritorna subbito" (Be careful and come back quickly). I wanted to go with him, but he said firmly, "No, you stay inside." As he went Mother repeated, "Be careful and come back quickly."

Father soon returned and said, "Everyone's already aware of what's happening. They have started taking people only two streets away from here." Then, "Let's wait and see what happens in the next few hours." The comfort and hope that the leaflets dropped by the aeroplane had given us had now been completely destroyed, returning us once again to the depths of fear.

"We'll stay inside and keep quiet so I can hear any noise outside," Father told us. I desperately wanted to see what was happening on the road outside, but as the attic had no windows and the doorway was on the side of the house, I could only see a lane about two hundred metres away through the spaces and cracks in the ancient door. Most of the time it was deserted; when I saw a person walking along it made me feel as if things weren't so bad after all. When I saw the armed soldiers go by I always called Father, who came to look through the gap at the top of the door. We were frightened they might come to get us, but we couldn't see if they were going straight ahead or turning into our road, so we remained by the door as if paralysed, listening for the sound of their boots over the stones and gravel on the road outside. Each time I felt that any moment I might hear the sound of their boots coming up the wooden stairway, but after a while we decided they had moved away from us. I strained my eyes looking through the gaps in the door hoping to see something good to tell Mother and Father about, but I didn't know what it was I wanted to see. Mother and Father kept telling me to come away from the door, but I would soon find myself peering through the narrow spaces again and be told off once more. I stood with my face pressed against the door for such a long time that the wind blowing through the cracks made my eyes hurt, but it was more frightening just to sit and stay quiet, hearing Mother and Grandmother praying and sighing deeply. I thought I was doing something good that might save us, yet Father kept saying, "Come away from the door. Come and sit here. Do you understand?" and reluctantly, I would go and sit down.

It was now towards the end of the day, just beginning to get dark, and, stretching and bending to look at the short way I could see along the lane, I suddenly became very frightened again as I saw men, women and children walking in single file flanked by soldiers wearing helmets and carrying rifles. The men were loaded with rucksacks and suitcases, the women carried bundles under their arms. No one seemed to be speaking, no one turned to look at one another. I immediately called Father. "Come and see, they are taking people away." Father jumped to his feet and looked through the gap at the top of the door. "I've already counted fifteen," I told him and Father said quickly, "Be quiet, be quiet", as if I'd said something wrong. "Ma che succede?" (But what's happening?) Mother asked, and Father replied, "Niente, non è niente, silenzio" (Nothing, it's nothing, hush), while Grandmother sorrowfully murmured, "Mio Dio, liberaci da questo inferno" (My God, liberate us from this hell). Since the door was low and narrow, Father stood immediately behind me, bent forward. I could hear and feel his deep breathing on my head as we both watched the horrifying scene motionless and in total silence.

When we couldn't see the line of people any more, Father took hold of my hand and said, "Now, go and sit down and don't come near this door any more. This is

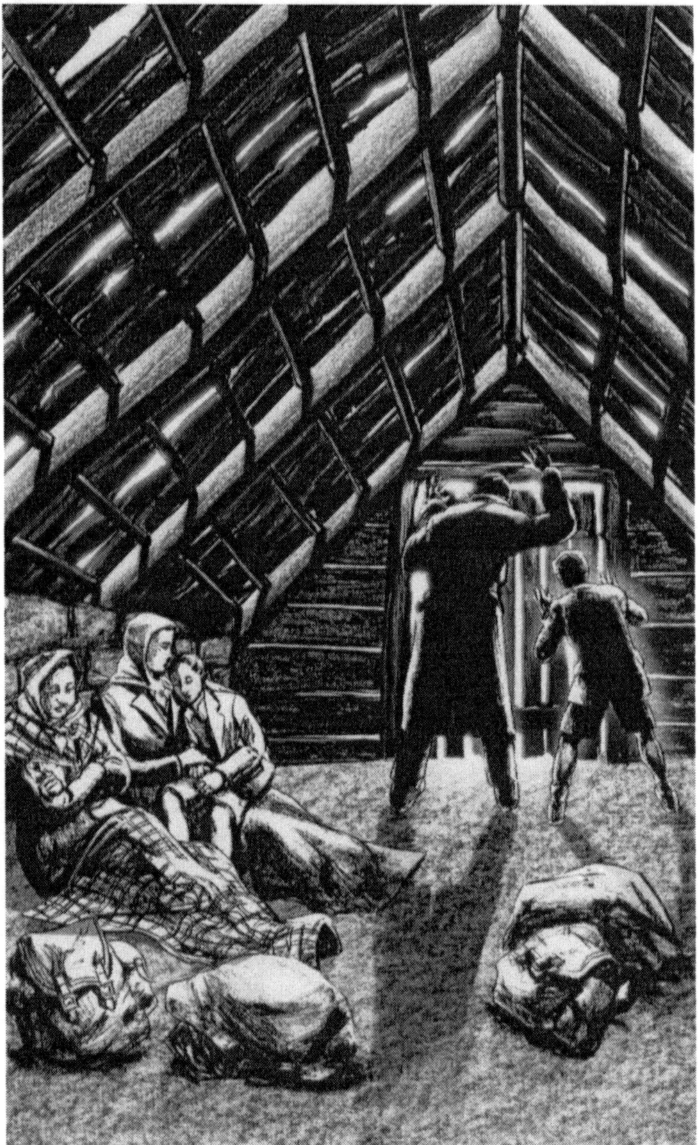

the last time I shall tell you." He stood before us and said, "Don't be frightened, soon it will be dark. They won't come this evening." Mother said, "Speriamo di no. Speriamo che Dio ci aiuta" (Let's hope not. Let's hope God will help us), while Grandmother murmured, "Gesù mio aiutaci" (My Jesus help us). Father continued, "The way people are speaking, I feel sure that in a day or two the Allies will come and we'll be liberated. What we have to do is go and hide somewhere until then. As soon as it's dark I will go and tell the rest of the family what we should do. Now let's pack our goods so we can leave this place at daybreak tomorrow, before they come."

Father started packing the huge rucksack and sack he always carried, then he and Mother organised the rest of our goods and piled them near the door ready for us to load up and leave. It was dark now and Father said, "I'm now going to tell the rest of the family we must all leave as soon as it gets light. Don't worry, I'll be back very quickly."

Father did return quickly, saying we would all meet on the road outside as soon as it began to get light. He then said, "Now we must get a good night's sleep, so tomorrow we'll go and hide on the hills where I've been going for firewood. They won't find us there. Go to sleep and don't worry, soon the Allied Forces will arrive and we'll be able to go home." Grandmother said, "Madonna mia aiutaci" (My Madonna help us), then she told me and my brother, "You pray to the Madonna too so she'll help us." Under the blankets we all tried to go to sleep to the murmuring sounds of Grandmother praying. I woke up many times that night. I was always pleased when it was still dark, because while it was dark they wouldn't come for us. I dreaded the ordeal of going to hide somewhere among the woods on the hills of Sora, fearing that when it got light we would be caught and taken away, but my biggest worry, what I feared most during that night, was that they would take Father away from us, because the many times I woke up Mother and Father were always talking and once I heard Mother say, "If they catch us we'll have to go, who knows where they'll take us?" Father said, "If they take me away, don't let them separate you from the boys", and Mother answered, "Gesù mio, mi devono uccidere prima" (My Jesus, they will have to kill me first). Father's voice was subdued. It sounded serious and frightening and I worried about how Mother, my brother and I would cope without Father. Who would carry our goods? Who would provide food for us? Now I feared them coming to take us away before daylight, thinking that any moment I would hear the sound of their boots coming up the staircase. I wished it wasn't true, I wished I could have fallen asleep. The night went on and on as if it was never going to end and yet the morning came too soon.

I began to see pockets of light seeping through the uneven roof tiles on the old bowed rafters. It sounded as if everyone was sleeping – yes, I could hear the sound of Father breathing; he was asleep. My eagerness to go and hide was all I could think of. I really believed they would come to get us that morning and take us away as I had seen the line of people being taken away the day before, and I thought of what Father had said, that if they took him away Mother shouldn't let my brother and me be separated from her. My mind was in turmoil and I longed to go. Why was Father still sleeping? Should I wake him? It was probably only a few minutes since I had woken up and seen the dawn light seeping through the tiles, but fear was tormenting me. Suddenly Father awoke, stood up and said, "Get up, get up. In just over an hour we'll be safe", then again, "Svegliatevi, presto, andiamo" (Wake up, quickly, let's go). Since we already had our clothes and shoes on, all we had to do was stand up and collect our blankets. Father took everything to the bottom of the staircase and Grandmother went to get Pee Pee in the cage under the outside staircase. We took up our loads and walked about twenty metres to the road, where we waited for the rest of the family. Father's parents, two brothers and two sisters were already there and groups of people passed us on the way to their hiding places. We stood close together with pounding hearts, looking at one another's faces for reassurance that we were all there. I felt guilty, as if we had to escape and hide again because we were bad, inferior people. I felt small, insignificant and worthless. Everyone around me looked in a trance. It seemed as if we were all guilty and our lives would be always the same. Soon the rest of the family came and one by one, all in line, we went on our way to our new hiding place. Father, Mother, Grandmother, my brother and I were five, Grandfather and Grandfather's brother and sister and their families numbered fifteen; there were twenty of us, all loaded with rucksacks, sacks, baskets and bundles, walking quickly after Father. It was getting lighter but it was still very early in the morning. Once again we were repeating what we had done so many times before, running in fear of our lives, except this time we were together as a big family, it wasn't cold any more and no shells or bombs were threatening us; however, the fear that we would meet German soldiers who would take us away was very real.

From the minor country roads we reached a main road where German lorries full of soldiers, tailing small guns, speeded towards the battlefront; they had no interest in us. We stopped on the grass verge until the lorries had passed then crossed the road and continued behind Father, trying to walk quickly through narrow paths and fields, without a word being spoken. It was hard going without a rest, especially for Mother, Grandmother and two aunts, go, go, go to reach a place where we wouldn't be found. Father found it difficult to turn round with the rucksack and the heavy sack on his shoulder, so now and again he asked Uncle, who walked behind him, "Turn round and see if everyone is following." Uncle always answered, "They're all coming, don't worry." Eventually we reached the foot of a hill where Father led us onto a path within the woodland where we were well hidden from view. Soon he put down the sack and took his rucksack off and everyone knew that at long last we were going to rest. We gathered together and sat on our packs, twenty exhausted bodies, eyes staring into nothing and deep in thought, trying to calm our breathing down. Many minutes passed with no sound except that of our heavy breathing, then Father stood up, took a few steps forward and said, "Datevi coraggio, fra pochi giorni ritorniamo alle nostre case, coraggio, coraggio" (Have courage, in a few days we will return to our homes, courage, courage). Then he said, "Tell me when you have rested enough, we have to climb this hill and go into dense woodland, we're sure to be safe there." There were a few moans from the tired women. "Dove, dove andiamo?" (Where, where are we going?). "Let's not go too high. The climb is too steep." "The sooner we get there the safer we'll be," Father answered, "then you can rest as long as you like. We'll go up slowly, but we have to go. Avete pazienza, non è colpa mia" (Have patience, it's not my fault).

It wasn't long before we were on our way loaded with our goods, slowly walking up a stony track that kept turning one way then the other. It was hard; the straps of my rucksack were hurting my shoulders and it seemed easier if I walked a little bent forward. My brother, who walked in front of me, kept turning to see if I was coming and copied the way I was walking. More than once he asked, "Is it far now?" and I answered, "I don't know". No one spoke; I felt sad and alone. We rested once, then left the track and went into dense woodland. After a short distance we found ourselves under a massive forward slanting rock with a small clearing in front of it, all surrounded by dense woodland. Father said, "We'll stop here for the night. We're safe now, they won't come here. Have a rest and then we'll work out the best way to sleep here".

Our journey hadn't been as bad or as long as many of our previous ones, but tension from the day and night before and the fast, non-stop pace to the foot of the hill with the fear we would be caught and taken away had exhausted us. We sat where we could. My ankles, knees and hips were sore and hot, my legs trembling. Everyone seemed far away and it was so silent that we were afraid to speak, or even look at each other. I still had a feeling of guilt, of shame, but I didn't know why.

We rested and ate some of the food we carried, bread and cheese. Some ate cold polenta, others cold boiled potatoes. There were heavy sighs and moans, "Let's hope they don't come and find us", "I hope we don't have to stay here too long", "Che vita, che vita, stiamo a vivere" (What a life, what a life we're living), "Let's hope God will help us". Some implored the saints for help. The twenty of us slumped on the stony, bumpy ground of the clearing, surrounded by a mass of thin, tall woodland trees that made the place dull and cold. The small portion of food each of us was handed quickly disappeared; it made our mouths water with real hunger.

In that miserable place I began to imagine that soon we would be able to return to our homes, and thought, "This isn't as bad as we've already been through." We were well hidden from the horrible soldiers who wanted to take us away. We weren't being bombed or shelled, and it wasn't cold like the terrible, terrible days when we were hidden in the cave, when for days and days I could feel the outline of my bones in my body because they were so cold. Yes, there was the danger of the soldiers finding us, but we'd been through so many dangerous times in the past that hiding on this hill, engulfed in the dense woodland, felt safe to me. The aeroplane that had dropped leaflets only three days before telling us to hold on and be courageous and in a few days we would be liberated gave me a real sense of reassurance and I began to have better thoughts. Having seen so many soldiers the day before in such turmoil as they loaded their carts or walked alone to the battlefront convinced that by noon the next day they would be killed told me that a massive effort was being made by the Allied soldiers to liberate us. I believed that soon we would be free, but for that night at least we had to remain where we were and sleep under the open sky.

After a good rest it was action time, preparing the ground to sleep that night. I wanted to stay by Father helping to clear the stones, but he wouldn't let me, saying, "Go and sit down. You don't have to do anything." I took my rucksack and went over to where Grandmother was sitting with Pee Pee squatted by her side. My brother soon joined us and the three of us stayed quietly together just watching the activity. The men cleared the stones to one side and broke branches to make an enclosure beneath the high rock. The women gathered piles of dry wood to make four fires, one for each family to cook potatoes, dried beans or make polenta, but the fires couldn't be started until nightfall so the smoke wouldn't be seen. Grandmother fell asleep, resting her elbows on her knees with her head bent forward. Each time Mother came back with a bundle of dry wood in her arms she gave us a smile. Once she came and squatted in front of us, saying very quietly so as not to wake Grandmother, "Do you feel tired? Try to close your eyes and see if you can sleep like Grandmother. Don't be frightened, the war has nearly finished. We'll soon go home." Before approaching the hill Father had seen a farmhouse with a well in front and some of the men and women went cautiously for water, which they carried in buckets and cooking pots.

As the day went on, Father kept telling everyone to try not to make any noise and to speak quietly, in case the Germans should be looking for us. When we heard any kind of noise, a moving stone or voice, we remained still and quiet until we knew what it was. Each time, the noise turned out to have come from other groups of people who, like us, were passing along the path as they went to hide in other parts of the woodland. The men constructed a huge enclosure against the rock, with the branches close together to keep the wind out. It was like a sheep pen. That night the twenty of us tried to sleep on the hard ground wrapped in our blankets; the night air was cold, so we all kept our heads under the blankets. The next morning everyone was apprehensive about what had happened when the German soldiers went to find us and discovered no one there. Were they looking for us now? We hoped the Allied soldiers had arrived so we could finally go home. When voices were heard from other groups who had taken refuge in different parts of the hill Father went to ask if they had any news, but no one had.

Later in the day a man came to tell us that he had gone as far as he could towards the town without being detected, and the area was still occupied by the German army. Everyone looked disappointed and Father thanked the man for coming to tell us, saying, "Aspettiamo domani, forse se ne vanno domani" (We'll wait for tomorrow, perhaps they'll go away tomorrow). The man answered, "Speriamo, speriamo" (Let's hope so, let's hope), and as he walked away Father said, "Arrivederci e bunoa fortuna per domani" (Goodbye and good luck for tomorrow). Our situation remained the same. The news made me sad as there was still the danger we would be found and taken away. There we stood, a large, close family of twenty, looking at each other's faces, speechless, helpless and lost in our thoughts.

The third day on the hill, the man who had come to give the bad news the day before returned and said, "I Tedeski sono fuggiti via" (The Germans have run away), "the Allies are about to arrive." There was a cautious eruption of sounds, "Oh, oh, è vero, è proprio vero?" (Oh, oh, is it true, is it really true?), "Sia ringraziato Dio" (May God be thanked), "Ma è proprio vero?" (But is it really true?). Everyone gathered around the man, asking him for confirmation of his good news. Mother hugged me and my brother, saying, "Have you heard we can go home now? We're going home forever, we don't have to be frightened any more, all the bad times are over. Aren't you happy?"

Eagerly we started to descend the hill, returning to the places where we'd been staying, wanting to start the journey home the following day. There was a spring in my step as I made my way from one stone to another. Weak as everyone was, they chattered to one another. "We'll have to start to rebuild our lives again. What joy, what joy to return to our home", "When we get back I want to kiss the walls of my house", "The land will be overgrown with weeds and wild plants now", "Doesn't matter, doesn't matter".

Back in our attic and we were free, free, free – free to go outside, free from having to be on the lookout all the time, free to speak as loudly as we wished. No more fear, but the many months of mental conflict weakened by hunger meant we hadn't much energy left to really rejoice.

It was towards evening and our packs were all ready to start our journey home early the next morning. There was excitement on everyone's face. Just one more night of sleeping on the floor in our attic! We heard people speaking freely outside the house. Father went out, telling me to stay inside, but soon came back with an apologetic air and said, "Avete pazienza" (Have patience), "we can't go tomorrow. We have to wait until the Allied soldiers tell us when we can go." Father also told us that the Allied soldiers had arrived in the centre of Sora, where crowds of people had welcomed them with flowers and wine, but before they had captured the town several Allied soldiers were killed by two German soldiers hiding on the top of a tree. It made me sad, and Mother and Grandmother made the sign of the cross. I asked Father why, since the Germans had gone, we couldn't go back home. He told me that although we had been liberated the war was still going on; the Germans were still there. I was disappointed to learn this and to know there were people still suffering. I really thought the war had ended for everyone.

The Return

Daily we waited anxiously for the Allied soldiers to tell us we could go home. We watched other families returning to their towns but couldn't yet return to ours, whether because it was still occupied by the German army or because it was heavily mined or for some other reason, I don't remember now. A few days passed before we heard the good news that we too could return to our homes, but we were also told we couldn't use the main direct road. Bridges that hadn't been destroyed were being guarded by the Allied soldiers, who weren't allowing civilians across. We had to find other routes to take.

Early the next morning the whole family gathered on the road outside the house and we started on our journey. "We'll be home in two days," Father said. Having been forbidden to be in our homes for such a long time, our daily struggle and suffering made it difficult to believe we were now actually returning to our normal way of life. We longed to return home, but our spirits were subdued by the long wait and our weakness. Some were emotional, others grumbled about the two-day journey we had to endure. I was feeling weak; I just obeyed and followed Father. Since we couldn't use the main road, the journey was going to be long and difficult. Once again we were walking one behind the other, carrying our loads, passing through country lanes, walking along footpaths, crossing abandoned fields, in the direction of our town. As always, Father was the leader. He decided which way to go, when to stop for short rests and when to eat some of the food we carried. Sometimes we reached the end of a path and then struggled across overgrown fields; there were groans from the women when we had to jump over brooks or climb from one level to another, and when we had to walk along neglected footpaths where the undergrowth and thorns had grown across, tearing their dresses and making it difficult to get through without scratches. Father, at the front, just carried on. "We are going in the right direction," he would say. There were times when we all stopped for a short rest and then Father discussed with Grandfather and the uncles what direction to take next. Finding ourselves in desolate countryside it seemed we weren't covering much ground, but when we passed groups of houses I felt good, as if we were getting nearer to our home. Sometimes we met other families returning to their towns. Father and Grandfather would exchange a few quiet words, "Where are you from?", "Are you all one family?", always finishing with "Coraggio e buona fortuna" (Courage and good luck); some gave a nod or just a glance, but no one stopped, their minds too troubled, their bodies too tired, to offer more. We just kept on walking.

After a long, tiring day, as evening began to approach, Grandmother and the aunts moaned about their tiredness and asked Father, "When are we going to stop? We'd better find a place to sleep before it gets dark." Father answered, "Let's walk for a while longer and then we'll find somewhere." We came to a group of houses where we could have asked for shelter for the night, but I heard Father say to Uncle Benedetto, who walked behind him, "Let's go on. Then there won't be so far to walk tomorrow under the hot sun and we'll reach home before dark." As we passed the houses I heard the women grumbling about why we hadn't stopped for the night.

It began to get dark. We were walking on the crest of a hill when we saw a farmhouse with stables and a barn; we approached the place and Father knocked on the door. A man and a woman came out and Father asked if they could give us a place to sleep for the night. They asked us to go inside and gave us three rooms for the twenty of us. They apologised that they hadn't any blankets or straw and told us they had returned the day before and found the house almost empty of their possessions. Father, Mother, my brother and I slept in a small room at the very top of the house that was reached by a steep staircase. It was dark and there was no electricity. We slept on the floor with our blankets over us and the next morning I awoke very early. I felt dazed and my body as heavy as lead. We gathered outside and ate bread and cheese. The owner of the house drew a bucket of water from the well for us and Father told us to drink lots because we didn't know when we would next find water to drink during our journey. It was early, the sun hadn't come out yet, but soon we were on our way. Once again, tired and sleepy with aching joints, without a word being spoken, we all followed Father, walking, walking, walking.

It was just before midday on a stony country road when Father's mother collapsed and fell. Everything she had been carrying was scattered around. Everyone stopped and gathered around her. Grandfather and Father quickly unloaded their things, rushed to pick her up and sat her on the grass by the roadside. Grandfather's sister knelt by her saying, "Don't worry, don't worry, it's so hot", as Grandmother cried and cried, saying, "I can't go on, I can't go on any longer. My legs won't carry me any more. What am I going to do?" Grandfather tried to console her: "We all feel the same. We should have stopped for a rest long ago." Others said, "Don't worry, the worst has passed, our suffering is over and in a few hours we shall be in our homes. Have a good rest, we all need a rest." We sat on the verge under the shade of oak trees and rested for a long time. There was a bad feeling because of the incident with Grandmother. We all felt exhausted, it was very hot, no one spoke much, only a few mumbled words. This time, Father waited for someone else to speak and ask when we should start walking again. After a period of silence Grandfather's sister asked Grandmother, "How do you feel now? Do you feel better? Do you think you can manage to go on?" Grandmother answered in a quiet voice, "It's better if we go" and started to get up. Everyone got to their feet and started to load their goods; most of those Grandmother had been carrying were distributed among the others. The long rest had made me feel even more tired and my joints ached much more.

Because of Grandmother's collapse and the sun being so hot we walked at a slower pace, dispirited and in silence, forcing our bodies to do what they had to do, just keep walking.

After more than a day and a half crossing fields and walking along country lanes and overgrown footpaths, we came to the main road leading to our town. I soon learned why the Allied troops didn't want us to use it. There were tens of thousands of us from various towns, far too many, since the road was heavily trafficked by convoy after convoy of huge lorries. Some were full of soldiers, others were covered with canvas, all were speeding in the opposite direction from us. Then I remembered that somewhere the fighting was still going on and felt sad for those still hiding in fear for their lives. The loud noise of the speeding lorries was scary and made me feel as if I was alone; after one convoy had passed another would appear, then another, travelling close to one another at high speed. Though this was a main road, it was narrow for those big lorries and full of shell and bomb holes which the lorries had to swerve from side to side to avoid. We had to walk in line on the neglected verge with its long grass and thorns. The lorries rushed past making loud, strained sounds, as if they too were tired and sad; their big wheels came close to us and they looked vicious as they sped over the battered gravel road throwing up such a thick cloud of dust that we couldn't see ahead and it became difficult to breathe. The dust was gritty in our mouths and made us cough and cough. Many times we had to stop with our backs turned to the road, close our eyes tightly and

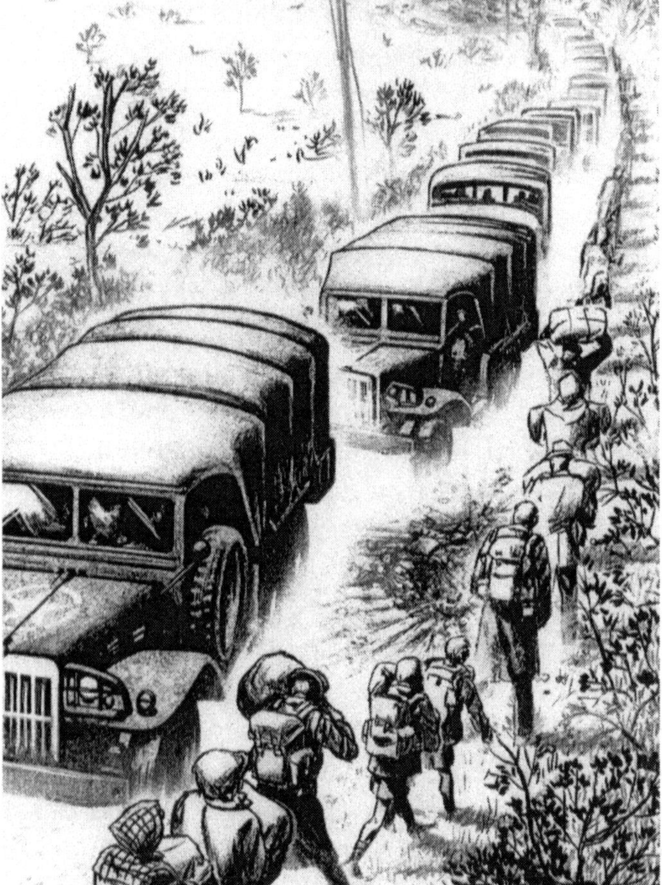

try not to breathe in until the thick powdery dust had settled, then we spat out the dust, but it still itched inside our noses. In some places there were fields full of tents, busy soldiers unloading lorries, and areas where lorries were being repaired. Now and again a jeep would speed by. It was very hot but we continued moving forward, exhausted, hungry and almost unaware of our bodies as we placed one foot in front of the other. We were too, too tired to think of anything except our eagerness to see our homes again.

It was late in the afternoon when I became aware that we weren't far from home. I recognised the place where we had found the barrow and, soon after, we turned left into the long empty road that would lead us to our town. The sight of this road brought back horrific memories of our outgoing journey and I found myself thinking of the sadness of that day. We kept on walking, always in line, following one another to avoid treading on mines, looking where to tread next. I was becoming excited at the thought of being back home.

After some time, we found ourselves turning a corner at the foot of the chain of mountains surrounding our town as if we were entering a gateway. Suddenly the familiar view of our town revealed itself. This was home. Seeing this familiar sight was exciting and I began to imagine seeing our neighbours and friends again, and especially a girl a little younger than me who lived next door. Her name was Rosina and she was Vincenzo's daughter. I looked forward to seeing my friend Bruno and my other school friends and wondered if they had returned before us. Though exhausted, we kept up a good pace as I thought about all that was to come. I became lost in a dream world and took little notice of the holes in the road, the battered houses we passed or what the others might be saying. I even forgot how exhausted I felt and our miserable state.

As we walked on, we passed the cluster of oak trees where there had been one of the huge German cannons. Now there were only mountainous piles of empty crates that had carried their powerful shells. We were about two hundred metres from our road. My mind was full of the joys of what it used to be like at home.

We turned into our road and after twenty metres or so found ourselves in front of our homes. I didn't want to accept what my eyes were seeing, my heart was pounding with dismay. It all looked abandoned, desolate, as if the place had been left centuries ago; the area had been massacred. All the houses had hundreds of holes made by the shells and bombs, huge areas of walls were on the verge of falling, roof tiles and rubble were everywhere, empty German ammunition boxes were littered around. The front door of Grandmother's house was open, while ours had no front door at all. Trembling with disappointment, we stepped over the rubble and cautiously entered our home. Rubbish and broken glass littered the floor. Only a dresser was left in the kitchen, only the bed with its mattress, the chest of drawers and the wardrobe were left in Father's and Mother's bedroom. The room that Father had filled with goods and bricked up, placing a dresser in front to conceal the new brickwork, had been discovered; all the best things had been taken. Father kept remembering so many things that were missing, including sheets, blankets, towels and saucepans. I also noticed that the wall clock with the pendulum wasn't there any more, nor the silk rug that hung on the wall with the picture of a camel; our gramophone and records had gone too. Even my pedal car that I had had since I was very small had been taken. It felt so strange and sad. The floor was littered with our clothes, books, papers and lots of our photographs, all of which had been trampled on. A nasty smell came from the room, rats were everywhere. It felt strange and evil. Was this because the soldiers who had stayed there had no souls? There was no joy in our return.

Father soon remembered the hand grenade that the German soldiers had placed on the bedroom windowsill to kill Mother. He said to us, "You three stay in the kitchen while I remove the grenade from the windowsill." Mother said, "Leave it, leave it now, you're tired. Tomorrow I'll ask the English soldiers to come and remove it." Father replied, "That's where the large bed is, it's the room where we'll all sleep tonight. You three stay here." We remained standing close together, tense, as Father went into the bedroom. He soon reappeared saying, "It's not there any more, we can safely sleep in that room tonight." Dazed with tiredness, the four of us were soon asleep.

When I awoke the next morning it was late and the sun was shining. Father was in the kitchen trying to make a replacement front door using wood from empty German ammunition boxes. Mother was cleaning. I stood by Mother with my brother while she removed the ash from the stove, using a small flat piece of wood to push it into a bucket. Then a hard object in the ash fell into the bucket. Mother put her hand in the bucket, brought out the object and shouted, "It's a hand grenade!" Turning to me and my brother she yelled, "Go, go away from here, go into the next room." Father immediately moved towards Mother. "Put it down, put it down, you go into the next room too, all of you, now." Mother pushed me and my brother towards the next room as she said, "They tried really hard to kill me." Father shouted, "Stay in there and don't touch anything, I'll be back soon, wait there till I'm back. I'm going to detonate it." The three of us nervously stood together waiting to hear the explosion and praying Father wouldn't be hurt. Mother made my brother and me stand side by side in front of her and placed her arms over our shoulders, her hands over our chests, holding us tightly against her body; I felt her nervous, heavy breathing. A few minutes later we heard the explosion then anxiously waited for Father to return, hoping he hadn't injured himself. Minutes later we heard Father's voice speaking to us loudly from the road, saying, "I am coming, don't touch anything". We remained in the room while he carefully searched in the kitchen and bedroom in which we'd slept in case of other possible traps. When he felt satisfied the two rooms were clear, he called us into the kitchen and gave us strict instructions, saying, "No one is to go into any room except the kitchen and the bedroom we slept in last night until the other rooms have been searched with a mine detector, and none of you is to go outside. Do you understand?" I asked Father if I could just pick up the photographs that were scattered on the floor in the other room. He said "No". Now we were even frightened of being in our own home.

The following day our next-door neighbours, Vincenzo and his family, returned – it was exciting to see them again. While Father and Mother spoke to Vincenzo and his wife I eagerly greeted their daughter Rosina, but it was a big disappointment because Rosina didn't recognise who I was and walked away from me to stand beside her mother.

At Home

Father was very strict with me and my brother; we weren't allowed to move away from the kitchen or the bedroom in which the four of us slept. Mother only went across the road to her mother's house. Father told us about some of our friends who had also returned, but wouldn't let us go to see them because of the danger of the ammunition left scattered around by the Germans. A few days later two English soldiers came with a mine detector, which looked like a thick frying pan with a long handle; they carefully went into every room and afterwards told us it was all safe. The soldiers stayed to talk to Mother for a long time as they sat on the empty German ammunition boxes that Father had collected to make use of their wood. They looked pleased to be speaking to Mother, who spoke English. It was my first contact with the English soldiers. They looked smart and important in their uniforms, they smiled, they were laughing, I could look them in the eye.

It was a treat when Father took me and my brother out of the house to visit his parents, brothers and sisters, whose house was about two hundred metres from ours. We had to stay by his side and he held our hands tightly as we walked in the centre of the road, avoiding the grass-covered roadsides in case mines had been planted there. Days passed, but Father's discipline never wavered. Even when he took us to where we stored our firewood, we had to remain by his side while he chopped the logs. Now and again he would turn to see if we were near him and say, "Don't move from where you are. Don't touch anything." He looked into every corner to see if explosives had been purposely left to hurt us. He was suspicious when he saw small patches of earth that had been disturbed and would tell us to move away as he carefully approached to investigate. Two or three weeks after we returned home we were still confined to our home. Those who visited us spoke only of the misery and fear of being injured or killed if one were to tread on the explosives that had been placed in so many unexpected places.

One afternoon Mother and I were alone at home. She asked me to go out with her and I was pleased to do so. We walked towards the main road, Via Roma. It was the first time since our return that I'd been more than a few metres away from our home. Everything looked so different, house walls full of holes made by the shells and bombs, piles of rubble everywhere. What attracted me most were the fields full of tents housing the Allied soldiers; two very long and high tents comprised their hospital, other tents were surrounded by lorries, jeeps and ambulances. Mother and I went amongst the tents and she told me she was going to ask if they had a job for her as an interpreter. We were directed to one of the bigger tents, where Mother spoke to a soldier in English. Although I knew what Mother was asking, I didn't really understand any of the conversation except the word 'interpreter'. The soldiers gathered around Mother, looking pleased to speak to her, and after a while she took my hand and said, "Ritorniamo a casa" (Let's go home). On the way I sensed that Mother was feeling happy; she spoke more quickly and cheerfully, and holding my hand tightly she told me that the soldiers had told her where there was a strong possibility she might be employed as an interpreter. Then she said: "I have invited them to visit us. They are coming this evening. It's sad that we've nothing to offer them." After a short pause she looked at me and added, "Do you mind if I go away for a while, so I can earn some money until things get better?" "Is it going to be very far?" I asked, and Mother replied, "I don't know, but if it is you can come to visit me." I could see the hope on her face, as if she'd already got the job.

We were almost home when I asked Mother if I could stay out for a while. She said, "Yes, but don't go too far and don't touch anything." Feeling as if I'd been unleashed for the first time, I went to the school playground where I could hear the sound of boys and joined them. They were much older than me, maybe thirteen or fourteen, and not my friends, but I knew them. They ventured further and further away and I followed, forgetting what Mother had told me – not to go too far or touch anything. It was my first taste of freedom and it felt good, as if I was a grown-up boy too, but without realising it I was increasingly distancing myself from home. As we walked along the road I was absorbed in looking at the destruction the bombs and shells had created. We passed an isolated villa on which I had actually seen a bomb being dropped in the days when we were hiding on the mountain. Now it was a huge heap of rubble and stones; only the pillars holding the two front gates remained. It was strange, scary and sad.

I was happy to be outside, but I also felt uneasy, because I knew Father wouldn't have allowed me this freedom. I wondered if Mother had wanted to please me because she was happy at the prospect of a job and wasn't concentrating when she permitted me to remain outside alone. I continued following the boys, though they didn't speak to me much. We came to a place where the Germans had set fire to their motorbikes and other goods before they left. Now and again we would see a pile of ammunition from which we walked away.

Eventually we reached an area at the foot of a hill where the Germans had dug into the hill, making caves for protection against bombs, shells and during air raids. Outside one of the caves under a tree was a pile of ammunition. I recognised chains of bullets for machine guns, some flares and a few shells, but what attracted my attention were some smaller objects with rings on them. I picked one up and tried to see if I could prise off the ring. One of the boys saw what I was doing and in a loud, angry voice he swore upon the Madonna, shouting, "Put it down, put it down" as another yelled, "It's an explosive device". They all ran away and I was left alone, trembling with fear. I realised how serious it was because the boy had sworn on the Madonna, which was a grave sin, and because they had all run off. I carefully placed the device on the ground and ran to rejoin them. They cursed me over and over again, telling me that if it had exploded in my hand I would have died and it would have made the rest of the ammunition explode too, then they would all have been killed. They were so angry, some still cursing me, that I became even more frightened than when I was holding the explosive device, I was so aware now of what could have happened had I not been stopped at that crucial moment. The boys started to walk home and I followed. They hadn't spoken to me much before and now they didn't want me in their company at all, so I walked a few metres behind them, but every few minutes someone would turn and give me a scornful look. I felt rejected, inadequate and scared.

I returned home pretending that I was happy, but inside I felt guilty and sad. That evening the three English soldiers whom Mother and I had met earlier that day came to our home. They sat with us and chatted a lot with Mother, who continually translated what was being said to Father. At times there would be bursts of laughter, but I was unable to concentrate on what was being said. I was burdened with fear about what had happened that day and worried for many days in case Father heard what I'd been up to.

A Visit to Caserta

Soon Mother did manage to get a job as an interpreter with the British Army, but she had to work a long way from home. I felt sad to see her go, but she assured me and my brother that as soon as she settled into her job we could go to visit her. Father went with her and returned after two days so we were left in the care of Grandmother. I felt miserable without Mother, there was an emptiness, something special was missing. When Father returned, he told us all about where Mother was working, where she stayed, and about the place itself. Father cooked our meals and I helped him prepare the food, did the washing up, swept the floor and many other jobs that I could manage. Father's sisters helped too, doing the washing and ironing. Father went to visit Mother once a week and brought back foods which weren't available in our town. On each of the visits Mother sent back special pastries for me and my brother, which Father took great pleasure in giving to us. He would hide some and a day or two later say, "Look what I've found, are they the ones I gave you yesterday? Didn't you like them? Shall I throw them away? Look! Here's another one."

My brother was taken to see Mother first and I went the following week. I learnt during my visit that it was one of the centres of the Allied Forces in Italy and that there was a big hospital where many of the casualties of the Battle of Monte Cassino were brought. The place was called Caserta. It had suffered war damage too, but nothing like the massacre our town had been through. There was a long train that had been hit and burnt out and was now tilted to one side of the track so that other trains could pass. It was a very large town, more like a city, with wide roads, tall buildings and palaces. The roads were full of army lorries and jeeps, with more jeeps travelling in all directions. The pavements were full of British soldiers; they carried no arms and wore no helmets. I watched them playing football; they were having a great time and looked very happy. The coffee shops were full of them. They were all smoking and I could smell the scent of cigarettes as we passed and saw the rooms full of their slowly rising smoke. The chairs outside the cafes too were full of soldiers, all with their packets of cigarettes on the tables.

It was great to be with Mother; she held my hand wherever we went. She had taken half a day off work and later in the day she took me to where she worked and the soldiers made a fuss of me. It was the first time that I'd seen any women soldiers; they looked very important, smart, tall and slim. One of them kept Mother talking for a long time and looked very serious. Later Mother told me she was an officer and was her boss. Father and I stayed the night in a room Mother shared with another woman. The next morning Mother had to leave early to go to her job and I felt miserable, as if a dark cloud had enveloped me. Later Father and I took the train home and I felt sad leaving my mother.

Having lost so much school time, our education had fallen very much behind and Father arranged for me and my brother to have a weekly private lesson to improve our reading and writing. We went to a man and wife, both teachers, called Pino and Amelia. When at home I would do whatever Father asked me to help run our daily lives. He kept my brother and me by his side at all times and we accompanied him if he visited anyone, even when he went shopping to the market in the next town. Father's discipline regarding my going to play with other boys remained unaltered. "No, no, no. It's too dangerous out there. There are still explosives in unexpected places. You can't go and that's it. Don't ask again," he would say.

People went about with sad faces, particularly those whose relatives had been killed or had died. Like Mother's mother, who lived across the road and was all alone now that Grandfather had died. Or Father's friend, who lived in the next group of houses; he and his wife were both killed as they returned home. Women who had husbands or sons in the army and hadn't heard from them for a long, long time travelled far to government offices, taking a whole day to enquire about them and returning exhausted without news or hope. The more days that passed, the greater the fear that they would never see their loved ones again. We too anxiously waited for news of one of Father's brothers. We hadn't heard from him for more than a year.

Sorrows

Food was scarce. Coupons were issued for the amount of bread and other foods each family could buy. People queued for hours waiting for the baker to bake bread and arguments often took place. On one occasion, after queuing for a long time, a heated argument broke out between the woman in front of me and the baker. (If I remember correctly, she was a war widow.) She wanted more bread than her coupons allowed and kept asking the baker loudly, "How can I feed my five children with this small amount of bread?" The baker answered, "I can only buy flour with the amount of coupons I present. If I give you extra bread, everyone else will want it." The woman went on and on, refusing to leave until the baker gave her more bread. A disease epidemic also affected a large number of families, probably due to malnutrition and the dead German horses and other animals left decaying above ground. I often saw the bones of animals by the roadside and in the fields. Medicines also were scarce.

Hearing and seeing people suffer was an everyday occurrence. Too often we heard the dreaded intermittent, melancholy sound of the church bell announcing another departed, followed the next day by the funeral procession on its way to the church then to the cemetery, the priest dressed in his funeral habit leading the mourners. Behind him walked the men carrying the coffin, followed by relatives, friends and neighbours, most dressed in black, praying aloud together and making a sad, muffled sound expressive of their sorrow.

My favourite uncle, Uncle Benedetto, Father's youngest brother, became ill too. He was twenty-three years old, always happy, and courageous. He had stayed behind with us to help as we moved from one place to another and suffered with us in the mountain cave. While we were in the town of Casalvieri he was beaten by the German SS soldiers for no reason. He became so ill that special injections were ordered from Rome, but every day his health worsened and the doctor told Father that my brother and I should not visit him in case we caught some disease. I was told Uncle continually asked to see me and my brother but each day excuses were made as to why we couldn't come. Yet we were less than two hundred metres from him. Sometimes when I passed the front of the house I heard his sad voice; it made me sad too.

Early one morning I was awakened by the dreaded deep, sad sound of the church bell and soon after I heard Father come in. He came straight to my bedside and said to me, "E morto zio Benedetto" (Uncle Benedetto has died). My brother and I were immediately taken to see him in his bedroom. His face had become very thin, his cheekbones were standing out, his eyes had sunk into his skull and he didn't look like my uncle any more. Soon, we went back home.

In the afternoon Father took me back to see Uncle's body. It had been moved to a room on the ground floor where it lay on a bed in the middle of the room. Many people were sitting on chairs and stools placed against the walls on either side of the bed. There wasn't a seat for me, so I went to sit on the wooden staircase that led to the first floor and from there I could see the whole scene. At times prayers were said collectively in a dull tone sounding more like a sad chant. Then all would go quiet as people just stared at the body. Often Grandmother would burst into tears and someone would comfort her. Others would refer to Uncle's wonderful qualities and say what a good-looking young man he had been. Then everyone would go quiet again. It was during a quiet moment that a man I had not seen before walked into the room and sat in the now empty chair next to Grandmother. He was of medium build, dressed in normal working clothes and had ruffled black curly hair and an unshaven face. He didn't say anything, but leant forward, resting his elbows on his knees, holding his face in the palms of his hands. Now I could only see the top of his hair. For a moment or two everyone continued to remain quiet, then Grandmother burst out crying again, saying, as she looked at Uncle's body, "My beautiful flower, why have you left me?" The man who had just entered raised his head and turned towards Grandmother, revealing his tired, tormented face. In a sorrowful voice he said, "Signora, consolatevi, consolatevi, consolatevi signora" (Signora, console yourself, console yourself, console yourself signora) "that you have your son in front of you in one piece. I was passing and heard of your misfortune. I am on my way to see the priest to arrange the funeral of my own son; he walked on explosives while we were working the land and was blown to pieces, I had to pick up parts of him and carry them home in baskets. Console yourself, console yourself, signora, your son is in one piece." The man then stood up, and without saying another word or looking at anyone, bowed his tormented face and left us. Everyone remained still and silent.

Time passed, but my mind remained in the same melancholy state. The devastation of the buildings was a daily reminder of what had happened to us. Worse was the grief in people's faces: those who had lost their loved ones, others whose husbands or sons hadn't returned from the war, people who had family members ill, without proper medication, and were unsure of their recovery, mothers who hadn't enough food to feed their children. It was an atmosphere of total gloom that kept alive in my mind what we had been subjected to, thoughts I found difficult to suppress. Often I found myself thinking of our time in hiding with barely enough food to survive another day, the exhaustion of walking, walking, walking, regardless of painful joints, the agony of the extreme cold, especially the days in the cave. I thought of when I feared so much that they would capture Father and take him away for ever, the many times we were traumatised by the bombardments and shelling, when I felt that horrific injuries and death were waiting for us, the screams of men beaten for no reason, the times we stood trembling on hearing the sound of boots coming and then being held in front of machine guns to face those merciless eyes under the ugly helmets.

As time went by, my sad thoughts about what we had suffered slowly faded, not because good things were happening, or through seeing happy faces or signs of a better tomorrow, but because of the horrifying tragedies that were still taking place, tragedies that destroyed all hope for the future, that tormented my mind and pushed me into a darker world, a world of pain, misery and sorrow, a stream of tragedies that imprinted more wounds and deeper scars in my mind. I was terrified because I thought something bad would soon happen to me too. Far too often I heard of people who had been injured or killed after treading on mines or were victims of exploding ammunition. It made me very sad to hear of these tragedies, but what affected me most was when they happened to people I knew well, boys who were my friends, and especially when I had been present at the time they were injured and had seen them suffer excruciating pain.

One mid-morning I was walking along the road, returning home from my grandparents' house, when I heard someone crying and saw two men supporting a boy coming towards me. I stood still as they passed by. I knew the boy well; it was Armando who lived nearby. His hand and arm were wrapped in a white cloth and blood was seeping through. Soon after I heard that part of his hand had been blown off. He was alone when it happened and had a long way to walk before reaching people who could help him. On another day, about sunset, I heard an explosion and within minutes three brothers, my friends, were carried to the area in front of our home. They were drenched in blood and screaming with pain. Both parents were crying too as everyone waited helpless. Someone had run to the British army hospital tent for help and two ambulances came and took them away. Two recovered fully, but one lost a leg. Another day, in the mid-afternoon, I heard another explosion. I went outside and moments later two young men, our neighbours, appeared on the road, both injured. One was supported on both sides, by his father and by another man, as he walked slumped forward with a towel over his head and face. The British soldiers had moved away from our town by then, so both of them had to be taken to the civilian hospital a long way away before they could receive treatment. I then heard that some of the injured were operated on on a marble table and had to be held down as the hospital had no anaesthetics and no medicines. Over the many weeks that one of the young men was in hospital he kept sending messages to us to pray to Santa Lucia, the patron saint for sight, because he couldn't see. Sadly, he never regained his sight.

Another day, towards evening, I saw a cart drawn by a donkey approaching. The cart, which normally carried firewood, stopped about fifty metres from me and I saw people gathering around it and heard crying, so I went to look. The cart was carrying the body of the woman who lived opposite my grandparents' house; her name was Anita and she had two boys a little younger than me and my brother. The men were discussing how they were going to lift the body out of the cart. There was much crying, despair and confusion and I was severely reprimanded for being there – "You go home immediately." I did go home, where I learned later that the woman had been gathering firewood on the edge of a field when there was an explosion. Father's cousin and another person heard her cries and rushed to help, but the woman died while they were there. The whole neighbourhood took turns in staying by the body through the night. Each tragedy left the neighbourhood in misery, sorrow and renewed fear, there were no happy faces to be seen and every conversation was full of sorrow. I couldn't sing. It was impossible to be happy.

Early in the afternoon of another day, I was returning home alone having been to a shop to purchase food. No one was about, it was sunny and all was calm and quiet, when I heard the sound of an engine. It was a van, the rear covered with a domed tent. It stopped suddenly in front of the doctor's surgery and I saw the driver jump out from the cab and rush inside. As I walked towards the van I heard cries and groans. The nearer I came to the van the louder the crying, and as I passed I turned to look inside, to be confronted by the most horrifying sight I had ever seen. It was a hell in there, crammed with injured people, some stretched out on the floor, some curled up as there was no more room on the floor, two standing as there was only space for their feet, holding on to the frame that supported the canvas cover. Most were wrapped in sheets and blankets, large patches of which were soaked in blood. The faces I could see were tormented with pain; a woman opened her eyes, looked at me and closed them again. Others tried to open their eyes but they remained closed. The moans, the crying, the groaning, the screaming, the horrific sight and sounds paralysed me so I was unable to move. I felt sad that I could only stand there and not help, I felt bad that the woman saw me looking at her, doing nothing as if I didn't care, I felt bad that they were suffering and I was all right. The driver rushed out from the surgery and came to the back of the van. Speaking quickly, his voice trembling, he shouted, "Il dottore ha detto che vi debbo portare direttamente all'ospedale" (The doctor said to take you straight to the hospital) "because he has no medicines, no bandages or injections. We should be there in about an hour." He opened the cab door, took out the starting handle, went to the front and bending forward desperately turned and turned the handle until the engine started, then jumped into the cab and slowly pulled away. My eyes went to one of the rear tyres, worn and patched up with pieces of other tyres held together with nuts and bolts. I remained still, looking at the van as it drew away from me, listening to the sounds of its spluttering engine and wondering if it would ever reach the hospital. I couldn't forget the horrifying scene, the mournful sounds, as if death was hovering over them deciding whom to take first.

I walked home devastated, overwhelmed by sorrow and fear. Father wasn't there. I was alone with no one to make me feel protected and I feared that life would always be tragic. I prayed and prayed to Jesus to keep me from being injured, because I could not bear such pain. In my prayers I asked Jesus to let me suffer in other ways, little by little, but not to suffer injuries like that because I would find the pain too, too unbearable.

We continued to survive day by day, hoping that the last tragedy was the final one, but the suffering, the fear, the horrors of the past made it seem that life had only sorrow to offer. It was difficult to believe that life would ever be good again.

Afterwards

Sadly, the struggle and the hardship continued in the months and years that followed. Food remained scarce as all the produce stored by the farmers had been taken by the Germans, together with the cows, donkeys, sheep, chickens and pigs. I remember so well how they searched high and low for pigs, as the farmers had taken them to remote places below the mountain. There was no 1943/44 harvest, of course, as every single person in the towns and villages in our area – 40,000 in all – had been forced to leave. The loss of the animals, as well as affecting our food supplies and the supply of future livestock, meant they were not available for transport, to plough the fields and sow the seeds. The basic essentials to sustain the population were no longer there, the rich, fertile fields of the past now deserted and full of bomb craters, the fruit trees and vineyards massacred by the shelling.

There was no electricity, and our light was now supplied by the fuel Father took out of the armoured tanks abandoned by the Allied forces at the foot of Monte Cassino, which he put into a small bottle with a wick. However, this could only be used sparingly as it created thick black fumes, in fact when I blew my nose it left big black marks on the handkerchief.

In spite of the politicians' many promises, nothing really changed. When the Allied forces left, Mother lost her job as their interpreter. Our meals were never sufficient, and there was misery, poverty and sorrow everywhere we looked. Time seemed to stand still while we waited month after month after month, then years, for a better tomorrow that never came.

Mother and Father's despair was evident in their looks, their voices, and in the discussions that led them to consider if we should emigrate to Glasgow, Scotland, where Mother was born and brought up and where her two sisters lived. In those days it was difficult, if not impossible, to come and live in Great Britain, but Mother still had her British passport. And so, early one morning, Mother set out to visit her sisters in Glasgow. She cried and I cried, and Father took her to Termini station in Rome, returning later that day.

After spending some time with her sisters, Mother went to London to visit Father's relatives, and it was from there that she made enquiries at the Home Office as to how Father, my brother and I could join her.

We arrived in London on February 12th, 1949. Our first address was in the centre of London – Tower Bridge Road, quite near the actual Tower of London with its famous bridge. Coming from a small country town and suddenly finding myself amid the hustle and bustle of a big city felt very strange. The cold weather, the dark, foggy days, the endless noise of the trams, the continuous honk honk of the barges in the Thames to avoid collisions in the fog and a language I did not understand all made my life even more confusing.

However, little by little I became accustomed to it all and eventually we found ourselves so satisfied with our new way of life that my father, brother and I applied for and were granted British nationality. My brother served in the Army and I joined the Royal Air Force.

God, let there not be another war

*Alberto Panetta whilst
serving in the Royal Air Force*

*Enio Panetta whilst
serving in the army*